Aesthetics of Equality

Aesthetics of Equality

Aesthetics of Equality

MICHAEL J. SHAPIRO

OXFORD
UNIVERSITY PRESS

Oxford University Press is a department of the University of Oxford. It furthers the University's objective of excellence in research, scholarship, and education by publishing worldwide. Oxford is a registered trade mark of Oxford University Press in the UK and certain other countries.

Published in the United States of America by Oxford University Press 198 Madison Avenue, New York, NY 10016, United States of America.

© Oxford University Press 2023

All rights reserved. No part of this publication may be reproduced, stored in a retrieval system, or transmitted, in any form or by any means, without the prior permission in writing of Oxford University Press, or as expressly permitted by law, by license, or under terms agreed with the appropriate reproduction rights organization. Inquiries concerning reproduction outside the scope of the above should be sent to the Rights Department, Oxford University Press, at the address above.

You must not circulate this work in any other form and you must impose this same condition on any acquirer.

Library of Congress Cataloging-in-Publication Data
Names: Shapiro, Michael J., author.
Title: Aesthetics of equality / Michael J. Shapiro.
Description: New York : Oxford University Press, 2023. |
Includes bibliographical references and index.
Identifiers: LCCN 2022034993 (print) | LCCN 2022034994 (ebook) |
ISBN 9780197670347 (hardback) | ISBN 9780197670354 (paperback) |
ISBN 9780197670361 (epub)
Subjects: LCSH: Equality—Philosophy. | Equality in literature. |
Equality in mass media. | Aesthetics, Comparative.
Classification: LCC JC575 .S4727 2023 (print) | LCC JC575 (ebook) |
DDC 320.01/1—dc23/eng/20220920
LC record available at https://lccn.loc.gov/2022034993
LC ebook record available at https://lccn.loc.gov/2022034994

DOI: 10.1093/oso/9780197670347.001.0001

1 3 5 7 9 8 6 4 2

Paperback printed by Marquis, Canada
Hardback printed by Bridgeport National Bindery, Inc., United States of America

For Hannah, with love, admiration, and gratitude

Contents

List of Figures ix

Acknowledgments xi

Introduction: The Grammar of Equality 1

1. Thomas Mann's Joseph Tetralogy: A "Musico-Literary Poetics" of Equality 18

2. A Right to the City: Toni Morrison's Literary Jazz 55

3. Sculpting in Time: Michael Haneke's *Caché* 89

4. An Egalitarian Istanbul: *Ethos*'s Cinematic Portraiture 122

5. Latinx Visibility: Architecture and Public History 159

Notes 191

Index 223

Figures

I.1	McNulty and Teenager	3
3.1	Alien staff, a Krysztof Wodiczko urban intervention	90
3.2	Laurent home bookcase in Michael Haneke's *Caché*	108
3.3	TV studio books in Michael Haneke's *Caché*	110
4.1	Grant Wood, *American Gothic*	128
4.2	Gordon Parks, *American Gothic*	129
4.3	Albrect Dürer's portrait of his father	131
4.4	Elisabet and Alma in Bergman's *Persona*	133
4.5	Meryem	135
4.6	Peri	136
4.7	Gülbin	140
4.8	Meryem at the mosque	141
4.9	The Hodja	143
5.1	Sam and Pilar at the drive-in in Sayes's *Lone Star*	189

Acknowledgments

I wrote Aesthetics of Equality under unusual circumstances. Stuck at home during the COVID-19 pandemic during the roughly eighteen-month period in which I worked on the manuscript, I participated in a series of virtual colloquia in which I shared a version of Chapter 3 (focused on Michael Haneke's film *Caché*). In addition to the several scholars who participated in those colloquia—the organizer, Fabiano Mielniczuk; Marta Fernández, Rohan Kalyan, Jessica de Oliviera, Sam Opondo, Lorenzo Rinelli, and Francine Rossone de Paula—there are several who have read and reacted to entire or partial chapter drafts or have lent an ear and responded as I discussed the project. Those include Arthur Bradley, Bill Connolly, Shree Deshpande, Brad Evans, Brianne Gallagher, Katherine Goktepe, Jairus Grove, Nicole Grove, Elisabeth Heradstveit, Robert Hopper, Sophie Kim, Sankaran Krishna, Chuck Lawrence, John Mowitt, Ali Musleh, Eliaquim (Ken) Reyes, Morton Rosenberg, Hannah Tavares, and Irmak Yaziki.

I am especially grateful to Angela Chnapko, my acquisitions editor at Oxford University Press, who welcomed the project from the moment I first sent a proposal and introductory chapter, conducted a timely review process at a time in which it was difficult to solicit reviews for manuscript drafts, and remained actively engaged throughout the production process. I want also to thank the production managers who kept in constant touch as they moved the manuscript along, Alexcee Bechtold of Oxford University Press and Ganga Balaji of Newgen Knowledge Works. Thanks are owed as well to Anne Sanow who did excellent and indispensable copy-editing. Finally, I am honored and grateful to my dear friend, the artist Barbara Benish who created the cover image, "In a Silent Way," a visual riff on a Miles Davis tune and a productive reception of Chapter 2's focus on jazz.

Introduction

The Grammar of Equality

Inspirations

A children's book and a television series are among the inspirations that shaped this book project. The former, Leo Lionni's *Frederick*, about a "chatty family of field mice" living in a stone wall and granary in an abandoned farm, narrates an egalitarian ethos, themed as an homage to the communal contributions of aesthetic work. As the story opens, all but the eponymous protagonist, Frederick, are busy gathering supplies—"corn, and nuts and wheat and straw"—for the winter. When the hardworking mice ask Frederick why *he's* not working, he says, "I *do* work; I gather the sun's rays for the cold dark days . . . and I gather colors, for the winter is gray." Later when they see him daydreaming, they ask if he's asleep. "Oh no," he says, "I am gathering words for the winter days are long and many, and we'll run out of things to say."

Once the winter days are upon them: the cold has set in, the supplies have dwindled, and "no one felt like chatting," they ask Frederick, "What about your supplies?" At that point Frederick makes his civic contribution. Telling them to close their eyes, he speaks about the "golden glow" of the sun's rays, and they begin to feel warmer. When they ask about the colors, he again tells them to close their eyes as he describes "the blue periwinkles, the red poppies in the yellow wheat, and the green leaves of the berry bush." They then "saw the colors as clearly as if they had been painted in their minds." And finally, when they ask about the words, Frederick clears his throat and "as if from a stage," delivers a lyrical soliloquy about the contributions of "four little field mice—the Springmouse who turns on the showers . . . the Summermouse who paints the flowers. The Fallmouse . . . with the walnuts and wheat, And the Wintermouse] . . . with little cold feet." He

Aesthetics of Equality. Michael J. Shapiro, Oxford University Press. © Oxford University Press 2023.
DOI: 10.1093/oso/9780197670347.003.0001

2   AESTHETICS OF EQUALITY

ends with the lines, "Aren't we lucky the seasons are four? Think of a year with one less ... or one more?"[1]

Composing a similar ethos, much of which is conveyed by the way it structures the visual field, the long-running HBO series *The Wire* (2002–2008) is distinctly different from the usual police procedural. In the opening scene of Season 1, Episode 1, the murder victim, an African American teenager called "Snotboogie" lies dead on a street in a West Baltimore neighborhood while the city police's murder squad is surrounding the body gathering clues. However, most of the camera's footage is on a peripheral conversation between one of the series' protagonists, detective Jimmy McNulty and an unnamed local Black teenager. They are initially filmed from the back left, conversing about what has gone down. McNulty initiates the conversation, asking the young man, "So who was Snotboogie." After responding, "I ain't goin' to no court," the teenager realizes that because McNulty is not assigned to the case—he's simply trying to understand the protocols of the local venue—he can speak freely. What then transpires is the enfranchisement of McNulty's conversation partner as a civic voice. As the camera swings around to a side view, we observe a scopic field with a paratactic configuration; the two bodies are in a nonhierarchical side-by-side position as the young man explains that there was no good reason to kill Snotboogie (Figure I.1). He tells McNulty that every Friday night there's a craps game, and each time Snotboogie is invited in as a player he grabs the pot and tries to flee with it, only to be apprehended and beaten. "Every time?" asks McNulty. "Let me understand, every Friday night he'd wait until there was cash on the ground then grab the money and run away ... you'd let him do that?" "We'd catch his ass and beat him," is the response. McNulty: "Then I gotta ask you, if every time Snotboogie grabs the money and runs away, why do you let him in the game?" The answer McNulty gets reflects the democratic, egalitarian mentality of the series: "Got to—this is America man!" Thereafter, the series devotes as much footage to the bodies, perspectives, and words of characters in West Baltimore's African American neighborhood as it does to the detectives working in the police precinct, the law enforcement hierarchy, and state and local political officials from the governor on down.

Figure I.1 McNulty and Teenager
Source: HBO Entertainment

Grammar and Method: The "And" and the "With"

Heeding that scene and several similar ones in analyses of diverse media genres at various points in my investigation, with an emphasis on the conjunction "and," I juxtapose the egalitarian implications of paratactic configurations to hierarchical, hypotactic arrangements in which one person or textual component is dominant. As I explain in Chapter 1's analysis of Thomas Mann's four-book version of the Joseph story, the tetralogy's equality-promoting ethico-political sensibility is affirmed and intensified by its paratactic structure. All the character's stories are arranged side by side, in contrast with a hypotactic structure that would have subordinated all other character's stories to Joseph's. The relevant grammatical figure for parataxis is the conjunction "and." To illustrate the substantive and methodological significance of that grammatical figure, I turn once again to an example from children's literature.

4 AESTHETICS OF EQUALITY

In A. A. Milne's Winnie the Pooh books, whose narratives follow relationships among Pooh and his anthropomorphized animal friends—Tigger, Piglet, Owl, Kanga, Roo, Rabbit, and Eeyore—there are frequent complaints by Eeyore, a notoriously grumpy donkey who feels that he is excluded from the conviviality enjoyed by the other animals. In the midst of a collective conversation he remarks, "I'd say thistles, but nobody listens to me, anyway,"[2] and most relevant to my analysis is his occasional use of the conjunction "and" to note his feelings of exclusion. In response to one of the animals saying "Hello everyone," he is prone to responding, "*and* Eeyore!" as if the greeting doesn't include him. His "and" is a demand for civic presence. Milne's scenarios and protagonists are forever frozen in time. The Pooh books are not Talmudic; they are not open to continual alteration through internal commentary. Eeyore will always have modeled a particular character type because he and Milne's other animal subjects are hostages to the verb to be. They will perpetually be what they have been.

The philosopher Gilles Deleuze bids to free such hostages. In a conversation with the journalist Claire Parnet, he addresses the stultifying effects of logical approaches to relationships that rely on the verb to be, "is," and advocates "thinking *with* AND instead of thinking IS." Offering an elaborated rationale for his grammar advocacy, he says:

> The whole of grammar. The whole of the syllogism, is a way of maintaining the subordination of conjunctions to the verb to be, of making them gravitate around the verb to be. One must go further, one must make the encounter with relations penetrate and corrupt everything, undermine being, make it topple over. Substitute the AND for IS. A and B. The AND . . . is that which subtends all relations, the path of all relations, which makes relations shoot outside their terms . . . and outside everything which could be determined as Being.[3]

Having noted the relevance of Deleuze's "and" to an egalitarian sensibility, I want gesture to the importance of the phrase that precedes his "and"—his expression, "thinking *with*"—because a reflection on that phrase provides an opening to the methods pedagogy that my investigation offers. While the "and" is crucial to my substantive

INTRODUCTION 5

focus on equality, the "with" speaks to the aesthetic method applied throughout the chapters. It underscores my attention to that with which the inquiry's textual objects of analysis think and as well that with which I think, the conceptual analytics to which I turn as I engage the texts. A remark by Michel Foucault about what he intends readers to derive from his inquiries captures what I want readers to take from mine. Referring to the kind of reception he intends in his analyses of prisons and asylums, he states, "*Je voudrais que mes livres soient une sorte de tool-box dans lequel les autres puissent aller fouiller pour y trouver un outil avec lequel ils pourraient faire ce que bon leur semble, dans leur domaine*" ("I would like my books to be a kind of tool-box which others can dig in to find a tool with which they can make good use, in whatever manner they wish, in their own area").[4] In accord with Foucault's remark, my hope is for a productive reception of my investigation. To make that hope apparent, in what follows I review aesthetic strategies, pointing to aspects of the "thinking with" inherent in the compositional styles of the textual objects of analysis, along with reference to my "thinking with," the idea systems I enlist to develop political insights from the texts. It's an approach to writing/thinking that approximates a method described by Cesare Casarino, who identifies it as "philopoesis," which "names a certain discontinuous and refractive interference between philosophy and literature."[5] It's a disruptive interference that enables critical thinking by confronting the experiential focus of literature, which Deleuze and Guattari refer to as its "affects and percepts,"[6] with the conceptual work of philosophy in order to open up "emergent potentialities that disrupt the status quo of the history of forms."[7]

The primary "withs" with which my main textual objects of analysis think are its protagonists who serve as epistemological subjects. Before turning to illustrations of some of those "withs," I want to share a brief reflection on what turned out to be the range of *my* "withs," the conceptually evoked aesthetic strategies with which I engaged the investigation's texts. Addressing what well-composed literary style accomplishes, the Czech novelist Milan Kundera states, "When you reach the end of the book, you should still find it possible to remember the beginning."[8] The temporal trajectory of my investigation violates Kundera's compelling suggestion, which presumes that the beginning

6   AESTHETICS OF EQUALITY

of a text should anticipate and have a regulatory force on what follows it. *Aesthetics of Equality* is not a book for which I planned to assert and illustrate an argument I had already developed. I deferred composing the introduction until I had completed the last chapter, because the political sensibilities that have resulted come from an inquiry that began without an elaborate set of presuppositions.

Aesthetics of Equality has been a learning text in which rather than imposing a well-developed conceptual agenda, I began with a broad question. I asked myself what one can contribute to equality issues by being attentive to aesthetic form in a variety of artistic genres that challenge institutionalized accounts of history. Broadening the "ethical terrain" of that question, Jill Jarvis adds a pertinent elaboration: "What would it take to write a history that takes up as truly authoritative the lost testimonies of all the dispossessed, detained, banished, forgotten, and disappeared?"[9] Refining the question as I worked my way into the diverse topics and texts featured in the book's chapters, I focused particularly on how diverse textual genres articulate political problematics through their compositional structures, what some theorists refer to as the "ideology of form" but is more elaborately expressed in Theodor Adorno's suggestion that the object of a literary text is not well understood through "the publicist aspect of art" and "still less through its ' 'message.'" By way of illustration, he points to Jean Paul Sartre's play *Huis Clos* (No Exit), in which "language jolts signification," indicating that what it contributes is less its "meaning" than the unsettling impact of the way it constructs a micro-world of associations.[10]

Thinking with Adorno's as well as the conceptual contributions of other philosophers and theorists, I focus on textual form. However, while aesthetic strategies articulated through attention to the forms of diverse media genres are a main aspect in my investigation, it is also shaped by substantive political concerns, particularly an attentiveness to persons and voices that tend to be civically invisible and unheard. Nevertheless, much of what emerged as I prepared myself to learn from the texts I selected for analysis are themes I had not fully anticipated. Among those is the issue of the right to space, an equality problematic (often raised by political geographers and urbanists) that is neglected in the dominant liberal/rationalistic methods deployed in mainstream political studies, which aggregate, either empirically or imaginatively,

INTRODUCTION 7

individual political attitudes and expressions (an approach to which Jacques Rancière refers as a "political arithmetic").[11] As I thought with Henri Lefebvre, who helped me shape my approach to an ethics of space, I focused on what he famously calls "The right to the city," which is at issue in the urban milieux I investigate. To implement his perspective is to heed disaggregation, a situation in which diverse ethnic groups, many of whom are migrants, struggle to manage an affordable and secure domesticity and varying degrees of social conviviality, against the incessant urban (re)designs of urban planning agencies.

Another crucial issue that came up continually regards historiography. I became increasingly aware that the equality lent to or demanded by diverse ethnic assemblages—by which I mean the acquisition of the material and symbolic resources needed to manage an effective civic presence—requires public recognition and legitimation of their stories, the narratives within which they situate their experiences in order to achieve historical continuity as an assemblage. In addition to requiring such an historiographic consciousness, which takes the form of what Foucault calls "counterhistory,"[12] an egalitarian commitment requires as well an acceptance of a wide variety of modes of existence, a recognition of a multiplicity of lifestyles and voices in order to broaden the bandwidth of what it can mean for diverse assemblages with cultural singularities to be civically in common. Thinking with David Lapoujade, who theorizes what he calls "lesser existences," I presume that "instead of a common world," there exists "a multiplicity of manners and gestures: manners of perceiving it, or appropriating it, or of exploring its potentials."[13] The texts I engage in each chapter disclose the parts of that multiplicity that tend to exist below the threshold of recognition. As the equality sensibility I have previewed briefly here is expanded and articulated through engagements with the diverse textual genres explored in each of the chapters, much of my approach to equality proceeds implicitly in the way I compose the chapters—with montages that juxtapose texts, concepts, and personae—instead of through explicit argumentation.

Rather than review the conceptual framing of the inquiries in each chapter, in which I draw from media theory, philosophy, architecture, photography, literature, and art history (they are noted as the investigation proceeds), I want to evoke once again the importance of the

8 AESTHETICS OF EQUALITY

"with," and illustrate a composition-oriented approach that thinks with its protagonists. For that I turn to a story whose scenario, bereft of an ideological metacommentary, exemplifies the kind of form-attuned equality advocacy that is composed throughout my investigation. Central to the story, Daniel Alarcón's "Collectors" is an intimate relationship between two cellmates, Rogelio and Henry, in a notorious Peruvian prison.[14] As the narrative begins, we meet Rogelio, who having lost his father at age eight, grew up emotionally attached to his older brother. Among what we learn about Rogelio is the equanimity of his personality, which his family found "disconcerting"; he loved his brother Jaime without showing concern for "whether Jaime loved him in return." Rogelio began "skipping school to spend hours walking in the hills above town." Although his lack of schooling had left him illiterate (in the usual sense of the term, unable to read books), he is literate in other respects, among which is "decent mechanical intuition." He and his brother, working on old "broken-down trucks," are able to "cajole those heaps of metal back to life." They perform "a complex and patient kind of surgery."

Rogelio precedes Henry into prison as a result of his devotion to his brother. He takes the rap when apprehended carrying drugs in the truck he uses for his brother's drug trafficking enterprise. Henry, who is super-literate in the traditional sense, follows Rogelio into prison eighteen months later for a very different kind of "crime." A playwright who has written and directed a play titled *The Idiot President*, Henry is arrested after one of the performances by "men in dark suits" and sent to Collectors, charged with the political crime of insulting the president. Rogelio takes pity on his new cell mate, a severely depressed Henry who hardly moves for three days after arriving. Telling Henry that he's allowed to move, Rogelio takes it upon himself to instruct him on what he must learn to survive in the prison culture. He explains that Henry has to become attuned to the prison's mood and gestural economy—specifically to learn to read body language. One of Rogelio's instructional remarks speaks to his possession of super-literacy: "There were moments in the day," he says, "when it was safe to be out, others when it was best to stay inside. The distinction depended not on the time of day but on the mood of the prison, which Henry had to learn to read if he hoped to survive."

INTRODUCTION 9

"How do you read it?" Henry asks. As Rogelio proceeds to explain that kind of literacy, he makes these detailed observations:

It involved listening for the collective murmur of the yard, watching the way certain key men—the barometers of violence in the block—were carrying themselves. Small things: Did they have their arms at their sides, or crossed in front of them? How widely did they open their mouths when they talked? Could you see their teeth? Were their eyes moving quickly side to side? Or slowly, as if taking in every last detail?

In addition to heeding Rogelio's advice, what ultimately contributes to Henry's survival is a status he acquires as a prison celebrity. He becomes a valued contributor to prison life after he stages his play in the prison, enlisting some of the most violent inmates as actors. His staging creates a new and ultimately contagious form of being-in-common in Collectors.

The story ends badly for Rogelio. Henry is released after serving a year and a half. Rogelio, who had become his lover, dies when the Peruvian army storms the prison and massacres hundreds in response to actual riots on which Alarcón's story is based. Crucially, apart from the story's genre as a piece of historiographic metafiction, which makes palpable the experience of those subjected to a violent historical event, is what it says implicitly about literacy. By elevating a character who cannot read printed words but is extraordinarily literate at reading body language, it deprivileges a class-coding practice that sustains meritocracy and legitimates inequality. Composing a challenge to a widely accepted aspect of meritocracy, Alarcón's "Collectors" *shows* the way an artistic work can unsettle institutionalized commitments to hierarchy. It's an instance of implicit artistic advocacy that elevates, grounds, and "confers legitimacy on a mode of existence" that is not ordinarily accorded civic value.[15] Although throughout my investigation I construct conceptual and compositional impositions that intervene in and radicalize the artistic texts that are the vehicles of the analysis—adding new angles of vision and staging encounters between concepts and affects and percepts—much of the egalitarian force I extract from the texts I engage is articulated through their casts of characters

10 AESTHETICS OF EQUALITY

performing in the scenarios the authors, artists, and filmmakers invent. Accordingly, I want to note the implicit advocacy in some of the chapters' main texts by attending to what I will call the Rogelio effect, the way that an egalitarian sensibility operates in the analysis in each chapter through the kind of dispositions and action trajectories allocated to characters who are ordinarily unheeded for purposes of civic relevance.

Rogelio Effects

Two of the characters in Chapter 1, whose main text is Thomas Mann's *Joseph* tetralogy (his four connected *Joseph and His Brothers* novels),[16] are exemplary: his versions of the biblical women, Tamar and Potiphar's wife. For Tamar, in contrast with the Old Testament scribes who treat her as a disruptive albeit genealogically relevant distraction and give her a brief walk-on part that occupies a mere thirty verses in Chapter 38 of Genesis (focused on her seduction of Judah with the intent of having her sons become part of the Israelite genealogy), Mann makes her a civically relevant subject. Turning her into a complicated "prototype of historical ambition," as he puts it, Mann expands her story to thirty-two pages and gives her a physiognomy and political sensibility.[17]

Mann's treatment of Potiphar's wife is a similar act of political subjectivization. Whereas she is reduced to being a resentful would-be seductress whose accusation delays Joseph's assent to prominence in Egypt in the Genesis account, Mann invents a complex persona with a name, lifestyle, and the experience of exquisite suffering. Explicitly regarding his novel as an egalitarian text, Mann undertook what he referred to as a "humane attempt to salvage a woman's honor by making a human figure of Potiphar's wife, by telling the painful story of her passion for the Canaanite steward of her pro forma husband."[18] In the Genesis version, Potiphar's wife lacks a name and occupies a mere half page (Genesis 39:7), where it's reported that she "casts her eyes upon Joseph" and attempts to seduce him; "lie with me," she says. In reaction to Joseph's refusal, she falsely accuses him of attempted rape. Unable to mount a plausible defense, he is sent to prison where he stays until he

INTRODUCTION 11

is summoned to help the Pharaoh by interpreting one of his enigmatic dreams.

Mann gives Potiphar's wife a name, Mut-em-enet, provides an extended narrative of her gradual descent into uncontrolled desire—covering one year of her hiding her feelings, a second as she reveals them, and a third as she attempts the seduction—embellishes the story with details of her appearance (describing the hours she spends on cosmetic and clothing), and gives the reader a keen sense of her suffering owed to Joseph's continual refusals. In her case, as with his version of Tamar, Mann opts for gender equality. He turns "Mut" into a protagonist rather than reducing her significance to her effect on Joseph's circumstances. His elaborate attention to both women contrasts with the priestly tradition whose focus is on the patriarchally oriented genealogy in which Abraham and his successors achieve a Yahweh-promised nationhood in exchange for their commitment to monotheism.

As is the case with Mann's Joseph story whose attention to peripheral characters decenters the Genesis account, Toni Morrison's novel *Jazz*, the main text in Chapter 2, lacks a central protagonist. Her novel contains an equality of coverage among its many voices and delivers its telling moments in fragments treating encounters that are figured as duets and solos. While the intimacy that survives in Mann's tetralogy involves reconciliation (between Joseph and his brothers), Morrison's novel is a love story composed in a bluesy jazz style in which her Black protagonists reconnect after episodes of estrangement. In addition to sharing structures based on musical idioms (while Mann's text mimics a Wagnerian motif structure, Morrison's is shaped as a jazz performance), the two texts share the issue of the right to space. The spatial issue in Mann's Joseph story is the right to the Holy Land, while in Morrison's it's the right to the city. As her diverse characters strive to achieve that right in the city of New York, their struggles are alternatively aided and impeded in varying degrees by nonhuman protagonists: music, personal history, the city, and the author's voice. For example, attributing the consequences of the Black experience in the United States to which Morrison refers as a history of "emotional disfigurement,"[19] *Jazz* articulates that history by materializing "disfigurement" through the conduct of one of the characters. Violet attends

12 AESTHETICS OF EQUALITY

a funeral carrying a knife with which she disfigures the face of the corpse, the eighteen-year-old Dorcas, with whom her husband Joe has had an affair before killing her.

In the novel the city is a protagonist that performs in a musical idiom. It impedes Joe's autonomy as he attempts to evince a right to an urban life. It has him "caught on a turntable with grooves" that have preceded him; "he is bound to the track. It pulls him like a needle through the groove of a Bluebird record."[20] Similarly, Dorcas's Aunt Alice, whose parents had been killed in a St. Louis race riot, "worked hard to privatize her niece" but is "challenged by a song more powerful than the personal song and dance she tries to negotiate with Dorcas." In the words of one of the novel's narrators, she is "no match for a city seeping music that begged and challenged each and every day."[21] Nevertheless music, as one of the novel's protagonists, plays an ambiguous role. Rather than a mere accompaniment to the city's relationship-shaping rhythms, it shelters and nurtures as well, at least in Black section of the city: "Up there, in that part of the City—which is the part they [Joe and Violet] came for—the right tune whistled in a doorway of lifting up from the circles and grooves of a record can change the weather. From freezing to hot to cool."[22]

Moreover, and crucial to how the novel works, Morrison as author is also a protagonist. She accompanies characters' voices, comping the novel's jazz performances. Near the end of the novel, while performing as the narrative voice, she wonders if Violent and Joe "know they are the sound of snapping fingers." As their "victrola plays in the parlor . . . The click of dark and snapping fingers" is driving them "into places their fathers have warned them about and their mothers shudder to think of."[23] At that point, a moment when Joe and Violent are restoring the intimate bond that had been broken, Morrison's (literary) fingers are also snapping to the tune.

The analysis moves from the aural to the visual in Chapter 3, whose main text is Michael Haneke's film *Caché*. As is the case with Morrison's *Jazz*, the cinematic text has nonhuman protagonists, among which is an unseen anonymous source continuously filming the Paris townhouse of Georges and Anne Laurent, and History, which is an allegorical referent of the film's personal drama. Those nonhuman protagonists compete with and decenter the human protagonist, Georges Laurent, who

INTRODUCTION   13

has a dark past that he tries to hide. During the first few times I watched the film, I paid little heed to Georges's and Anne's son Pierrot because most the film's drama follows Georges's growing agitation and dissembling reactions to receiving anonymous videos and drawn images at home and at his workplace. During his first appearance onscreen Pierrot performs the role of a typical disaffected teenager, showing up late for dinner and responding to his parents' queries about his day in impatiently delivered monosyllables.

However, as the film narrative progresses, focused primarily on the relationship between Georges and his former foster brother, an Algerian immigrant Majid, whom he had conspired to have expelled from the family and sent to an orphanage, Pierrot's role becomes increasingly significant. Among other things, he enters the film's scopic field as a witness, doubling the surveillance effect created by the anonymous videos. In several scenes he watches as his parents are disingenuous about the emotions that they're experiencing in reaction to anonymous videos delivered to their home, and he becomes especially disaffected after peering through the window of a café where he sees his mother looking intimate with a male coworker whom he suspects is a paramour. Ultimately, his estrangement from his family is allegorical. A younger generation's witnessing of parents hiding personal experiences reflects allegorically on the film's witnessing of France's failure to confront the historical and contemporary abuses of its postcolonial, immigrant population. The film's compositional structure implies that a younger generation is on the verge of forming a fraternal bond across ethnic lines, an alliance that would obviate the effect of the cultural difference-dissolving "fraternity" in the French motto, which has stifled the possibility of hospitality toward postcolonial cultural pluralism. In the last scene Pierrot is standing side by side with Majid's (unnamed) son. Paratactically posed and appearing convivial, their positioning implies that their generation might displace France's amnesiac paternalism.

Chapter 4 devotes much of its space to the Netflix series *Ethos*, which is shot as a series of cinematic portraits, while its main theme is a juxtaposition of Western European psychoanalysis and traditional Islamic spiritual therapy. The therapeutic divide is one among several aspects of the series' exploration of the ongoing tensions between secular and

14 AESTHETICS OF EQUALITY

religious cultural allegiances, played out in the city of Istanbul. At the center of *Ethos*'s narrative are encounters between the headscarf-wearing religious fundamentalist, Meryem, and her secular, psychoanalytically trained therapist, Peri, who confesses to *her* therapist that she cannot help associating her client with a moral claustrophobia visited on Istanbul by fundamentalists. The secular–fundamentalist divide between Meryem and Peri is repeated within families, most notably within the family of Peri's therapist, Gülbin, a secularist violently confronted in several scenes by her fundamentalist twin sister, Gülan (a micro version of the fraught cultural conflicts within Turkish society) and within the family of the Hodja, a religious Iman/teacher whose daughter drifts away from her father's religious influence.

Much of the analysis is focused on the series' visual language. The chapter locates *Ethos*'s cinematic portraiture within a historical trajectory of portraiture that has moved on from its historical preoccupation with elites to allow ordinary people to rise above the threshold of recognition. *Ethos* actualizes that sensibility with many face shots of Meryem, whose work as an apartment cleaner reflects her low social status. Hilmi, a spiritual assistant in the Hodja's mosque, another character who occupies a relatively low social status, is also featured in a few portrait-like framing shots. Although he is on camera in only a few scenes, he functions as someone with more civic significance than would be expected from one with his vocation. *Ethos* constructs him as a primary epistemological subject.

The first few shots of Hilmi show him struck by Meryem's beauty. A close-up of his face shows a man experiencing love at first sight. However, while in early scenes the emphasis is on the hopelessness of Hilmi's attraction to Meryem (who under her breadth refers to him as the "ugly little man" who is unable to "admit that he likes me"), in later scenes the film narrative redeems him as much by subtle changes in his cinematic portrait as by his words. What began as a diffident and awkward expression becomes an assertive one that accompanies his narrative assignment in which he becomes a civically relevant persona who delivers two of the series' critical perspectives. First, he mediates the tension between psychoanalytic and spiritual forms of healing. In a conversation with Meryem he explicates the Jungian version of psychoanalysis, which merges psychological and spiritual forms of therapy. The lesson he expresses to Meryem is about fashioning a self no longer constrained by fundamentalist inhibitions. Providing a cultural mediation that the religion-aversive Europhile Peri was unable to offer, he points out that according to Jung the second part of one's life is no longer about proving oneself; what has been repressed is no longer in control of one's destiny. In a later conversation, he states what I suggest is the ethos of *Ethos*, which the series has implicitly articulated with its images. Suggesting that one should treat life as a festival, he delivers an implicit advocacy of a less divisive temperament, an acceptance of a pluralistic recognition of the society's many modes of existence.

Chapter 5 on the Latinx experience in historical and contemporary California and Texas is articulated through an architectural narrative thread that runs throughout the analyses of the chapter's several featured texts. Among the protagonists are a freeway interchange and a historic building. Here I will confine my illustrations to two seemingly minor sites and their proprietors in the cinematic text with which the chapter closes, John Sayles's film *Lone Star* (1996). As I note in the chapter, although the film's superficial narrative genre is a whodunit— the Texas border town, Frontera's new sheriff Sam Deeds is pursuing a murder investigation—the story's political significance emerges from the way the film connects personal and collective histories associated with the historical trajectory of Anglo-Latino conflicts. As is the case with characters I select for attention in some of the other chapters, the two seemingly peripheral characters I treat in Chapter 5—Chucho, a Mexican owner of a tire repair shop across the US border in Mexico and Wesley, a Native American proprietor of a tourist gift shop on a highway on the periphery of Frontera's business district—are epistemological subjects. While within the whodunit narrative the film gives them roles as informants for Sam's murder case, it also enfranchises them as knowledge agents who inform the viewers about the historical unfolding of the region's ethno- and geopolitics.

When Sheriff Sam Deeds plans his excursion to the Mexican city across the border to interview Chucho, he refers to a visit "to the other side," an expression that has several resonances. In addition to referring to a trip across the bridge separating the two border towns, it refers to a geopolitical divide owed to an historical event (the US takeover of the

16 AESTHETICS OF EQUALITY

Texas territory and the forced movement of Latino North Americans southward). And most relevant to the political sensibility that the film narrative conveys is the presentation of a different perspective from the institutionalized Anglo views of personal and collective history. Although Chucho had been a witness when the former sheriff, Charley Wade, killed his friend Eladio Cruz (Wade is the murder victim whose killing Sam is investigating), the conversation's larger significance inheres in what Chucho has to say about geopolitics and the relationship of space to one's discursive eligibility. Parodying his mundane economic status, which he implies may hinder the legitimacy of his observations, he begins by referring to himself as "*El Rey de las Llantas* (King of the Tires)." He then launches into a geopolitical lesson. Drawing a line in the sandy soil outside his shop with the neck of a Coca Cola bottle (notably a product with cross-border distribution), he points out that Sam's policing authority disappears as soon as he crosses a geopolitical line. "When you step over that line," he says, you're "no longer the Sheriff of anything."

While Chucho's voice "from the other side" challenges the hierarchical assumption that the legitimacy and cogency of a voice depends on the power associated with its geopolitical location, a different value issue emerges during Sam's visit to the Native American tourist shop on the outskirts of Frontera. With the shop proprietor, Wesley's commentary the film warrants the value of a voice that has been historically disqualified *within* the same geopolitical space. Serving as an informant about local and personal issues, Wesley tells Sam about his late father, Buddy Deeds's, extramarital relationship with Eladio Cruz's widow, Mercedes. However, the political significance of his voice—one among the many indigenous voices that have been historically disqualified—is allegorical. When Wesley jokes about the location of his shop on a "stretch of road that runs between Nowheres and Nothin' Much," the historical referent is clearly the valueless spaces of the reservations allocated to Native American peoples (who were once nations occupying extensive territories). And when he disparages the value of the artifacts he sells to tourists, which once had cultural value for Native American nations—for example Buffalo chips and curios from Texas history that are reduced to kitschy icons—he's an interpretive voice in behalf of the film's theme about the consequences of Anglo

INTRODUCTION   17

dominance. Most notably, when he refers to one of his sales items, "a wooden radio carved to resemble the Alamo," he is articulating the film's explicitly stated theme, "forget the Alamo" (flashed onscreen at the film's conclusion).

The Chucho and Wesley sites—the tire shop in Mexico and the Native American gift shop in Frontera, respectively—are countersites that disclose a counterhistory. The voices of the sites' proprietors challenge the perpetuation of the Anglo hegemony-supporting Alamo myth. The politics of aesthetics immanent in the use of such voices in Sayles's *Lone Star* (as well as throughout the textual genres within all the chapters) is effectively summarized in Gayatri Spivak's remark about the value of fictional voices. "The protocols of fiction," she writes, "give us a practical simulacrum of the graver discontinuities inhabiting . . . the ethico-epistemic and ethico-political . . . an experience of the discontinuities that remain in place in 'real life.'"[24] Rancière offers a similar observation: "Literary fiction—or avowed fiction in general—is not so much the object that social science has to analyze as it is the laboratory where fictional forms are experimented as such and which, for that reason, helps us understand the functioning of the forms of unavowed fiction at work in politics, social science or other theoretical discourses." What distinguishes avowed fiction, as Rancière points out, "is not the invention of imaginary beings in contrast with solid reality. Like non-fiction, it provides 'sense of reality' by cut[ting] out a frame and plac[ing] elements within it so as to compose a situation and make it perceptible."[25] As I engage the fictional texts in the chapters that follow, my compositional and conceptual interventions—the frames I cut out by engaging the frames the texts cut out—work to unsettle the interpretive practices that obscure a pervasive discontinuity, that between egalitarian pretentions and the realities of structures of domination and exclusion. I emphasize how those texts make visible and audible—in short, enfranchise—politically disqualified persons and assemblages in order to lend them civically relevant recognition.

1
Thomas Mann's Joseph Tetralogy
A "Musico-Literary Poetics" of Equality

Prelude: The "I Am"

There is no more moving moment in the Old Testament than in Genesis 45:3–4 where Joseph reveals himself to his brothers, saying initially "I am Joseph" and then more elaborately, "I am Joseph your brother, whom ye sold into Egypt."[1] Thereafter, it becomes evident that Joseph's "I am" has initiated a process of reconciliation aimed at the consolidation of a people headed toward the fulfillment of Yahweh's promise to the patriarch Abraham. Hence Joseph's last "I" (Genesis 50:24) is in the sentence " 'I die': and 'God will surely visit you and bring you out of this land unto the land which he swore to Abraham, to Isaac, and to Jacob.' " In Thomas Mann's tetralogy *Joseph and His Brothers*, which stretches a Joseph story that occupies a mere 14 chapters in Genesis to 1492 pages (in the 2005 Everyman edition), Joseph's "I am" (and "I am he") is a persistent leitmotiv punctuating the musically figured story in several places. However, the Old Testament scribes' theologico-political agenda—reconciliation and consolidation for purposes of a Yahweh-granted territorial acquisition—was not Mann's. Throughout his epic tetralogy, Joseph is never the same "I am" or "I am he." Although doubtless, Joseph's the oft-repeated "I am" is an oblique reference to the Old Testament's most famous "I am"—Exodus 14:3, which has Yahweh's statement to Moses, "I AM THAT I AM"—Joseph's frequent "I am" is parodic rather than reverent. Mann's Joseph subject, an experiment in the multiplicities of identity, is not given an authoritative, fixed self. As I will be emphasizing, throughout his Joseph tetralogy Mann's text is ambiguous with respect to "what meaning to impute to the Joseph subject in that always shocking phrase 'I am he.' "[2] Inasmuch as Mann privileges no one version of the "he," the persona he lends Joseph is

---

Aesthetics of Equality. Michael J. Shapiro, Oxford University Press. © Oxford University Press 2023.
DOI: 10.1093/oso/9780197670347.003.0002

a dispersion. As Mann narrates his story, interspersed with essayistic reflections on the grammar of the self, he sides with no particular version of the self and with no singular construction of the various political cultures through which his Joseph moves. I engage Mann's text to extract its nonjudgmental egalitarian structure, which is articulated through its form as much as through its themes. It is a text that invites close attention to compositional structure.

The Hebrew Bible as Writerly Text

In his treatment of texts as "methodological fields" from which one can extract their "subversive force in respect to old classifications,"[3] Roland Barthes famously privileges "writerly" texts. Meant to engage a reader conceived as a producer who extends or reinflects the implications of the text, "the goal of literary work (of literature as work)," according to Barthes, "is to make the reader no longer a consumer, but a producer of the text."[4] The Barthean active reader is especially enabled by texts whose compositional structures resist interpretive closure. "To interpret a text," as a producer rather than passive consumer, is to "appreciate what *plural* constitutes it."[5] One would presume that the Hebrew Bible is what Barthes calls "readerly" rather than writerly, where a readerly text engages a reader assumed to be a consumer for whom "reading is nothing more than a referendum."[6] Erich Auerbach addresses the kind of "referendum" that the Old Testament was composed to stage, an allegiance to a covenant theology. As he explains, the writing style of the biblical text is devoid of the concrete details one finds in Homer's elaborate description in *The Odyssey*, specifically the moment when Odysseus, who has entered his former home as a stranger, has to hush the maid Eurycleia, who is about to cry out after recognizing him because of the scar on his leg sustained in a boar hunt (Homer provides the details of the "whispered threats and endearments").[7]

The Homeric text, as Auerbach describes it, features "an externalization of phenomena in terms perceptible to the senses."[8] It's a "style" that "knows only a foreground, only a uniformly illuminated, uniformly objective present."[9] In contrast, what is distinctive about biblical stories is "not [the attempt] to bewitch the senses ... because the moral,

20 AESTHETICS OF EQUALITY

religious, and psychological phenomena are their sole concern."[10] "The Scripture stories do not, like Homer's, court our favor . . . they seek to subject us, and if we refuse to be subjected we are rebels."[11] The reader that the text enjoins is one who is summoned to a pious form of interpretation. What Auerbach shows convincingly is that the intent built into Scriptures distinguishes it from genres designed to "represent reality." The aim is not to entertain by making experience palpable but to assemble an interpretive/theological community.

Nevertheless, there are productive readers who have rendered Scripture as writerly. For example, rather than interpreting a portion of the text in order to participate in the Covenant, the Dutch art historian, Mieke Bal interprets it rebelliously from a feminist perspective. Unfixing the bible's Rabbinic-sanctioned tradition, she reads the Book of Judges to provide what she calls a "countercoherence" to the traditional patriarchal narrative in which one man, Abraham (under Yahweh's sanction), becomes a nation. Deflecting attention from traditional exegeses whose narrative coherence is based on "the geography of the land to be conquered," Bal elevates the significance of women in the biblical story. The countercoherence she constructs renders the household as a political arena, disclosing "how deeply a violence is anchored in the domestic domain."[12] Going beyond merely interpreting that violence—in which patriarchal judges, Jephthah among others, murder female family members—Bal subjectivizes a woman that has been left nameless.

In the biblical narration of the story, in return for Yahweh's grant of a victory over the Ephraimites, the judge, Jephthah promises to kill the first person that greets him after his victory. It turns out to be his nameless daughter. In order to lend Jephthah's daughter/victim a subject position, Bal gives her a name, Bath Jephthah, and connects her fate with those of other female victims in the domestic spaces that canonical readings pass over in order to tell a geopolitical story that valorizes the deeds of heroic men. Bal's refocusing of spaces and diegetic agents tells a different political story, one in which women in the domestic sphere achieve the recognition of which they are deprived in the dominant exegetical tradition of bible scholarship. Shifting the story from the land to be conquered to the houses that are conquered, Bal focuses on the places where the interaction between the political and the domestic is located. Her reading emphasizes places where "daughters . . . meet there undoing," that is, are murdered by Israelite "heroic men." Among the consequences of Bal's reading is an alteration in the value attributed to the kinds of lives that can be seen as politically qualified rather than being regarded (in Giorgio Agamben's terms) as mere "bare life," life that can be destroyed with juridico-political impunity. On Bal's reading the domestic space takes on a political significance that it lacks in canonical readings. Women who live nameless, politically unqualified lives become recognizable political subjects.

By way of transition, I want to suggest that in his novelistic version of the Joseph story, Mann performs a similar diegetic shift. However, his intervention is best characterized as a "countersong" rather than counter coherence because his style is parodic and musically figured.[13] Mann is explicit that he composed his Joseph story as a song, referring for example to "My song of Joseph," in the introduction to the single volume edition.[14] And his "Prelude" has explicit musical references; it's composed as a musical motif with six repetitions of Joseph's name within two paragraphs. Thereafter the composition of the text contains several musical thematizations. In the chapter where Jacob meets Joseph at "the well," Mann refers to their dialogue as a "duet," while Jacob performs some of his remarks as a "chant," and Joseph expresses his desire to "sing to the Lord of Hosts with a nimble tongue."[15] And perhaps most tellingly, while in the well where he was cast by his brothers, Joseph's "thoughts" are figured as a "musical composition."[16]

Mann's "song of Joseph" unfolds within a demanding political context. To recreate Joseph's story and give it contemporary resonance he had to both preserve the political tone of its historical moment and, contrapuntally, work it against a contemporary tone by obliquely referencing his own politically fraught historical moment (the tetralogy is composed during the rise of fascism between 1926 and 1942). As he states in his 1943 Library of Congress lecture, the tetralogy is "not only the product my individual time and stage of life, but that of the time at large, *and* in general *our* time of the historic convulsions."[17] The dual temporality to which Mann refers resonates with a contemporary reflection on a "fraught historical moment [of the COVID-19 pandemic]." Noting that "surviving 2020 has meant living, simultaneously, in two incompatible timelines," the writer, who is attuned to what

22 AESTHETICS OF EQUALITY

Auerbach ascribes to Mann's "time perspective," a concern for "the symbolic omnitemporality of events,"[18] says, "There is on one hand the relentlessness of the present moment. 'Now! Now! Now! Now! Now!' 2020 screams in our faces, constantly, like a bullying mindfulness coach. And yet we can also feel ourselves being pulled out into the deep stretch of history."[19]

Yet Mann, who also figured his pull back into history in terms of depth (referring to the past as a depth to be plumbed), was nevertheless optimistic about what he referred to as *our time*. He counted on the spirit and influence of American democracy to defeat the fascism gripping much of Europe and thereafter shape a freedom-realizing global future. That too he figured with a song motif. In the lectures he delivered while traveling around the United States in 1938, "The Coming Victory of Democracy," he referred to "your American statesmen and poets such as Lincoln and Whitman who proclaimed to the world democratic thought and feeling, and the democratic way of life," and added that "Whitman . . . knew better than any other writer or thinker how to elevate a political idea into 'intoxicating song.'"[20]

Given the nature of his temporal lens and parodic style, Mann's musically figured language functions within a genre constraint. The compositional structure of the Joseph story fits within what Linda Hutcheon famously calls "historiographic metafiction." As she puts it, "Historiographic metafiction works to situate itself within historical discourse without surrendering its autonomy as fiction . . . it is a kind of seriously ironic parody that effects both aims: the intertexts of history and fiction take on parallel (though not equal) status in the parodic reworking of the textual past of both the 'world' and literature."[21] Within that genre Mann constructs a "double-voiced discourse with both the deep seriousness of biblical authors [and characters] and the ironic distance of the literary author."[22] In parallel with the dialogues he creates among his characters is the implicit dialogue that irony lends to the text, Mann's dialogue with himself. Irony, as Georg Lukács notes, is "the novel's dialectical reflection."[23]

Within his self-conscious parody, Mann accomplishes a reinflection of Old Testament politics that accords with Bal's reading. Creating an imaginative version of the Judah–Tamar encounter, for example, he tells a story that emancipates Tamar from her enclosure within the text's preoccupation with an Israelite genealogy (oriented toward acquiring the right to the land promised by Yahweh). He transforms and expands Tamar's "story from a few sordid verses of the Old Testament narrative" in which, disguising herself an intercepting harlot, Tamar becomes "against Judah's will the mother of Judah's sons and an ancestor of David."[24] Whereas the Old Testament scribes construct Tamar as an inconvenient albeit genealogically relevant distraction—Judah notices her, assumes she is a harlot (because of the way she has disguised herself) and (as it's put in a decidedly unromantic passage) "came in unto her, and she conceived by him" (Genesis 39:18)—Mann gives her detailed attention and lends her a political sensibility:

> She was beautiful in her way, indeed not pretty but simply beautiful in an austere and off-putting way—that is, she seemed angered by her own beauty, and rightly so, for there was something bewitching about her that left men no rest, and to counter such unrest she had set those creases between her eyebrows . . . She had remarkably beautiful brown eyes that spoke with great urgency, almost circular nostrils, and a proud mouth . . . Tamar was a seeker. The creases between her eyebrows expressed not only anger at her own beauty, but also a strained effort to find truth.[25]

Like Bal, Mann performs a literary act of political subjectivation, turning a woman with a small walk-on part (roughly one page, the thirty verses of Chapter 38 in Genesis) into a major protagonist who occupies an entire thirty-two-page chapter.

Why did he turn to Tamar with such extravagance? In his 1948 preface, Mann reports that he wanted a female character for the *Joseph in Egypt* book (volume 3) that "could match the Rachel of Volumes 1 and 2"; "It was Tamar . . . whom I turned into a disciple of Jacob, into an Astarte-like figure with added characteristics from the Book of Ruth, and, in the same semicomedic style that informs the whole, developed her into the prototype of historical ambition."[26] That the treatment of Tamar serves the text's politics as well as its poesis is affirmed by the way Mann also invents an extravagant version of Potiphar's wife. He reports that "*Joseph in Egypt* seemed to me the poetic high point of the work, if only because of my humane attempt to salvage a woman's honor by

24 AESTHETICS OF EQUALITY

making a human figure of Potiphar's wife, by telling the painful story of her passion for the Canaanite steward of her pro forma husband."[27] In the Old Testament, the wife of Joseph's Egyptian master, Potiphar (in whose sight "Joseph found grace" as an overseer of the household, Genesis 39:4), is unnamed and given a mere half page. Enamored of his good looks and bearing, she "casts her eyes upon Joseph" and attempts to seduce him; "lie with me" (39:7) she says. When Joseph refuses her invitation, she falsely accuses him of attempted rape. Unable to mount a plausible defense, he ends up in prison where he's held until summoned to help the Pharaoh by interpreting one of his enigmatic dreams.

In contrast with the little attention Genesis allocates to the episode, Mann gives Potiphar's wife a name, Mut-em-enet, and gives the reader an extended narrative of her gradual descent into uncontrolled desire, spending one year hiding her feelings, a second revealing them, and a third attempting the seduction. Where the Old Testament provides a mere statement of fact, Mann provides a drama with details of the woman's beauty and hours spent on preparing her appearance—cosmetic, clothing, the helping role of her handmaidens—and gives the reader a sense of her exquisite suffering owed to Joseph's continual refusals. As is the case with his version of Tamar, Mann opts for gender equality as he turns Potiphar's wife into a protagonist. Rather than reducing her significance to her effect on Joseph's circumstances, she like Tamar is described at length with details of both her appearance and inner life. Mann's creative reimagining of the two women's roles is part of the egalitarian sensibility he composes throughout the tetralogy as he decenters the familiar Joseph story by elevating other characters and expanding their stories.

An important narrative thread begins in Part One of *Joseph in Egypt* and proceeds to chronicle the process through which Joseph slowly learns that his story is one among many. Affected by encounters, he gradually becomes attentive to other's stories. As one commentator puts it, "Joseph must outgrow an inclination to see himself as a youthful nature-god, whom others must love more than themselves."[28] It is through a concentration on Joseph's growth that his part of the story is composed as a *Bildungsroman* (a novel concerned with a protagonist's moral growth).

THOMAS MANN'S JOSEPH TETRALOGY 25

The novel's initial version of Joseph, a naïve otherness-insensitive youth, is introduced in the *Young Joseph* book (volume 2) at a moment in which he summons his brothers and unadvisedly regales them with the details of a dream he's had (after pressing them, despite their protests of disinterest, to listen): "I have had a dream," he begins, followed by several attempts to get their attention—for example, "I really want to tell you the dream that I dreamt during my nap"—before he gets them to listen.[29] When he finally has their ears, he narrates a dream in which they had all bound their harvest sheaves, left them in the field, "and walked away . . . and behold: my sheaf is standing in the middle, straight up, but yours, gathered round it in a circle, bend low to it, bend low, bend low, but mine stands upright."[30] Not surprisingly, Joseph's dream report enrages his brothers, who were already jealous of his favored position with their father Jacob. It's the final provocation leading to the well-known fate his brothers arrange for him. Despite Reuben's attempt to protect him from the wrath of the others, "the dreamer" is cast into a "pit" (described as a dry well) and then sold to nomadic merchants after they decide not to slay him. When the brothers return home with sheep's blood on Joseph's famous coat of many colors, they say that it's Joseph's and tell a distraught Jacob that he had likely been dragged off and killed by a wild animal.

Except for the more elaborate dialogue Mann supplies for the angry and quarreling brothers (and details of a blow-by-blow fight that removed Reuben's protection), that part of Joseph's story closely follows the biblical account. However, as is the case with Mann's style throughout his literary corpus, the scene contains a critical repetition with changing resonance. Wells function as an important motif, showing up in other contexts, one of which is metafictional. Mann, figuring the historiography of the fictional rendering of the Joseph story, begins his "Prelude" with the sentence, "Deep is the well of the past. Should we not call it bottomless?" Pursuing that figuration, he adds, "the deeper we delve and the farther we press and grope into the underworld of the past, the more totally unfathomable become those first foundations of humankind, of its history and civilization, for again and again they retreat farther into the bottomless depths, no matter to what extravagant lengths we may unreel our temporal plumb line."[31] Thereafter Mann's deep probing into the "well of the

26 AESTHETICS OF EQUALITY

past" projects his drama into several well scenarios. For example, *The Story of Jacob* (volume 1) has a lengthy chapter, "At the well," in which Mann, concealing "himself... behind his characters,"[32] uses a dialogue between Jacob and Joseph to rehearse the theological issues arising in Genesis. Reflecting on what that book has disclosed, Mann intervenes at the beginning of the next chapter with an essayistic reflection on the difference between the biblical and his contemporary thought world. It's a prelude to a section in which he discusses "Who Jacob Was":

> Ultimately, the idea of individuality stands in the same chain of concept that includes unity and entirety, totality, universality; and the differentiation between human spirit in general and the individual spirit has not always had anything like the power over the mind than it has in today's world, which we have left behind to tell of a different mind, whose mode of expression provided a faithful image of an understanding, as when for notions of "personality" and "individuality" it knew only more of less objective terms like "religion" and "confession."[33]

The sense of that Jacob is as much captured by who Jacob was not (he was less a spiritual force than a kind of voice). Mann's novelistic aesthetic articulates a politics of discourse rather than the political theology that the scribes—Elohists and Yahwists—composed. The tetralogy thus fulfills the perspective that M. M. Bakhtin famously accords to Dostoyevsky's approach to language. For Mann, as is the case for Dostoevsky, "the human world exists as an ongoing dialogue in which multiple languages and chronotopes [time/space figures] engage and reshape each other perpetually."[34] As Bakhtin puts it in his egalitarian approach to discourse, the novel is distinguished by its lack of a "verbal ideological center";[35] "in Dostoevsky almost no word is without its intense sideward glance at someone else's word... there are almost no objectified words in Dostoevsky, since the speech of his characters is constructed in a way that deprives it of all objectification."[36]

Among the exemplary places where Mann accords equal recognition to his speaking protagonists, giving Joseph's words a "sideward glance" at another's words, is a conversation between Joseph and

Mai-Sakhme (his jailer after his ill-fated sojourn on Potiphar's house) on their first encounter. After Mai-Sahkme hails Joseph as the "former steward of Petepre," Joseph responds, "I am he." As I have noted, it's the phrase he repeats throughout the tetralogy but with altered meaning each time; the changing Joseph is never the same "I" or "he." Mann then adds (in a subjunctive grammar that destabilizes subjective coherence), "He could have replied with a 'so you have said,' or 'my lord knows the truth,' or even the more flowery 'Ma'at speaks from your mouth.'" Or "'Your servant,' or I true abasement, 'This servant here.'" Through the way he shapes the dialogue, Mann is stating that there is no single context one can privilege as definitive. That assertion acquires veracity from what immediately follows: "But worse still, the 'I' itself played an alarming role, for in connection with the 'he' it raises a value 'suspicion' as it destabilizes the Joseph subject." What Mann suggests is that "old, familiar phrase . . . I am he" carries with it complicated and contestable historical resonances, which he renders with a Bakhtin-like acknowledgment of the political implications of the dialogic context of language.[37]

Mann lends an extensive cultural geography as well to his Bakhtin-like perspective on dialogue. By the time the novel moves to the fourth book in the tetralogy, *Joseph the Provider*, it had become evident to Mann, who by then was writing in California, that "what the entire opus offers above all else, is a work of language on whose polyphonic sounds of the Near East are blended with something very modern, with the accents of a fictive scientific method, satisfied with how it delights in changing linguistic masks the way the hero changes the masks of the gods—the past of which has something strikingly American about it."[38] As Mann notes, with the linguistic form to which he refers he has sought to "emulate [Richard] Wagner with language alone." He construes the "governing principle" of Wagner's compositions as a "concealment of the production process through the appearing product." However, affirming the parodic mood of his style, Mann adds that his own "work" has been too honestly "ironical" for total emulation: "I have always taken pleasure in compromising the act of productivity in some humoristic fashion or other."[39]

Before I rehearse more elaborately the Wagner effect in Mann's compositions, I want to pick up and reflect on Mann's reference to

28   AESTHETICS OF EQUALITY

"gods" (in the plural), which provides a strong hint about both Mann's implied reader and his own ironic detachment. Taking the "gods" reference along with Mann's essayistic meta statements into account, especially one with which he closes his epic story—"And so ends this invention of God, this beautiful story of *Joseph and His Brothers*"[40]—it's evident that the novel imagines a notably different reader from the one that Auerbach posits for the Old Testament (one who as noted reads the biblical text to be enlisted as a participate in the Covenant). What for example can one make of the expression, "this invention of God?" in that closing sentence? I suggest that it's a moment of biting irony that evokes Nietzsche's parodic treatments of the biblical Yahweh, for example his observation, "It was a piece of subtle refinement that God learned Greek when he wanted to become a writer, and that he didn't learn it better."[41] Playing on the word "invention," Mann's antitheological perspective accords with Nietzsche's implication that God is a media personality, an invention of the biblical scribes. Moreover, he is Mann's (re)invention, a character in a parodic Joseph story in which he (Mann) develops a subversive religious sensibility that he articulates through Joseph. Joseph is "one," Mann writes, "who did not discover God, but knows how to 'treat' him, one who is not only the hero of his stories, but their director, even their poet, and who embellishes them; one who still participates in the collective-mythical, but in a witty-spiritual way, playful, purposeful-conscious way."[42] Mann does his own embellishing in the "Prelude" to the volume of the tetralogy, *Joseph the Provider*. In a Nietzsche-like passage he does a parody of the presumption of God's omnipotence. Suggesting that a "mere 'Let there be' carries 'risks' and 'may have been insufficient to prevent ... blunders and highly otiose effects,'" he proceeds to ponder (turning yet again to the subjunctive) whether it would have been better to create "angelic beasts" rather than separating "angels from beasts."[43]

Crucially, while serving as a relay for the ironic distance that Mann evinces from a religious sensibility, the textual Joseph explicitly conveys that aspect of Mann's style. In a response to his jailer, Mai-Sakhme's mood management of the jail—"keeping a happy medium, respect tinged with gloom"—Joseph replies, " 'I'm not much of a master of gloom,' . . . 'Perhaps one could lend the respect a tinge of irony.' "[44] Joseph also serves as a voice to explicate Mann's compositional style in which various motifs are repeated. When he is summoned to interpret Pharaoh's enigmatic dream, he explains the pattern of his falling and rising (Mann's "well" motif) to Pharaoh's "runner," who has been charged with bringing Joseph to the palace: " 'You can see my friend,' 'how things stand with me,' Joseph says . . . 'They are hastily releasing me from this hole and pulling me from the well according to an old pattern.' "[45]

Political Obligations and Sensibilities

As Michael Minden infers, the tetralogy encourages more of a contemporary political rather than religious sensibility. He attributes the political sense it promotes to its genre (the romantic novel): "The novel is consumed in private but addresses the public sphere." Within that framing, the political obligation that the novel solicits applies to citizen subjects rather than religious adherents. Instead of assembling a collective that is allegiant to a Covenant, it "confirms the reader's membership" in that public. It thus participates in the diverse modern media genres with which one or another public sphere is assembled.[46] To contrast the novel's and the biblical text's readers in this way is to recall the important historical period that J. G. A. Pocock identifies as the "Machiavellian moment," which associates Machiavelli's writings with the emergence of Atlantic Republicanism. That ideational event was an ontological shift in the temporality of human existence. Unlike the "theocentric" view of time as eternal, "The republic was not timeless . . . it did not reflect by simple correspondence the eternal order of nature . . . The thing most clearly known about republics was that they came to an end in time";[47] they were subject to historical rather than eternal time, which translated as a political obligation assigned to citizenship in the dominant political venue of the period, the city. If people are to be understood as historical beings rather than eternal ones, they have civic responsibilities. Instead of merely exhibiting a morality that will guarantee their salvation—as they are required to exhibit within a (Christian) theocratic understanding—they are enjoined within Machiavelli's embrace of republican historical time to exhibit civic virtue.

30   AESTHETICS OF EQUALITY

Given that he writes in a post–Machiavellian moment, Mann's reader is already constructed as a citizen subject. Because his novel therefore addresses a potentially acting rather than a piously interpreting reader, a politically engaged approach to the Joseph tetralogy requires an assessment of what it does as well as how it means. Operating in an era of dangerous mentalities (during the emergence of fascism), Mann's tetralogy turns to mythic archetypes to look for and model humanity's better civic selves. And ironically, as Mann lengthens Joseph's story (inspired by Goethe's remark that the biblical story is "most charming, only it seems to short, and one feels inclined [to] put in the detail"),[48] he provides a Joseph who "represents the essence of humanity . . . because he embodies a *shortened* [my emphasis] version of human history."[49]

As I have been suggesting, the main political effect of what Mann's text does is owed to the compositional, grammatical and rhetorical structures with which it unsettles hierarchies and instills an equal eligibility for moral solicitude for all of humanity. It is arguably an effect that belongs to the development of the novel as a genre in general. In his analysis of Auerbach's contributions to novelistic realism, Jacques Rancière makes that case. Attributing an equality-promoting effect to the genre, he notes that whereas within the classic Aristotelian "division of poetic genres" they were "classed . . . according to the dignity of the subjects represented . . . Elevated genres—tragedy or epic—suited only elevated characters, kings and heroes [while] . . . The representation of lessor people was the job of low genres, comedy and satire [and] "novelistic realism broke that 'taboo.'"[50] Mann's Joseph tetralogy is exemplary in that respect; it elevates all its characters to equal status with an equality-promoting ethico-political sensibility that is intensified by its paratactic structure. All the character's stories are arranged side by side, in contrast with a hypotactic structure that would have subordinated all other character's stories to Joseph's.

As for how the novel thinks, I want to suggest that Mann's literary approach to equality articulates with the musical forms he mimics. The music-inspired compositional structure that organizes Mann's prose— a tonality in which every note has an equal value—migrates into what Rancière refers to as novelistic equality in which there is "the equality of subjects and the availability of any word or and phrase to build the fabric of any life whatever."[51] It is an aesthetically delivered equality;

"not the molar equality of democratic subjects, it is the molecular equality of micro-events, of individualities that are no longer individuals but differences in intensity."[52] The egalitarian force of Mann's text is clearly articulated in the tetralogy's most telling micro-event, a crucial conversation during which Joseph is disabused of the illusion that he sits at the center of his story. It's a dialogue about centers, framed as a politics of discourse in which Joseph's words and his perspective on his location in the story lose their privilege.

Joseph's Centers

Part 1 of the third volume of Mann's tetralogy begins with Joseph's question to Kedma, one of the nomadic Ma'onite traders who purchased him after his brothers had decided to sell rather than slay him. "Where are you leading me?" Joseph asks? Kedma responds, "Where are we leading you? So we're leading you, is that it? We're not leading you at all! You happen to be with us because Father bought you from harsh masters, and you're traveling with us wherever we go. You can't very well call that 'leading' you."[53] After Joseph persists in his assumption that the Ma'onites are part of his story but he adjusts his locution, "No? Well then, not . . . I only meant: Where is God leading me by having me travel with you?" Kedma responds, "You have a way of putting yourself in the middle of things that leaves a man not knowing whether to be amazed or angry. Do you suppose, Hey there, that we journey simply so that you may arrive somewhere your god wants you to be?"[54]

Joseph tries to hold onto his center imagery, at least as far as *his* story is concerned. Responding to Kedma's last remark, he offers a pluralistic version by suggesting that there are multiple circles and admitting that although he is not in the center of Kedma's, he is in his: "But behold, the world has many middle points, one for each creature . . . I . . . am in the middle of my own circle."[55] By the time he has met Kedma's father, the head of the nomadic trading family, his reputation for topological narcissism has preceded him. The merchant's first words are, "I hear . . . that you have said you are the navel of the world?"[56] After Joseph repeats his "many mid points" perspective, the merchant

32 AESTHETICS OF EQUALITY

responds that his pluralization "amounts to the same thing . . . What do you suppose would happen if every dunce and dullard in the great muddle of mankind were to walk about regarding himself as the navel of the world, and what would we do with so many middle points? [and adds with heavy sarcasm] . . . was that well then the world's holy middle point?"[57]

At this stage in the narrative, Joseph is perceiving the world through what the novelist, Milan Kundera, calls a "median context," a universal impulse by which "every people in search of itself thinks about where to locate the margin between its own home and the rest of the world."[58] Unsettling that tendency in Joseph, Mann's novel imposes three effects on the Old Testament's biblical story. One is through parody; the ironic remarks of the Maʾonite creates a "countersong" to the more heroic version of the scribes. Another is articulated by Mann's geographic ontology; through the discursive recalcitrance of Joseph's interlocutors, his perceptual topography is unsettled. A third is compositionally delivered; as noted, the novel is structured as a *Bildungsroman* that chronicles the growth of a character's awareness of the world's complexities, giving us a durational Joseph who ultimately retreats from his original mapping of space as he cedes legitimacy to other topological ontologies.

Here once again Auerbach's genre insights help us appreciate Mann's novelistic (and biblically observant) way of constructing the "great figures" in the Old Testament stories. Distinguishing the treatment of those figures from the classic Homeric heroes, Auerbach points out that whereas the Homeric heroes "have no development . . . their life-histories are clearly set forth once and for all," the "figures of the Old Testament [are] more fully developed"; their lives are "fraught with their own biographical past" and what they become "proceeds gradually, historically, during the earthly life upon whom [Yahweh's supposed] choice has fallen."[59] Auerbach's genre perspective accords with what Bakhtin suggests about a novel that features a *Bildungsroman* narrative (at least in the case of an "incomparably rarer type"). It "provides an image of man in the process of becoming"; it's a "novel of human emergence."[60]

Because Mann's tetralogy is structured nonchronologically, it emphases how the past persists in Joseph's unfolding present. In

THOMAS MANN'S JOSEPH TETRALOGY   33

addition, the treatments of Joseph's changing self-understandings have a temporal complexity. Displaying uneven temporal rhythms, the tetralogy represents the growth of Joseph's self-awareness gradually and intermittently. His story is punctuated occasionally by strikingly episodic effects, for example at a point in which Mann introduces an epiphany rather than a more gradual departure for Joseph's escape from his biographical past. Moderating the charge levied against Joseph by Kedma, the account suggests that the charge "ignores," the effect of "those three black days [in the well] that had preceded Joseph's rising anew. They and their cruel pains had forced him to see the fatal error of his previous life and to renounce any return to it; they had taught him to affirm his brothers' trust in death."[61] Having "foresworn his juvenile self-centeredness,"[62] Joseph had already decided that his prior self was no longer among the living. As Mann puts it in an essayistic intervention, "If to be 'dead and gone' means to be bound to an inviolable state that permits no backward wave, no greeting, not the slightest resumption of relationships with one's former life; if it means to have vanished ... then Joseph was dead."[63]

Joseph's alterations, a dispersion through which his story shares the textual space with many others whose similar multiplicities receive detailed coverage (they all have more than one name)—men and women, the economically and attributionally exalted and the low borne—to constitute the political sensibility that the novel articulates. It's a political perspective that deviates markedly from the geopolitical framing that the biblical scribes compose. The canonical narrative begins with Yahweh's promise to Abraham: "And I will give thee, to thy seed after thee the land wherein thou art a stranger, all the land of Canaan, for an everlasting possession" (Genesis 17:8), and proceeds to use the biblical protagonists to legitimate the possession of the land. However, to construct that legitimation, the scribes had to manage a contradiction, a structural complication that the anthropologist Edmund Leach has identified.

Given that "the *Old Testament*, as a whole, asserts that the Jewish political title to the land of Palestine is a direct gift from God to the descendants of Israel [Jacob]," the Israelites have to practice endogamy to legitimate the promised inheritance. However, as is well known, they "and their 'foreign' neighbors intermarry freely."[64] The common

34   AESTHETICS OF EQUALITY

practice of exogamy was based on security policy rather than the requirements of ethno-national coherence. Intermarriage created the alliances through which the Israelites sought to protect themselves from their enemies. In order to overcome the contradiction the scribes strive—in the verses that treat non-Israelite women—to turn them into Israelites in order to maintain the "common descent" necessary to be "the divinely ordained owners of the whole promised land."[65] As a result, the stories of the women whose sons are supposed to be part of the legitimating descent—Tamar, Rachab, Ruth, and Bath-Sheba, and Abagail—have to be reinvented as Israelites. As Leach points out the "five stories" in which they are featured "keep harping in a single theme which centers on the question of whether it is possible for a "pure blooded Israelite to beget legitimate children from a woman who is not Israelite, or conversely for an Israelite woman to bear an Israelite child after cohabitation with a man who is not a pure Israelite."[66] The structure that Leach extracts in his reading of the biblical stories has had a persistent historical life. In modern times it has been the basis for the much-contested "Jewish" claim to the "right to the city" of Jerusalem—a "right" issue famously addressed by Henri Lefebvre (to which I turn more elaborately in subsequent chapters).

In contrast with the land title legitimation that Leach's reading sketches, Mann's politics of place is a critique of the privileging of central stories, the collective one (the Israelite's ascension to a title to the land) and an individual one (Joseph's). In particular, his treatment of Joseph's story deconstructs the very idea of a center. As I have noted elsewhere, the form of Mann's novel comports well with critical cinematic approaches.[67] His text is a literary actualization of what Gilles Deleuze ascribes to cinema: "Cinema does not have subjective perception as its model," he writes, "because the mobility of its centers and the variability of its framings always lead it to restore vast acentered and deframed zones."[68] Having constructed his approach to the Joseph story as a film-like literary montage, Mann turns to poetic and musical figuration and reports that his novelistic treatment of the biblical Joseph allowed him to gloss a world of diverse styles (what he calls "lyricisms") and positions that were in flux, a process of merging from the many to the one. Describing that distribution of lyricisms, he states, "all that is Jewish, throughout the work, is merely foreground,

THOMAS MANN'S JOSEPH TETRALOGY   35

only one style element among others, only *one* stratum of its language which strangely fuses the archaic world and the modern, the epical and the analytic," and adds that the poem in the last volume, "the song of annunciation (sung by a child to the aged Jacob) is an old composition of psalter recollections and little verses of the German romantic type, a musical fusion that is an example of the character of the whole work, which seeks to blend a great many things, and because it imagines everything human as a unity, it borrows motives, memories, allusions, as well as linguistic sounds from many spheres."[69]

As he resists subordinating characters to a single narrative thread, Mann practices another cinematic method, the long take characteristic of "slow movies."[70] For example, in a section in which Joseph is in "the second pit" (the imprisonment to which he is assigned after the accusations of Potiphar's wife Mut), Mann breaks into the story with a rationale for his long take-like focus on personalities. Referring to the even temperament of Mai-Sakhme, the warden of the prison holding Joseph, Mann writes that to illuminate the qualities of "the jailer," he is "intentionally . . . in no hurry." He is letting the "spotlight . . . rest on him long enough for you [the reader] to have time to imprint his essential humanity—previously as good as unknown to you—on your minds; for a not insignificant supporting role . . . has been reserved for him in the story."[71] That method, a "long take style," as the Russian film director Andrei Tarkovsky describes it, gives the viewer "an opportunity to live through what is on screen as if it were his own life, to take over the experience imprinted in time on the screen."[72] As Mann suggests, it's the opportunity his style gives his reader. Mann's slow deliberative construction of Mai-Sakhme is exemplary of his writing style, which is homologous with his normative mentality. Stylistically as well as thematically the tetralogy articulates an egalitarian, democratic, ethos. Within its nonlinear progression, the narrative gives equivalent attention to disparate characters and their life worlds.

Especially notable in that respect is Mann's elaboration of the different ways that religion connects with politics for Israelites versus Egyptians. Setting up the comparison he remarks (within the narrative), "One fails to recognize the unity of the world if one considers religion and politics as two fundamentally different things that have nor should have anything to do with each other."[73] As the tetralogy

36   AESTHETICS OF EQUALITY

progresses, it becomes evident that the theologico-political imperatives differ markedly for the two nations. The Israelite, Yahweh-imposed politics is aspirational. Treating that onto-political culture, Mann's narrative follows Genesis's preoccupation with the genealogically legitimating issue of the title to the land that Yahweh promises Abraham. In sharp contrast, he features Egypt as an already consummated kingdom preoccupied with displaying its grandeur. It's a kingdom of light in which the Pharaoh is figured as radiance, as one "symbolized by the early morning sun."[74] Mann allows those two opposing systems to sit paratactically side-by-side, "suspended in mutually exclusive equipoise" without implied judgment,[75] while his Joseph serves as a mediator, situated in both his family's legitimating genealogy and (ultimately) in a position of command as an official in Egypt. After an experience of the sublime—Joseph is initially overwhelmed while being led through the golden city of On while on his way to meet the Pharaoh, "a city whose outward appearance made all eyes blink"[76]—he recovers from his mental "disarray" (Kant's famous expression for the initial effect of an encounter with the sublime) and is able to comprehend what is characteristic of Egypt's preoccupation with display and ornamentation. It was a kingdom whose architecture and decoration served Egypt's theological politics. Joseph observes that "the young Pharaoh," in whose administration he is to be employed, "had made the pictorial ornamentation of the world the object of his eager, indeed zealous attention, had done so . . . in complete accord with the efforts he expended in conceiving and advancing the god Aton in all his truth and purity."[77] Managing an aesthetic rather than an aspirational polity, those governing Egypt had shaped its visual expressivity. Viewing an abundance of that expressivity, especially Egyptian statuary, as he moves through the country—"forbidden things"[78] for the Joseph that is Jacob's son—Joseph is forced to reflect on his disjunctive situation. Belonging initially to a people who practice the imperative, "Thou shalt not make to thyself any graven image," he has been assimilated into a world that was "speaking in the language of aesthetics."[79]

As Joseph's sojourn ends with his assimilation as an Egyptian— "both his flesh and bodily garment were of pure Egyptian stuff."[80] Mann has him standing athwart the two political cultures. The once self-centered Joseph has been culturally dispersed. No longer anchored in the singular self he had performed as "the dreamer," he has had to take over the scripting of a continually unsettled life that he has learned to endure. A Bakhtin observation captures Joseph's situation: "Authors are open to themselves by seeing themselves as 'unconsummated,' as subjects who are always becoming, who are axiologically yet-to-be."[81] Settled in Egypt and thus living under "the sun of his adopted land," yet unsettled as regards the lingering responsibilities associated with his Israelite heritage, Joseph finds himself managing a dual life as he carries out his responsibilities to his two different peoples. He is explicit about the complicated authorship of his story. Pondering his role as "provider"—how to manage his family's pending arrival—he consults Mai Sakhme (his former jailer who has become his steward), saying, "'I don't know how to proceed with them and wanted to ask you for advice and support—you my steward, whom I have taken into this *story*'" (my emphasis).[82]

Mann thus composes a dual authorship, his and his main protagonist's. Within his story of Joseph, he has his Joseph character participate as an author of his own story. It's an authorship enabled by the way Joseph draws on the perspectives of those whom he has encountered after being displaced from his familiar place (e.g., Kedma and Mai Sakhme) and on *what* he has encountered, especially the materialization of the Egyptian aesthetic ontology. For example, "the sight of the Sphinx," as Mann tells it, "made on him . . . more impression that all he had hitherto seen in the land of Egypt."[83] Here Jacques Rancière's insight about the political consequences of such aesthetic experiences is apropos: "Aesthetic experience has a political effect to the extent that . . . it disturbs the way in which bodies fit their functions and destinations . . . It has a multiplication of connections and disconnections that reframe the relation between bodies, the world where they live and the way in which they are 'equipped' for fitting it."[84] To put it in the context of Joseph's itinerary, what enabled that political effect was his geographical displacement. Addressing that effect elsewhere, I've put it this way: "To be displaced is to be invited into an aesthetic experience, into a reorientation and reframing of one's sensible world. From the point of view of a radical politics, a displacement-engendered aesthetic experience disturbs authoritative distributions of social identity."[85]

38 AESTHETICS OF EQUALITY

Significantly for Mann's interest in a displacement story, he shares the ideational effect of Joseph's exilic condition. In Mann's case it was an America effect that registers itself clearly in the fourth book in the tetralogy, "Joseph the Provider," which he wrote while in exile in California. However, Mann's experience of exile, ensconced as he was among much of Germany's exiled intelligentsia residing in close proximity (many in frequent conversation) with him in California, his exile had not left him eager for a homecoming. As he put it in a letter to the Hungarian classicist Karl Kerényi (also in exile nearby), " 'Exile' has become something wholly different than in the past; it is no longer a condition of waiting oriented for a home-coming but a foretaste of a dissolution of nations and a unification of the world."[86] With a political mentality that migrated from an early "intoxication with nationalism," through a growing cosmopolitanism while moving through his exile, first in Switzerland and then in the United States, to his ultimate attachment to the version of democratic equality he witnessed during the Franklin D. Roosevelt administration, his changed political sensibility is registered in his last version of Joseph as the "provider." It's a version of Joseph fashioned as a bicultural character with a modern democratic sensibility (a reviewer in *The New York Times* refers to the Joseph in that book as "A New Deal Man in Egypt").[87]

Along with Mann's attachment to Roosevelt's political initiatives was a turn—subsequent to his Joseph work—in his musical investigations. He supplemented his Wagnerian emphasis on motifs with atonal musical effects, owed to a musical trajectory running from late Beethoven through Schoenberg, where atonal composition eschews "the subordination of notes to the hierarchical key system in tonal music" and gives every note the same value. "In political terms," as Evelyn Cobley suggests, "this strategy aspires to be radically egalitarian."[88] My suggestion is that Mann's egalitarian impulses, thematically and formally, were incipient in his Joseph novels but lacked the acute conceptual sensibility that he was to develop later in his adoption of atonality as a compositional inspiration.

To appreciate the influence of the turn toward atonality in modern music, which shapes Mann's thoroughly musically oriented later work, *Doctor Faustus*, is to recognize that like his Joseph (whom Mann has consult with Mai Sakhme, to cope with his exilic challenges), Mann

THOMAS MANN'S JOSEPH TETRALOGY 39

relies on an adviser who shares his (Mann's) exilic situation. In his case it's the philosopher/musician/critical theorist, Theodor Adorno, an influence that was both indirect (Mann carefully read his *Philosophy of Modern Music*), and direct; through correspondence and face-to-face encounter Mann solicited advice from Adorno about how to implement modern musical form in his Faustus novel. Remarking that Adorno "knows every note in the world," Mann credits his Nietzsche-like "searching criticism," which helped him "rediscover a long familiar element in" himself and achieve the "mental alacrity" he needed to think through the music-politics relationship that modernist musical composition encourages.[89]

While exploring that music-attuned political thinking, which ultimately shaped Mann's egalitarian ethos, asserting itself first in the decentering effects throughout his Joseph tetralogy, I draw inspiration from Mann's grammatical playfulness and in the spirit of Barthes's "productive reader," I enact my own grammatical intervention to situate critically the musical influences running from Wagner through Schoenberg. I first locate Mann's approach to the Joseph work in a past tense, exploring the way Wagnerian form is infused within his writing in a trajectory from his early novels through the Joseph tetralogy. Then turning to a subjunctive grammar, I imagine how the Joseph story *might have been* had it been shaped by modernist musical form, the primary compositional effect shaping his *Doctor Faustus*. An earlier familiarity with that musical development could have inspired Mann to compose his Joseph work in ways that would have more adequately fulfilled the egalitarian democratic aspirations toward which the tetralogy gestures.

Wagner's musical innovations set the stage for later atonal compositional approaches. They enabled a musical progression culminating in Schoenberg, who (as Adorno puts it, "achieves . . . a 'transcendent negation' of tonality . . . meant to disturb and unsettle us as we listen, whereas Wagner's art [acording to Adorno] practiced a comparatively shallow method of 'representing passions.' "[90] Schoenberg testifies that Wagner's musical innovations were a condition of possibility for the emergence of the atonality and the emphasis on dissonance that were to be his (Schoenberg's) compositional signature. "Wagner's harmony," he states, "had promoted a change in the logic and constructive

40   AESTHETICS OF EQUALITY

power of harmony . . . tonality was already dethroned in practice, if not in theory [participating] . . . in what I call *the emancipation of dissonance*."[91]

The Wagner Effect: From *Buddenbrooks* to the Joseph Tetralogy

To situate the inspiration that Wagner's music provided for the compositional structure of Mann's early writings, I want to locate the innovative compositional aspects of the Wagner effect as it was articulated in other literary work by reviewing David Michael Hertz's comprehensive narrative of the literary emulations of Wagner's musical form. The Wagner effect expressed itself in a "new approach in which plot loses is command in favor of linguistic play."[92] As for what of Wagner Mann emulated, the affected literary practice was inspired by Wagner's disruption of a traditional "tonal text," encouraging a writing style that shuns ordinary "ordering constraints" and uses an "open-ended paratactic, and elliptical" compositional structure. "Parataxis (placing side by side)" contrasts with "hypotaxis (arranging under)," where the latter (as Hertz notes) "requires a clear hierarchy of events."[93] To substitute a paratactic compositional structure for a hypotactic one is to practice what Adorno refers to as "judgmentless judgment."[94]

Central to the Wagner effect was the fracturing of the traditional quadratic form, which disrupted the "cultural code of expectations that is mutually understood by the composer and [her]/his listener" and inspired compositional innovations among both composers and writers.[95] Where Wagner's compositions deliver a series of a "*cadence rompue[s]*" (Schoenberg was later to refer to them as "sense-interrupting" effects[96]), the literary implementations of those effects are realized as texts punctuated by aesthetic breaks. Thus, Stéphane Mallarmé, influenced by the way "Wagner sews a new motif into the heart of cadence [so that] . . . Musical punctuation is defunct at the expense of organic continuity,"[97] picked up the challenge with similar punctuation. In his verse, he obfuscated "the syntactic hierarchy of the poetic line" by interspersing silences (effectively like musical rests) with "blank space[s]."[98] His "language is used to create startling,

THOMAS MANN'S JOSEPH TETRALOGY 41

arresting effects."[99] Similarly, Gustave Flaubert, writing in the midst of a Wagner-influenced French musical milieu that valued asymmetry, strove to avoid "the old symmetrical rhythm of poetry," which he did by listening to his words—"shouting out his prose in his apartment."[100]

That Wagner effect, a paratactic concatenation of motifs that defy narrative symmetry and continuity, is also abundantly evident in Mann's early novels. While in his first novel, *Buddenbrooks* (1901), the Wagner-inspired musical effects are apparent in the overall composition with its recurring leitmotifs, those effects are more explicit in his novella *Tonio Kröger*, published two years later. His protagonist, Tonio, explicitly cites Wagner's *Tristan und Isolde* in a section in which he refers to "the bliss of the commonplace," in close juxtaposition with a reference to "awe-inspiring, holy Russian literature." Here, as in the Joseph novels, a protagonist relays Mann's perspective (Mann had explicitly stated that Wagner satisfies sophisticated needs and "commonplace ones"). In a 1933 lecture he presents that view, in which he attributes to Wagner both "dilettantism raised to the level of genius" and the ability to "persuade even the unmusical to listen to music."[101]

Along with the novella's explicit thematization of Wagnerian themes is its Wagnerian musical form. Like a Wagner opera, the novella has a musical structure that J. A. Kelly appropriately describes as a "perfect triptych": "We have first the exposition, Tonio's youth, then, preceded by lyric-philosophic intermezzo . . . the crisis, the hero's unhappy visit to his old home . . . another transition, the storm [here one sees a Beethoven effect as well, viz. the storm in his *Pastoral*], and finally the dénouement, his awaking in Denmark. The parallels between the last part and the first are many and striking."[102] Throughout the novella there are the kind of leitmotifs that Mann was subsequently to implement pervasively in the Joseph tetralogy, a frequent repetition and changing of names (to which I have referred). For example, there's a moment in which complicated attractions and problematic disclosures have the character Hans calling Tonio by his family rather than given name.[103]

By the time Mann wrote his 1924 novel, *The Magic Mountain*, his compositional approach was more pervasively Wagnerian. More explicitly symphonic than his Buddenbrooks, it's the novel in which

42 AESTHETICS OF EQUALITY

Mann frequently has a "musical phrase . . . serve as a 'veritable leit-motif' for a character—or for one character's perception of another."[104] As he testified,

> the novel was always for me a symphony. A work of counterpoint, a web of themes. Whereby the idea of musical motives is important . . . I myself have drawn attention to the impact of Richard Wagner's art in my own works . . . I especially follow Wagner in the use of leading motive carried into the narrative . . . not just in a merely naturalistic manner or reductionist treatment, but instead in the symbolic representation of music.[105]

As is well known, much of the novel's storyline mimics dramatic events in Wagner's *Parsifal*, which is a "music," to which Mann referred to as "the zenith of modernity and nor surpassed by anyone else."[106] While the novel picks up various Wagner motifs from *Parsifal*, for example the motif of wounding—there is *Parsifal's* Amfortas, the leader of the "Grail Order," who suffers a wound that won't heal, and *The Magic Mountain's* Castorp, who is portrayed as about to die of his wounds in battle—Mann's motifs are reversals; his *Magic Mountain*, like his Joseph tetralogy, has ironic transformations. While wounds signal moral impurities in *Parsifal* and are thus religiously allegorical, in *The Magic Mountain*, the wound motif is geopolitical. The willful ignoring of illnesses by individual characters serves as an allegory for Europe's failure to confront the militarization that a leading it toward World War I.

Mann's allegorically expressed critique of Europe's militarization was shared by his contemporary, the novelist (and fellow California exile) Herman Broch, who expresses his similar concern with an essayistic intervention on the wearing of uniforms. Referring to the soldier in a "generic" military uniform, he writes, "the soldier has no need to think deeply . . . for a generic uniform provides its wearer with a definitive line of demarcation between his person and the world; it is like hard casing against which one's personality and the world beat sharply and distinctly and are differentiated from each other; for it is the uniform's true function to manifest and ordain order in the world, to arrest the confusion and flux of life."[107]

I draw from the clothing motif in Broch's novel because it is a frequent punctuating motif in Mann's Joseph tetralogy, serving as one of the ways in which the work implements Wagnerian form. That motif begins with attention to Joseph's coat of many colors; proceeds to the garment left behind to be used by Potiphar's wife, Mum, to incriminate Joseph; is followed by the required change of clothes Joseph is given to meet the pharaoh in proper attire; and ends with details of his Egyptian wardrobe. In his last incarnation (as noted), "both his flesh and bodily garment were of pure Egyptian stuff" (which bespeaks the Egyptian identity Joseph ultimately performs along with his still deeply felt Israelite connection). Like the well motif, the clothing motif marks the transformations that constitute Joseph as a multiplicity—or as Mann suggests, as a multitonal "song" that locates him in many different musically figured biographical/historical situations. There is no one Joseph to be discovered. As Mann sequentially removes and replaces Joseph's masks (or often his garments), he does not deliver an ultimate, singular Joseph.

From Joseph to Doctor Faustus

Early in his *Doctor Faustus*, Mann's narrator, Serenus Zeitbloom, who has begun his literary account of the life of the composer, Adrian Leverkühn (the novel's protagonist who sells his soul to the devil in exchange for twenty-four years of musical creativity), introduces the musical idiom that is to pervade the novel. In contrast with a mere song—Mann's characterization of the narrative of the world of his Joseph story—Zeitbloom refers to the "tonality of life."[108] Thereafter the modernist musical idiom shaping the novel delivers its atonality, a dissonance-infused micropolitical sensibility. Where the Wagnerian framing of the Joseph tetralogy shapes a more or less progressive narrative that moves toward reconciliation, his *Faustus* is more Schoenbergian, a compositional strategy in which "the rational organization of the artistic processes of production—is broken up into disparate entities."[109] Early in the novel, Leverkühn—affected by the teaching of "the stutterer" Kretzschmar, who offers a radicalized view of Beethoven's sonata form (which sets the stage for further musical

44   AESTHETICS OF EQUALITY

innovation from Wagner forward)—composes in a Wagnerian style in an opera version of Shakespeare's *Love's Labor's Lost*. However, by late in the novel Leverkühn's composition the *Apocalypse*, which strikes the fearful Zeitbloom as a "pandemonium of . . . infernal laughter . . . the mocking laughter of hell," is Schoenbergian with its rhythmic upheavals and counterblows . . . "a dreadful mayhem" of alarming sounds, a musical commotion that appears as "a reprise of the Devil's laughter."[110] And importantly, from the point of view of what Schoenbergian form does, the work (explains Mann through his narrator) produces an "emancipation of dissonance from resolution, so that dissonance achieves absolute value, as can already be found in some passages in late Wagner [and in terms of it egalitarian metaphorical implications] . . . every cluster of sound can prove its legitimacy to the system."[111]

That expression of the Schoenberg effect showed up in other artistic genres, such as in the painter Wassily Kandinsky's attempt to render on canvass what he refers to as Schoenberg's radical "acts of mind." Kandinsky equated the "blotches, which have become fixed in [Schoenberg's] music," with compositional aspect of "his pictures."[112] Picking up on the homology, Adorno suggests that the Schoenbergian musical equivalent of a blotch "challenges music's façade of self-sufficiency."[113] However, I want to invoke a more radical expression, which accords with the description of Leverkühn's *Apocalypse* composition. In his analysis of Vermeer's canvasses Georges Didi-Huberman emphasizes blotches, which he suggests are enigmatic signs that because they lack a descriptive role, create a "catastrophic commotion" for the viewer. They disrupt closure with respect to what the painting depicts.[114] Schoenberg's music enacts a similar disruption. It picks up and extends what is resident in late Beethoven sonatas, which (as explicated by the novel's musical instructor, Kretzschmar) disrupt traditional categories and suspend the dynamic of "recapitulation" in way that is "subversive to [a traditional practice] of *social hierarchy* [my emphasis]."[115] Accordingly, I want to suggest that what Kandinsky discerned was the micropolitical potential of Schoenberg's compositions. As the novel's juxtapositions make evident, in its macropolitical sensibility Mann equates Leverkühn's pact with the Devil (his ultimately catastrophic bargain) with Germany's "national catastrophe," as the narrator Zeitblom puts it.[116] Elaborating, Zeitblom conveys Mann's purpose in using the Faustian biographical genre to lament the National Socialism catastrophe, which had, states Zeitblom, "turned Germany into an arena of war." "Such," Zeitblom adds, "is the background of my biographical effort."[117] In contrast, at a micropolitical level, the novel's form creates a *positive* political catastrophe. It "turns down" commitments to traditional sociopolitical hierarchies that privilege particular ways of voicing one's feeling and being ("catastrophe" from the Greek—καταστροφή—translates as the trope, to "turn down").[118]

My suggestion then is that while the novel's macropolitical sensibility is developed by equating Leverkühn's fall into illness with Germany's national sickness—after referring to "the period in which [Leverkühn's] health was at its nadir," Zeitblom points (on the same page) to "the collapse of Germany's authoritarian state"[119]—the novel's micropolitical sensibility is articulated in dissonant dialogic encounters that legitimate linguistic dispersion rather than imposing reassuring resolution. They mark Mann's migration from a Wagnerian to a Schoenbergian compositional form. Adorno succinctly captures the difference. He discerns an ontology of chaos underlying Schoenberg's works that distinguish them from Wagner's: "What was still unified and progressive in Wagner's composite work of art . . . unified by the rational organization of the artistic processes of production—is [to repeat the above quotation] broken up in disparate entities in Schoenberg's compositions."[120]

In one of those entities, there are vestiges of the Joseph story. Composing the Devil's encounter with Leverkühn, Mann turns again to a clothing motif and has the Devil changing shape and clothing styles throughout their conversation. Moreover, as is also the case with his use of Joseph, Mann has his Devil offhandedly explicating the novel's ironic style. The Devil affirms the novel as a parody at a point at which he credits his appearance changes to "mimicry . . . the mumchance of and conjuring of Mother Nature, who always keeps her tongue in her cheek."[121] However, for purposes of illustrating my primary concern with the novel—the Schoenberg-inspired micropolitical level of *Faustus*—rather than treating the conversation with the Devil

46 AESTHETICS OF EQUALITY

more extensively, I want instead to focus on what I regard as the novel's more exemplary conversation. At a moment in which Zeitblom and Leverkühn are discussing the latter's musical adaptation of Shakespeare's *Love's Labor's Lost,* the conversation turns to a wedding they had just attended. In an ironic mood, Leverkühn remarks that he was pleased that the Pastor's "wedding homily has been short and plain" and goes on to say he was positively impressed by the bridegroom whom he describes with a Nietzsche-like parody of devout Christian discourse:

Good eyes . . . good stock, an honest, sound, tidy gentleman. He was permitted to woo her, gaze upon her, covet her—covet to make a Christian wife of her, as we theologians say with justifiable pride at having smuggled the Devil out of the union of flesh by making a sacrament of it . . . [it's] really comical, how what is natural and sinful has been taken prisoner by the sacrosanct . . . one must admit that the domestication of what is naturally evil, of sex, by Christian marriage was a clever makeshift.[122]

Scandalized, Zeitbloom charges Leverkühn with "handing nature over to evil," to which Leverkühn replies, "You never get the joke. I was speaking as a theologian." The conversation, which is dialogic in Bakhtin's sense (every word is looking sideways at another possible word), is atonal in Schoenberg's. Metaphorically, there is no central musical key, or in a discursive idiom there is no commanding discursive space with which perspectives on the object of their conversation can be shared or reconciled. Zeitbloom reports that he was himself in the process of courting and is perplexed with respect to how to locate the love-sensuality binary under discussion within an appropriate discourse. In response, Leverkühn continues his reflection on the wedding ceremony, mentioning that the pastor had left out the passage, "And shall be one flesh." He then remarks, "Of course there is no way to separate sensuality and love," and goes on to complicate the subjectivity involved in the tension between Christian/moral and psychological discourses on the issue of sensuality. Interarticulating pious religious and psychological discourse—in effect staging an encounter between the apostle Paul and Sigmund Freud—Leverkühn says, "Lust

THOMAS MANN'S JOSEPH TETRALOGY   47

for another person's flesh means one has to overcome the resistance already blocking it, which is based on the strangeness of the *I* and the *you*, of the self and the other."[123] Although Zeitblom is put off by that remark, regarding it as tactlessness on Leverkühn's part, he finds himself nevertheless interested in what he is hearing and rejoins that Leverkühn is speaking "more as a humanist than a theologian." To that Leverkühn responds, "Let us say as a psychologist." "And how," asks Zeitblom, "would it be . . . if we were to speak now on a quite simple, personal bourgeois level?"[124]

It becomes apparent that the conversation has been aping a scene from Leverkühn's opera version of Act Four of *Love's Labor's Lost*. It's a work that had just "served for our jests," says Zeitblom, followed by Leverkühn remarking that he plans to instill counterpoint, a statement that affirms the musical frame within which Mann has staged the conversation. Speaking to the novel's micropolitical level, the dialogue suggests that there is no foundational discursive space within which to judge the tension between love and lust (or anything else). The staging of the conversation accords with what Jean-François Lyotard famously refers to as a "differend," a fight of phrases. In place of Immanuel Kant's figuration of philosophy as a 'tribunal,' where 'critical philosophy is in the position of a juridical authority,' Lyotard substitutes the "battle-field."[125] Citing what Kantian philosophy misses, "the negative events that engender 'the exploding of language into families of heterono-mous language games,'" encounters of incommensurable positions without recourse to a universality with which they could be reconciled, Lyotard insists that one needs a "philosophy of phrases rather than one of the faculties of the subject."[126] A Lyotardian take on the conversa-tion accords with what a Schoenbergian atonality implies, the absence of a stable frame of reference and thus a recognition of a fundamental dissonance (the essence of Schoenberg's compositions). It is thus ap-ropos to note Slavoj Žižek's analysis of the ethos that is immanent in the novels of Henry James (and applicable to Mann's), "the lack of a fixed frame of reference," as he puts it, "far from simply condemning us to moral relativism, opens up a new 'higher' field of ethical experi-ence, that of intersubjectivity, the mutual dependence of subjects, the need to not only rely on others, but also to recognize the ethical weight of others' claims."[127] Of course, that presumes a social arena open to

48 AESTHETICS OF EQUALITY

hearing and giving equal weight to all the claims, an issue to which I return.

Joseph and His Brothers, Reinflected

Returning to Mann's Joseph tetralogy to fulfill my promise to speculate about how it might have been composed had Mann been cognizant of the musical innovations in Schoenberg's compositions, I want to begin by conceding that the seeds of Mann's later compositional form in his *Faustus* had already been planted in his Joseph novels. They are apparent specifically in the decentering dialogues between Joseph and the Ma'onites, conversations that challenge what I called Joseph's narcissistic topology (locating him in the center of his story and his story in the center of his time). They are also apparent in the subjunctive grammar with which Mann imaginatively revises Joseph's possible responses to Mai-Sakhme's identity query during their first encounter (composed as a series of could-have-saids quoted above); they are even more apparent in what I referred to as Mann's intervention with a Nietzsche-like speculation that undermines the notion of God's omnipotence, where (to repeat the quotation) Mann suggests that such God talk as "let there be . . . may be insufficient to prevent . . . blunders and highly otiose effects," and proceeds to ponder whether it would have been better to create "angelic beasts" rather than "separating angels from beasts."[128]

That the text fails ultimately to live up to those more radical language- and authority-contesting moments is doubtless owed to Mann's adherence to a version of polyphony that (as he said in his Library of Congress lecture) yields a composition that is a "musical *fusion* (my emphasis) which seeks to blend a great many things . . . because it imagines everything human as a unity." Had he been familiar with the "disjunct atonal style" he later gleaned from Schoenberg (through Adorno) and implemented it in his later *Faustus*,[129] the democratic sensibility articulated in his Joseph tetralogy *might have been* articulated differently. To actualize that "might have been," I suggest a way that one of the dialogues *could have been* composed more dissentually. When Joseph's sojourn in the "second pit" is ending, because a courier

THOMAS MANN'S JOSEPH TETRALOGY   49

has been sent to bring him to the Pharaoh, the conversation opens with Joseph describing his unfortunate situation to a man who is concerned only with his delivery task. Joseph's initial response to the courier, after being hailed by one of his many names, is "Your name is Usarsiph?—is his oft repeated, 'I am he.'" After then being told that he must accompany the courier, who identifies himself as Pharaoh's "first runner," Joseph wonders, "How can that be? I am too lowly for that."[130] There follows Joseph's further remarks to the courier and then to his jailer, Mai-Sakhme. Both are observations that serve not only to manage the particular interactions (operating at an interpersonal level in the narrative) but also to explicate the compositional style of Mann's tetralogy because they operate at a meta level.

To the courier Joseph says, "I was placed in this prison . . . though to be sure due to a misrepresentation, after having been stolen, so to speak, and brought down here. But here I lie as a slave condemned to hard labor, and though my chains may not be visible, they are there. How could I depart with you through these walls and gates to board your express boat?"[131] Then, once the courier has asserted his authority to extract him from his prison, to Mai Sakhme he says (here I'm repeating a passage quoted above), "You can see, my friend, how things stand with me and what is being done with me after three years. They are hastily releasing me from this hole and pulling me from the well according to an *old pattern*" (my emphasis).[132] While to the courier Joseph is explaining not only his condition but also the kingdom's structure of punitive servitude, to Mai Sakhme he is providing much more; he is explicating two of the tetralogy's motifs, that of the oft appearing well—a nodal point for character encounters throughout the tetralogy—and that of the casting down and raising up of his situation, the tetralogy's most persistent motif. As a commentary addressed to the tetralogy's Wagnerian compositional structure states (which captures the complexities of Joseph's parting remark to Mai-Sakhme), there is first "the simple recurrence of leitmotivs" followed by the "subsequent equation or merging into complexes."[133] Lest the reader miss the significance of the recurrences, Joseph helps by referring to "an old pattern."

I too want to extract Joseph, albeit from his *double* servitude—from the moments when he verbally capitulates to the forces controlling

50   AESTHETICS OF EQUALITY

him at each stage of his journey and from his acquiescence to being the character fashioned to serve Mann's Wagnerian narrative, expressed in those moments when he validates its structure and rhythms with theme-supporting remarks. To render Joseph as a more "unpredictable subject" with a dissonant voice (in the manner that the atonal compositional style of Mann's *Faustus* renders its voices) we have to have him resisting the way he is serially (mis)interpellated as he is hailed in the intersubjective moments that reflect his alternative names.[134] Mann has him already on his way toward resisting the first form of servitude. By merely speaking about his situation, he has retrospectively turned the trajectory of his spaces of servitude into political zones, a result of his being a voice rather than a mere set of laboring hands. He has thereby symbolically stepped out of the spaces that others have allocated to him.[135]

However, in a commentary reflecting on his tetralogy, Mann obscures that insight. Referring to his account of the changing Joseph, he invokes a Freudian idiom to conceive his character's emergence as a subject, referring to "the birth of the ego out of the mythical collective."[136] That conceptual construction yields a subject with potential for political participation as a self-understood individual but one without an intersubjective positioning, whether consensual or dissensual. Rather than treating the I-subject as an accomplished ego, ready to operate within a consensual social order, we can heed Gilbert Simondon's concept of individuation, a process of becoming without resolution. In contrast with a Freudian narrative in which the ego achieves comfortable coherence to the extent that it works its way successfully through a fixed narrative of stages, Simondon substitutes contingency. His preindividual exists as a domain of potentialities containing within it the possibility for alternative individuations. Within that framework, we can note how Mann has mapped Joseph's "theater of individuation,"[137] a becoming he has been undergoing throughout his binational encounters that have preserved the tensions in the dispersal of his "I am" rather than (as is suggested in Freudian ego psychology) moving him toward an accomplished stability, having resolved earlier traumatic phases. Within Simondon's approach to individuation, a movement from the contingencies afflicting the preindividual to those shaping the process of individuation, we observe a subject that is recalcitrant

THOMAS MANN'S JOSEPH TETRALOGY   51

to one merely pertinent to traditional liberal egalitarianism. Heeding that model of the emerging "I," we can reinflect the tetralogy toward an aesthetics of equality that incorporates an intra-subject and intersubjective dissensus, which lends Joseph more *im*pertinence.

For that imaginative recreation, we can have Joseph sound more like Kedma, who resisted being hailed as a minor character in Joseph's story. For example, summoning a neo-Althusserian perspective on interpellation (James Martel's reinflection of that Althusserian concept), we can reconsider the moment in which Pharaoh's courier hails him as Usarsiph and heed Martel's suggestion that "we have never been the subjects we thought we were . . . [and] are not in fact utterly determined and controlled by those identities we receive."[138] Accordingly, Joseph (sounding like Kedma) could have said, "Oh, so now I'm Usarsiph for your purposes" and then have added, "I have never been him for my own." And he *could have* followed up with, "I now understand that even in my first incarnation as 'Jacob's son' I was incarcerated in someone else's story" (one invented by the Old Testament scribes and repeated frequently by the novelist, albeit with parodic irony). Then, after Joseph presents his soliloquy on his physical incarceration ("having been stolen") and is told that his past is irrelevant because an aesthetic occupation (in many senses of the term) awaits him and cannot be resisted ("nothing stands before Pharaoh's beautiful will,"[139] rejoins the courier), Joseph has to capitulate to the summons and enter a world "with certain sanctified pictorial understandings," where even though he thrives in it, he is in someone else's story. To the extent that he will have had a hand in *his* story, it is one that must be *con*sonant with the way the Old Testament scribes and subsequently Mann have composed it.

So, I will give him one more opportunity to be *dis*sonant, noting the place where Mann has him utter his most complicated "I am," which, late in his territorial and identity journeys, testifies to what has become his binational and bigenerational identities (Israelite and Egyptian, son of Jacob and father to the young Pharaoh). It's the place where, shortly after Joseph has revealed himself to his brothers, he has to overcome their initial skepticism that he can be both the brother to whom they did evil and a "prince" who manages a vast kingdom and is bidding to be their savior. Here Mann once again invokes the clothing motif in a

52 AESTHETICS OF EQUALITY

passage that is clearly meant to mirror the Doubting Thomas episode in John 20:24–29 in the New Testament. However, whereas Thomas, to verify a resurrected Jesus, wants to see the "print of the nails" and to thrust his hand into the side wound a Roman spear had made during the crucifixion, the brothers take a gentler verification path: "Two or three of them actually touched him, gingerly stroking a hand along his garment." Then one of them, Issakhar, asks which body are they seeing, a prince or "only our brother Joseph." In response, Joseph recounts his duality: "Only? . . . That is surely the most of who I am. But you must understand me rightly; I am both." Another brother, Zebulun, then chimes in, "one surely cannot say that you are only the one and not the other, but instead must say that you are both in one."[140] Having experienced "the violent oscillations that overwhelm an individual," while having sought initially "only his own [ultimately 'unlocatable'] center," he finally recognizes that "an identity is essentially fortuitous . . . [that] a series of individualities must be run through each of these oscillations, so that as a result the fortuitousness of this or that particular individuality will render all of them necessary."[141]

I want to reset this scene and change Joseph's response to Zebulun in order to take advantage of a possible fraternal moment by imagining Joseph and his brothers' bodies arranged paratactically rather that hypotactically (i.e., side by side rather than in a subordinate-superordinate arrangement) and render the interlocutory encounter with Schoenbergian atonal dissonance, so that each voice/tone has the same value and as a result Joseph's voice is not a central tonic (a repeating major tone). Instead of Joseph and Zebulon accepting the "both," which renders Joseph as the all-powerful provider/prince and his brothers as the suppliants, thereby repeating the Old Testament scribes' and Mann's interpellation of Joseph as the oft repeated "Jacob's son," we can heed the tetralogy's title and stress the copula, *Joseph AND His Brothers*. Accordingly, Issakhar could have asked what body Joseph wants them to see, and Zebulon could have said, "can you choose between brother or prince so we can decide whether our burden should be that of the guilty or of the suppliant." Joseph in turn *could have* said, "I'd rather be either both of them and at various moments neither; let us assume that we are all of us free to share in the invention of how our past should be acknowledged and how our world-to-be should be composed, freed from the strictures of Yahweh's promise that our father has had us observe and freed from the other legacies of our family's history." We could then engage each of us in our own way in mutually supportive self-fashioning. We could for example liberate Reuben from his ignominy, a humiliating demotion in which he has dwelled since he bedded our father's concubine. Thus freed from the patriarchal burden articulated through the story's privileging of heredity, the normative mentality of Mann's work could have resulted (in Jacques Rancière's apropos terms) in "fraternal community... won in combat against the paternal community... destroying the portrayal of father, which is at the heart of the representational system... [to] open the future of a fraternal humanity."[142] "Democracy," Rancière suggests, when understood as not merely a particular kind or regime, "consists in [among other things] the act of revoking the law of birth... in the attempt to build a common world on the basis of... contingency."[143] Mann found a music compatible with such an egalitarian vision years after his Joseph had been left to remain in a song dominated by paternal motifs.

Nevertheless, there are places in which that song registers moments of antiphony that militate against a primarily patriarchal story. As I've noted Mann's attention to Tamar and Potiphar's wife stand out. However, I want to emphasize an earlier moment where there was a hint of Joseph's break from the congeniality he displayed in his conversation with Jacob in the "at the well" scene. Their "duet" (as Mann calls it) progresses harmoniously throughout most of the conversation as together they "rattle off" generational connections that locate their understanding of their obligation to the covenant for which their people (genealogically consolidated) has been chosen.[144] It is a conversation that Joseph understands as "fine discourse,"[145] a recitation of "things already known." However, near the end of their duet, Joseph recounts a dream he has "dreamt many thousand times," which foretells his being thrown into "the darkness of the pit" before being rescued by the Lord and being "made great among strangers." It's the kind of moment to which, Schoenberg, as I've noted above, refers as a *cadence rompue*. Sensing that break, Jacob is taken aback by Joseph's dream report, saying that the words are "imposing, but do not accord with reason," although Joseph passes off his dream report as merely an exercise of his "desire to say something grand for our lord."[146] It is the first sign of a break in the genealogical cadence of what otherwise would be a wholly paternally oriented version of Joseph's story. I want to figure that moment musically as a dissonant break in the novel's harmony, an atonal departure from the dominant tonic to which the tetralogy repeatedly returns. Hence, in order to imagine the tetralogy's egalitarian potential, I have rewritten a section to amplify resistance to Genesis's paternal sensibility, a resistance already intoned at moments *within* Mann's "Joseph song."

2

A Right to the City

Toni Morrison's Literary Jazz

What Can Music Say?

At roughly the same time that Thomas Mann was composing his "song of Joseph," using Wagnerian leitmotifs to structure the world of the Old Testament's Genesis chapter and (allegorically) his contemporary world, the composer Igor Stravinsky was saying, "I consider that music is, by its very nature, powerless to express anything at all, whether a feeling, an attitude of mind, a psychological mood, a phenomenon of nature. If . . . music appears to express something, this is only an illusion and not a reality."[1] Although Mann's Joseph story is a work of literature rather than a musical score, Mann convincingly appropriates the "meaning potential" of music, which is available to be "actualized within specific social [as well as historical] contexts."[2] While Adorno, from whom Mann learned to appreciate the nuances of atonality, expressed the view that aesthetics is autonomous rather than directly socially or politically relevant—"the function of art" for Adorno is to be "nonfunctional," as one commentary puts it[3]—he nevertheless shared with Mann the suggestion that what Schoenberg's atonality gestured toward is "life under late capitalism," while he saw Stravinsky's compositions as evasive with respect to "the conditions of modern life."[4]

In contrast with Adorno's ambivalence about music's autonomy from sociopolitical issues, there are compelling contemporary challenges to that position. One such challenge belongs to the development of jazz, which in both implicit and explicit ways has provided a political articulation of the historical conditions of the African American experience. The bebop version for which Charlie Parker was the major innovator "was [implicitly] more than just a set of musical procedures;

Aesthetics of Equality. Michael J. Shapiro, Oxford University Press. © Oxford University Press 2023.
DOI: 10.1093/oso/9780197670347.003.0003

56 AESTHETICS OF EQUALITY

it was also a musical vehicle for expressing Black dissatisfaction with the status quo."[5] As for the explicit, there is no more comprehensive treatment than Duke Ellington's *Black, Brown, and Beige* composition (1958). Inventing an aesthetic subject, Boola, Ellington has him beginning in Africa (in the "Black" segment), suffering through the Middle Passage, and ending up in America. After becoming a Christian, Boola is drawn by music to a Black church where he hears a hymn, "Come Sunday," orchestrated as a bluesy jazz version of a spiritual. Containing "short, lyrical statements by solo trombone and trumpet [that] introduce[s] a song" whose structure is a "typical blues style . . . 'flatted fifths,'" the hymn resonates with the emotional timber of a Black religious assemblage, which is kept outside the church but is vocally participating in the worship in progress inside: "The music holds still, catching its breath [as] the Blacks outside grunt/Subdued approval."[6] When the composition moves to the "Brown" section, "the rhythms and tonalities of the spiritual follow its historical and musical migration to the blues [as it] features the traditional twelve-bar blues structure . . . and by the time the composition moves to *Beige* . . . [it has been transformed] from a 'weary blues' mood to a hopeful one, reflected in the intellectual contributions of the Harlem Renaissance and the patriotic contributions of Black America's participation in the war effort."[7]

As for other explicit political articulations of jazz, notable is Lee Blanchard's soundtrack for Spike Lee's Hurricane Katrina documentary, *When the Levees Broke* (2006). In contrast with Ellington's interarticulation of musical and Black history, which sticks to a linear narrative, the Lee-Blanchard rendering of the Katrina event moves back and forth in both musical and Black history. As it elucidates the political economy of the Black experience in New Orleans, the film's music-image composition has the rhythms of the soundtrack match the rhythms of Lee's scene editing. As Ernest Callenbach puts it, "The rhythm of the music and the rhythm of the cutting concur."[8] Composed to capture the mood of an event, the music is a realization of the phenomenology of the storm. Blanchard punctuates the composition with silences to represent the aftermath of the storm and captures the effect of the wind with high-pitched jazz that mimics its howls. Figured variously as a "tragic symphony," as "a mass for the dead," and as a "requiem," the soundtrack is a vital part of the

A RIGHT TO THE CITY   57

documentary's meaning-making, which explicitly references aspects of African American musical history. It embeds the Katrina event in musically realized local Black history.[9]

More generally, to assess the most notable implicit music-politics connections in jazz we have to heed the way compositions have "fused form and content to deliver a political sensibility" (as I have put it elsewhere). Exemplary in that respect is "John Coltrane's *Alabama*, a composition with musical resonances of the rhythms of Martin Luther King's eulogy at the funeral of the four young African American girls who died when 'dynamite Bob' blew up a Black church in Alabama."[10] The piece "opens with Coltrane's saxophone interpreting the preacher, with [McCoy] Tyner's heavy, sad [piano] chords responding like the congregants. A third of the way into the five-minute song, there's a pause, a deep inhale, a moment to deal with the emotions, to gather sad thoughts. The four players [there is also Jimmy Garrison on the double base and Elvin Jones on drums] then go in conversation with the meanings and nuances of King's speech."[11]

Thelonious Monk's jazz compositions/performances are implicitly political as well, albeit in a different way. They feature "the creative pause"[12] ("Monk makes hesitation eloquent," as Nathaniel Mackey puts it).[13] Although his jazz contains no direct political statements and (unlike Coltrane's 'Alabama') reference no particular historical events, Monk's jazz politics operates through the way it partakes of "the fundamental oppositionality of a pervasive approach to language intelligibility of much of the African American assemblage."[14] His music functions like "Black talk," which has been an expression of an African discursive heritage. The counterintelligibility he performs mimics a "coded form of discourse developed among people who have not, in varying degrees and at different historical moments, been free to express themselves directly [or to participate] in mainstream . . . civic expression.'"[15] Monk's music thus engages what Paul Gilroy refers to as "a partially hidden public sphere."[16] Form wise, his musical realizations of the counterintelligibility practiced in that "fragile" Black public sphere proceed by restructuring the intervals in the original versions of popular songs.[17] Employing a resolution-deferring "microsyntax," they "contain a distinctive 'metapoesis'. . . [which] engages a 'very specific addressee or set of addressees'; as they recreate a 'Black vernacular

58   AESTHETICS OF EQUALITY

orality'" practiced by an assemblage able to manage the "structural hearing" necessary for effective reception and able to "feel" what Geneva Smitherman refers to as the music's "'tonal semantics.'"[18] Playing to those abilities, Toni Morrison, whose novel *Jazz* is the primary object of textual work in this chapter, strives as she has stated to make her sentences "speakerly."[19]

Why Jazz and Why Morrison?

As performed, jazz features polyphonies, atonalities, and innovative (mostly modular) harmonies, embodying the equality effects I attribute to Mann's realizations of Wagnerian and Schoenbergian compositional form in Chapter 1. What is added by turning to Morrison's *Jazz* is a novelistic realization of the way modern jazz—especially a free, improvisation version—articulates the African America urban experience. As one who has been concerned with recovering and reinflecting the Afro-American "presence in American literature,"[20] Morrison turns in *Jazz* to a cultural genre in which African Americans have been always already abundantly present. Sharing that presence, her musically figured literary composition operates on "the fringe of contact between music and language."[21] Her writing mimics a jazz performance as it animates Black voices, moving them from the margins of a white-dominated social order to give them a vocalized civic presence in American urban life.

There is a figurative bridge from Mann's Joseph tetralogy to Morrison's *Jazz*. Both contain well motifs. However, while Joseph survives being pitched into a well, in *Jazz* a well is a space of death; it's a place where the protagonist Violet's mother kills herself. Most significant for purposes of comparison, Morrison's novel, like Mann's tetralogy, is composed as a musical score, albeit a more improvisational one which comports with the free jazz structure inspiring it. As she explains in the Foreword, "Jazz is the engine" of my "compositional drama . . . I had written novels in which structure was designed to enhance meaning; here the structure would *equal* meaning . . . I didn't want simply a musical background, or decorative references to it. I wanted the work to be a manifestation of the music's intellect, sensuality, anarchy, its history, its range, and its modernity."[22]

A RIGHT TO THE CITY   59

There are other similarities between Mann's Joseph story and Morrison's *Jazz*. Form-wise, what is most notable is the way characters' voices are rendered musically in both texts. As I note in Chapter 1, by the time Mann wrote his 1924 novel *The Magic Mountain*, his compositional approach was more pervasively Wagnerian. More explicitly symphonic than his earlier Buddenbrooks; it's the novel in which Mann frequently supplants a character with a musical motif. Similarly, Morrison is explicit that her *Jazz* is a collection of musical voices. Mann and Morrison also share a visual aesthetic, ascribed to their respective venues. Just as Mann renders Egypt as an aesthetic kingdom, manifested in expressive architectural and decorative displays, Morrison renders her Harlem aesthetically, in her case through attention to body culture. Among her protagonists are the married couple Violet and Joe Trace, the former running a hair salon in her home and the latter selling "Cleopatra" cosmetics door to door (a brand name that links Morrison's novel with the Joseph story's last venue). There is also a similar use of characters. As I've noted, throughout the tetralogy Mann's Joseph explains the author's use of irony. Adopting a similar strategy, Morrison uses her character Violet to explain the text's jazz-mimicking, improvisational style; "What's the world for if you can't make it up the way you want it," she says at one point.[23] Finally, crucial to the comparison is the nature of the antiphonal musical forms that shape the poetic expression of their egalitarian sensibilities. To prepare for my reading of her novel, in which nameless narrators intervene in the text, adding voices to Morrison's textual jazz ensemble with temporal observations that render the musical text as historiographic, I draw inspiration from Morrison's meta narration and engage in my own interpretive intervention to amplify what the meta level of Morrison's novel discloses; it illustrates how a literary realization of a jazz performance can articulate an egalßitarian perspective.

Free Jazz and Its Egalitarian Ensembles

Recalling my intervention into a section of Thomas Mann's Joseph tetralogy in Chapter 1—the words I put in the mouths of Joseph and his brothers during their encounter near the end of *Joseph the Provider*—I

60   AESTHETICS OF EQUALITY

initiate my analysis by repeating a similar intervention. Inspired by listening to the way a composition developed through improvisation when Miles Davis joined Cannonball Adderley's quartet to perform *Autumn Leaves* (the first cut in the album *Somethin Else*), in a previous investigation I invented a discursive version of their musical performance:

ADDERLEY ET. AL.: "Here's how we imagine an introduction to the tune."
DAVIS: "OK; here's how I imagine its melodic mood."
ADDERLEY: "Thanks for that, here's how I am inspired to continue."
"OK, after that, I want to come back this way."
JONES, JONES, AND BLAKEY: "We're with it; does this bring us all together?"[24]

Gregory Clark, who sees that Davis-Adderley encounter as an expression of "civic jazz," reads the performance in a similar way, as a dynamic of consensus building from an initial dissensus:

> Playing together, they all five begin to sound something like the way people sharing the same car on a train might look; each one deep in his own thoughts and feelings . . . In this "Autumn Leaves," as each musician engages the others in the differences that divide them, they are bound inexorably together by the time, place, and purpose they share.[25]

Emphasizing the tensions between the ensemble's dissensual and consensual impulses, Clark adds that the musicians both "challenged and supported each other . . . the two primary soloists, Davis and Adderley, found ways to make what they had to say something they could say in this song together."[26] Figuring the performance as a conversation, I suggest that it begins with what Maurice Blanchot refers to as a third kind of relation. It is not appropriative in the sense that it creates a generalized sameness, nor is it a matter of fusion in which each person's distinctiveness is lost (his first two kinds of conversational interaction). Rather, it is founded on "leaving it still unfounded" what he calls "the *strangeness* between us: a strangeness it will not suffice to characterize as a separation or even as a distance."[27] It's a form of civic encounter that exemplifies a mutual recognition that does not extinguish individuality. Each of the conversation partners are acknowledged for their distinctiveness as the addressees all seek to learn from each other without losing themselves.

Among what is distinctive about such episodes of "jazz work" is the structural setting of the ensemble.[28] In contrast with the hypotactic (subordinating) structure of players in a symphony, where a group of already hierarchically differentiated musicians (e.g., the first, second and third violins) face a conductor who leads them, free jazz ensembles are typically arranged paratactically, in a leaderless structure spaced to facilitate serial interventions among the musical voices, as the musicians respond to each other to build toward a provisional collective statement. As one commentator puts it, "it's like a conversation . . . one guy will create a melodic motif or a rhythmic motif and the band picks it up. It's like sayin' that you are all talking about the same thing."[29]

Exemplifying that ensemble effect, Duke Ellington, who as I've noted elsewhere, "was keenly sensitive to the interrelationships among his players,"[30] organized the performance of his compositions to assure recognition of both the individuality of each musician and the dynamic rapport of the ensemble. For example, to lend attention to the contribution of an individual musical voice in his saxophone section, rather than "wasting . . . [Harry] Carney's very personal tone," in his band's version of *Tishmingo Blues,* he gave him "important notes [within the C-ninth] chord that specifically determine the quality of that chord."[31] The antiphony-embracing democratic ethos informing Ellington's construction of an alternating consonance and dissonance in the delivery of his compositions is exemplified in a moment of antiphony in his *Creole Love Call.* In that performance he "superimposes over . . . three sustained clarinets a short figure that momentarily clashes with them," a "precursor," as Gunther Schuller puts it, "of a long line of such harmonic clashes."[32] The Adderley-Davis et al. performance of *Autumn Leaves* exemplifies the Ellington egalitarian ethos and mix of harmonic consonances and dissonances. While substantively the piece is about how it feels to have lost love, at a meta level it's about what musicians playing together can learn from each other about how to engage in dialogue about it musically and achieve an

62   AESTHETICS OF EQUALITY

"unpredictable musical chemistry."[33] Paratactically (side-by-side) and alternatively consensual and rivalrous, the musicians generate "paired tonics," giving their composition a Schoenbergian quality. For Schoenberg (as expressed in a commentary that applies well to such jazz performances), "paired tonics" carry more importance than a "progression from one to the other," because, as he says, "the tonic 'admits the rivalry of other tonics alongside it.'"[34]

To further situate the improvisational nature of such performances, noting especially their many antiphonal moments, I turn to a Nathaniel Mackey commentary, which deftly captures the difference between the mid-twentieth-century large jazz bands that simply played a musical score and the improvisational versioning approach of an African American free jazz ensemble thinking/talking its way through a set. The (largely white) big "jazz" bands played a musical score in a way that went from "verb to noun," a translation that Mackey refers to as an "erasure of Black inventiveness by white appropriation." They play a music that "on the aesthetic level, is a less dynamic, less improvisatory, less blues-inflected music."[35] In contrast, Black jazz versioning is a "privileging of the verb"; "the movement from noun to verb, linguistically accentuates action among a people whose ability to act is curtailed by racist constraints."[36]

Houston A. Baker Jr. provides a similar commentary. Figuring African American jazz versioning as a form of action, he invents a neologism. It's a "go(uer)rilla action in the face of acknowledged adversaries,"[37] he suggests. And for James Snead, jazz versioning is an oppositional practice of repetition that cuts and breaks rather than smoothly progressing (the latter an aesthetic orientation of a Euroculture's preoccupation with material progress); instead of a dialogue about a history already past, African American free jazz performances function as ethno-historiography; they dwell on the past by "re-staging it."[38] Moreover, and crucially as regards its adaptability for structuring a novel, jazz's polyphony is compositionally homologous with the modern novel, which as M. M. Bakhtin puts it, exhibits "many contending voices."[39] Whereas in "homophonic music" "one voice becomes dominant" or "hegemonic" voice while "other voices become subordinated . . . not equal to the dominant voice, and not melodically meaningful in isolation—they become meaningful only in relation to the dominant voice"[40]—polyphonic music elevates other voices to equal status. As I note in Chapter 1, when a composition is atonally and/or antiphonically composed—or as is often the case for free jazz, structured with a modular harmony in which all chords are equal so that the music lacks a tonal central[41]—the decentering effect metaphorically translates to an egalitarian representation of social life. "In political terms," as Evelyn Cobley suggests, the decentering effect of atonality is a "strategy [that] aspires to be radically egalitarian."[42]

Ethnohistorical Roots and Jazz as Archive

Heeding the formal characteristics of modern free jazz prepares us to appreciate how a jazz-structured literary composition can recover an obscured past and articulate that temporal trajectory within an egalitarian ethos. The music history on which such a political aesthetics is based begins with European colonization of the African continent, when political domination was accompanied by the imposition of a "tonal language" that kept "Africans trapped in a prisonhouse of diatonic tonality," as Kofu Aguwa puts it.[43] However, despite all the resources European colonists put into effacing the prior cultural coherence of African peoples, some African composers resisted being "submerged entirely in that tonal world."[44] Preserving the dissonances among interacting voices that colonial domination failed to over code, their compositions, combined European tonalities with distinctively African modes of tonal thinking, yielded a musical hybridity that was later to be articulated by African American jazz musician/composers.

The atmosphere resulting from the violent oppression of the colonial era within which African composers worked was reproduced within a subsequent era, the slavery through Jim Crow period within which American jazz compositions were given their initial musical inspirations. With both their blues intonations and their performance styles, modern free jazz as performed constitutes a historical archive that reaches back to both eras.[45] To appreciate that assertion—that jazz performances function archivally as a historiographic medium—we need to think outside of the tradition image of archives and their referents. The dominant story of official archives is a nation-state story.

64   AESTHETICS OF EQUALITY

As Rodrigo Lazo points out, "The history of the modern archive is inextricable from the establishment of nation-states . . . Archive and nation came together to grant each other authority and credibility."[46] Suggesting an alternative, he states, "A personal archive has the potential to challenge the authority of the national building."[47] Achille Mbembe offers a similar observation, pointing out that traditionally "the term archives refers to a building, a symbol of a public institution," and to "a collection of documents—normally written documents— kept in this building," so that "the status and power of the archive derive from this entanglement of building and documents." Consequently, to open a space for the archives of assemblages that have lacked publicly recognized building-housed historical documents, one needs to "refigure" the concept of the archive.[48]

There are creative events with lasting resonance in jazz performances in which both the personal and collective challenges to the archival thinking to which Lazlo and Mbembe refer take place. For an illustration I turn to a fictional jazz performance that Nathaniel Mackey describes in his epistolary novel *From a Broken Bottle Traces of Perfume Still Emanate*, a text that (in his words) "builds . . . on the correspondence between music and verbal discourse."[49] During the performance, the author (as one of the musicians) is joined by the other ensemble members. They are arranged in an egalitarian spatial positioning characteristic of free jazz ensembles; the players—"Aunt Nancy on violin, Lambert on tenor, Penguin on oboe, me on saxello"—stand in "a semicircle around the same mic, leaning toward it as if in a huddle," as an extraordinary event takes place. "Aunt Nancy began to do something which gradually altered the music's course . . . she embarked on an increasingly complex run."[50]

As that complex run proceeds, the text provides two critical insights about what jazz routines can do. First, what is evinced is a musical conversation in which the rest of the group enters as the run continues. Picking up on the significance of Aunt Nancy's musical legacies, they hear Jack McDuff's "Jive Samba," "Paganini's Caprices," and "Ayer's Ghosts," and thus edified and inspired, run with Aunt Nancy, adding a "ditty hop" anthem (Lambert), alternative tones (Djamilaa's "Indian Insinuations") and Ayer's Ghosts melodies (by Penguin), as they all collaborate to produce "a wailing structured rush of sound."[51] Second,

A RIGHT TO THE CITY   65

it is because of the way a variety of musical legacies emerge in their musical conversation that jazz reveals itself as a historiographic medium. Drawing on disparate musical traditions, the performance dynamic of Mackey's fictional ensemble delivers an Afro American political aesthetic, shaped by a history of encounter between different tonal worlds. In contrast with the tonal "prisonhouse" (to which Agawu refers), erected during the colonization of Africa, this imagined musical event generates tonal liberation. There is no dominant tonal world directing where the run must go, no single voice dominates the group, and there are no protocols for how the set must end. Each of the players contributes in their own way to participate in the calls and responses as the group as a whole enacts a provisional, dissonant, and antiphonal community of sense, which because it emerges durationally as the piece progresses, reveals an articulation to which Mackey refers as "time and telling."[52] As a dynamic composition takes shape, it challenges the conceit that an archive is restricted to the static "entanglement of building and documents" (*pace* Mbembe). The event elevates an Afro-American archive to equal status with the familiar, building-situated Euro-American archives.

A Coltrane Interlude

What Mackey's fictional ensemble achieves in that imagined episode is characteristic of John Coltrane's jazz work. As has been pointed out in many commentaries, there is a consistent chord structure that references diverse ethnic musical tonalities in Coltrane's jazz performances. While some hear a mere wall of sound, others hear systematically combined (albeit rapidly moving) underlying chord systems that reach back to both African and European tonal worlds. The chord tones are organized in consistent narratives as Coltrane performs a multivoiced polyphony with tonic-altering modulations.[53] That compositional effect operates I is also the Morrison's literary jazz as well. The novel has a well-organized underlying musical structure that is recoverable. Noting (among other things) her repetitions, especially the different way in which "love" is a primary reoccurring tonic (which compares with the systematic repetitions in for example

66 AESTHETICS OF EQUALITY

Coltrane's "Love Supreme"), we observe a structure within which it repeats with continually altered significance. What characterizes the experiences of all of Morrison's characters are their attempts to secure loving intimacy in struggles with a structure of oppression—narrated in musical idioms—that restrict opportunities and render precarious their attempts at extracting themselves from impoverished life worlds. And importantly, in bringing the different voices/songs into lyrically expressed, call and response encounters, Morrison fashions an egalitarian sensibility, acknowledging in musical idioms each of her character's attempts to cope with a world of racist containment that has shaped Black musico-literary political aesthetics. Morrison's *Jazz* is a jazz performance that extends over decades. It's an unfolding story that features the complex temporality that Mackey accords to free jazz performances, "the connection between 'time and telling, timing and telling,' which, he suggests, "obviously applies to a piece of fiction [as well as] a piece of music (rhythm, sequence, pattern, pace, etc.)."[54]

What, then, are the Coltrane resonances in that story? Lars Eckstein provides an answer. Discerning the musical strategies in Toni Morrison's earlier novel, *Beloved,* he likens many of Morrison's musically structured passages to Coltrane's jazz compositions, pointing out for example that in many of the novel's passages, for example, one that begins, "In the beginning there were no words," the musical form has implications that are more historical than metaphysical. Functioning as historiography, the music references the Black experience over time.[55] As Eckstein points out, Morrison's "jazzthetic" writing mimics "the sound and rhythms of Black music [which is] a source of narrative content."[56] He goes on specifically to connect Morrison's musically shaped textual strategy with Coltrane's 1964 studio recording of "the four-act suite" *A Love Supreme* in which he sees him translating the verbal language of Black talk (especially its emotional resonances) "into instrumental music."[57] He likens the coordinated interaction of the different voices of Coltrane's players—Coltrane on sax, Elvin Jones on drums, McCoy Tyner on piano, and Jimmy Garrison on bass— to the voices of Morrison's characters. As is the case for the quartet's playing of *A Love Supreme*, in "the collective chorus of *Beloved*, the individual voices retain their distinctive qualities." The Coltrane effect that Eckstein sees in Morrison's *Beloved*, provides a formal frame to read Morrison's more explicitly jazz-structured novel. Morrison explicitly evokes John Coltrane in connection with her search for "whatever ineffable quality is that is curiously black and finding the only analogy [in] music."[58]

Jazz

Morrison's earlier novel *Beloved* (1987) initiated the thinking that is articulated through the tonal structure of her *Jazz*. As she puts it in the foreword,

> *Beloved* unleashed a host of ideas about how and what one cherishes under the duress and emotional disfigurement that a slave society imposes. One such idea—love as perpetual mourning (haunting) led me to consider a parallel one: how such relationships were altered later, in (or by) a certain level of liberty. An alteration made abundantly clear in the music. I was struck by the modernity that jazz anticipated and directed, and by its unreasonable optimism . . . the music insisted that the past might haunt us but it wouldn't entrap us.[59]

Morrison's version of jazz evokes its historical legacy; it's a bluesy jazz, where the "the blues is not a style of phase of jazz, but its heart."[60] The story's opening in 1926 with the main narrator stating, "Sth, I knew that woman. She used to live on Lenox Avenue," is linked to *Beloved*, which follow's Sethe's life during slavery. Doubtless the venue choice and musically figured style is inspired by Langston Hughes's 1926 poem "Lenox Avenue: Midnight," whose first two lines captures the novel's musical ontology and venue:

> The rhythm of life
> Is a jazz rhythm.

Although the jazz rhythm shaping Morrison's story is composed to give extended attention to each voice in the novel's ensemble, much the way African American jazz ensembles feature each of the musician's contributions during a set, there is nevertheless a musical

68 AESTHETICS OF EQUALITY

voice that transcends the musical contribution each character makes. As one of the novel's narrators puts it, it's "the music the world makes," a music that "has no words."[61] The city, as part of that music-making world—performing as part of what Morrison calls "the voice of the talking book"[62]—is a player that dominates the novel's ensemble of characters. In the words of the urban theorists Amin Ash and Nigel Thrift, the city is "a kind of force field of passions that associate and pulse bodies in particular ways."[63] The character Dorcas (and her generation) surrenders to "the City's seductive call . . . to the 'illusion' of the music's 'secret drive: the control it tricks them into believing is theirs,' "[64] and although Joe Trace, who came from a small southern town before moving up to Harlem, "thinks he is free" as he works on fashioning his own voice and choices in a seemingly more liberating milieu, he is caught up in that force field. Voicing a song of his love for Dorcas, he intones, "I *chose* you."[65] However, "the city," as a narrator puts it, "makes people think they can do what they want and get away with it."[66] It has Joe caught on a turntable with grooves that have preceded him: "He is bound to the track. It pulls him like a needle through the groove of a Bluebird record . . . You can't get off the track a city lays for you." The passage continues right up to *Jazz's* main tonic, "love" (repeated and reinflected throughout the novel): "Whatever happens, whether you get rich or stay poor, ruin your health or live to old age, you always end up back where you started: hungry for the one thing everybody loses—young loving."[67]

The "emotional disfigurement" to which Morrison refers—suffered by an oppressed and (mis)interpellated Black assemblage—is apparent at the story's outset. It is expressed palpably early in the novel when Violet attends a funeral in order to disfigure a dead girl's face, the eighteen-year-old Dorcas with whom her husband Joe has had an affair before killing her. Thereafter that disfigurement is articulated in repeated sequences that mimic the modal harmony of modern jazz performances. Morrison substitutes the linguistic mechanism anaphora (repeated words at the beginning of successive clauses) for chordal changes in repeated musical phrases. Describing Violent' assault on the dead girl face with a knife, the sequence begins, "*that* Violet not only knew . . . ," and is followed by "*that* Violet knew . . . *that* Violet had to push aside . . . *that Violet* unsatisfied, fought . . . a power *that* Violet had not lost . . . *That* Violet should not have let the parrot go . . . *that* Violet was strong and had hips."[68] She also composes what jazz musicians call "double-takes," "re-reports" of scenes "with slightly different details from the first version," for example a place where a fireplace is described as "clean, set for a new fire" in a second version after having earlier been described as having "a heap of ash" in the first.[69]

The changing "that" sequences and double-takes are typical of Coltrane compositions, exemplified in his version of "My Favorite Things" (from the Rodgers and Hammerstein musical, *The Sound of Music*). Although the content of the original piece might make Coltrane's performance seem to convey "the unreasonable optimism" that Morrison ascribes to much of modern jazz, it is arguably instead a performance that appropriates what is trivial and banal to hold it up for critical appraisal. It is what I have elsewhere called one of Coltrane's semiotic encounters, "staged between a system of meaning characteristic of African American culture and the institutionalized referentiality of the dominant white culture."[70] Rather than follow the song by merely representing its statements with the original harmony, which would affirm the value attributed to the "things" that are the song's referents, Coltrane, like Morrison in her "*that*" and double-take sequences, performs an elaborate series of reinflected repetitions: "To the original tune, he adds seven bars in E minor and twenty-three in E major, repeating the melody within different chordal harmonies."[71] Playing in what Deleuze calls "the theater of repetition," Coltrane mobilizes the affective force of the "apparatus of repetition['s] . . . terrible power."[72] Similarly, Morrison's literary appropriation of "themes of canonical texts" of Euro-American writers, which she interlaces with her characters' songs, is an improvisation which, like Coltrane's, involves "turning an original version on its head such that its vapidity or ridiculousness is exposed."[73]

In the novel, Violet's song shares the literary space with songs of the other main characters, all of which reach back into the pasts of the three main protagonists, Violet, Joe, and Dorcas. The three are aesthetic subjects whose biographical trajectories interweave "rural memory" with an "urban present."[74] As their songs are interwoven they are comped by the songs of the polycentric narrators, who perform alternatively as "a neighborhood gossip, a jazz balladeer, and

70   AESTHETICS OF EQUALITY

New World griot."[75] At a micro level, the narration's temporal structure renders their songs as a series of call and response duets and antiphonal solos, while at a macro level the characters, having moved North from southern venues, belong to a large chorus known as "the Great Migration" (Chorus imagery abounds for Morrison who likens the songs and chorus of Greek tragedy to "Afro-American communal structures").[76]

With its jazz structure, the novel's macro level song references the movement of precarious Black bodies—fundamentally stories of escape from the original "emotional disfigurement" to which Morrison refers—and haunts the micro level duets and solos, each of which is an antiphonal series of alternations between moments of violent abjection and loving approach. Exemplary in this respect is Violet's duet with the deceased Dorcas. After having disfigured the face of Dorcas's corpse with a knife at her funeral, Violet seeks to get intimately close to Dorcas's life. Having "lost Joe to a dead girl . . . she wonders if she isn't falling in love with her too."[77] Keeping a picture of Dorcas she's taken from her aunt's home, she looks at it obsessively, displacing her lost love for Joe on Dorcas: "When she isn't trying to humiliate Joe, she is admiring the dead girl's hair; when she isn't cursing Joe with brand-new cuss words, she is having whispered conversations with the corpse in her head; when she isn't worrying about his loss of appetite, his insomnia, she wonders what color were Dorcas' eyes . . . In the photograph . . . the girl needed her ends cut. Hair that gets fraggely easy. Just a quarter-inch trim would do wonders, Dorcas. Dorcas."[78]

Exemplary as well is a contrapuntal duet featuring Joe and Malvonne, whose apartment Joe seeks to borrow for his trysts with Dorcas. To Joe's first remark, "Can I step in? Got a proposition for you?" Malvonne counters, "I don't have a nickel, Joe." Once the conversation is well into a call and response motif, that proposition is antiphonically negotiated. Joe continues: "A favor you might say," to which Malvonne counters, "Or I might not say." And once Joe suggests details—"It wouldn't be every day, Malvonne," followed by Malvonne's "It wouldn't be no day"—the song ends with a deal: "two dollars every month" is finally accepted after several back-and-forth suggestions and rejections and a space for "outlaw love" has opened up. Like a free jazz

A RIGHT TO THE CITY   71

session, the intensity abates as the clashing tonics are repeated until, exhausted, they fade into a shared tone.[79]

The novel is punctuated as much by solos as it is by duets. Like Duke Ellington solicitous and egalitarian treatment of each band member, Morrison lends her characters individual riffs. This solo by Joe is particularly revelatory with respect to the way her protagonists adjust to the changing pressures and precarities in alternative milieux:

> The first day I got to school I had to have two names. I told the teacher Joe Trace [his parent had "disappeared without a trace"] . . . The second change came when I was picked out and trained to be a man. To live independent and feed myself no matter what . . . Then I got a job laying rail. I was twenty-eight years old and used to changing now . . . I changed up again a fourth time . . . And I thought I had settled into my permanent self, the fifth one when we left the stink of Mulberry Street and little Africa.[80]

As the duets and solo riffs proceed, performing diverse versions of emotional disfigurement punctuated by moments of hope, the narrating voices perform what Morrison attributes to the literary language of her work as a whole, a "deft manipulation of voices." As a performer in the story, Morrison is doing what in jazz talk is called comping. Sensing the tones she lends to her characters, she provides the accompanying back up riffs (which are usually allocated to the pianist). Put linguistically, her "choices of language," as she testifies, express her "reliance on a full comprehension of codes embedded in Black culture." Accordingly, her narrator's voices also function as historiography to "transfigure" what has been a disfigured, "Afro-American presence" in American history and literature.[81] The musical idiom for Morrison's refiguring of Afro-America's emotional disfigurement is apparent at one of the most telling points in the novel where a narrator speculates about the emotional resonances of the week's seven-day cycle. If we heed the importance of the rhythms of consonance and dissonance within the story while noting that dominant seventh chords, which are the most dissonant chords in music (adding an extra, fourth, voice and including extended intervals) and are among the most frequently used for blues, soul, and jazz, this

72   AESTHETICS OF EQUALITY

passage conducted by the city reveals itself as a meta commentary on the novel as a jazz performance: "The City thinks about and arranges itself for the weekend—perhaps there is something so phony about the seven-day cycle the body pays no attention to it, preferring triples, duets, quartets, anything but a cycle of seven that has to be broken into human parts."[82]

What is performed by the macro level music of the narrators? While love remains the novel's main tonic and is thematized in many of the novel's duets and solos (the word comes up continually in varying contexts), violence is the underlying motif of much of the macro-level song performed by the narrators. For example, Chapter 3—mainly devoted to Dorcas—adds her to the flow of bodies into New York and to the legacy of violence that shapes the way they cope. While she is living with her Aunt Alice because her parents had been killed in a race riot in St. Louis, Alice tries to keep her out of trouble: "she had worked hard to privatize her niece" while challenged by a song more powerful than the personal song and dance she tries to negotiate with Dorcas. However, Alice was "no match for a city seeping music that begged and challenged each and every day."[83] By way of explication of Dorcas's unruly Harlem existence that Alice cannot control, there's a telling episode with Dorcas at a public dance hall.

After being approached by two brothers (in both senses of the term), who on closer inspection decide to turn away, her emotional disfigurement, a profound lack of a feeling of self-worth (doubtless a legacy of the violence that took her parents), is told by a narrator (in musical idiom):

> Dorcas has been acknowledged, appraised, and dismissed in the time it takes for a needle to find its opening groove. The stomach jump of possible love is nothing compared to the ice floes that back up her veins now. The body she inhabits is unworthy. Although it is young and all she has, it is as if it had decayed on the vine at budding time ... So by the time Joe Trace whispered to her through a crack in a closing door her life had become almost unbearable. Almost. The flesh. Heavily despised by the brothers, held secret the love appetite soaring inside it.[84]

A RIGHT TO THE CITY   73

Like Dorcas, Alice copes with a violent legacy, also dating back to the 1917 race riot in St. Louis, which was precipitated by a reaction to the racism faced by disgruntled veterans who had fought in all colored units in World War I . . . and came home to white violence more intense than when they enlisted. A member of Alice's family experienced the consequences. "Her brother-in-law was not a veteran, and he had been living in East St. Louis since before the War. Nor did he need a white man's job—he owned a pool hall . . . he wasn't even in the riot; he had no weapons, confronted nobody on the street. He was pulled off a street car and stomped to death."[85] Although Alice's Harlem neighborhood provides a respite from New York's City's brand of violence, Alice cannot avoid a more subtle version. She's not pulled from a street car, but she is humiliated on one; "she had begun to feel safe nowhere south of 110th Street, and Fifth Avenue was for her the most dreadful of all . . . where women who spoke English said, 'Don't sit there honey, you never know what they got,' and women who knew no English and would never own a pair of silk stockings moved away from her if she sat next to them on the trolley."[86]

Although Alice is robbed of her dignity in parts of the city, the bodies the novel moves northward are headed into a racial/spatial order where there are reprieves from the intense and pervasive racist oppression in the South. One such reprieve surfaces for Violet and Joe, who are described in a telling moment with respect to the problem of dignity. It was Violet that chose Joe, although it was simply circumstances that brought them together, the contingency of proximity: "They were drawn together because they had been put together [working in the same cotton field], and all they decided for themselves was where and when to meet at night."[87] As they head north to move to Harlem from (the fictional) Vesper County in Virginia (where they had met under a walnut tree), they experience some of breaks in the racially marked and policed cartography. Once Morrison has them on the train, part of the Great Migration, America's Black population's social transformation from a rural proletariat to a largely urban and industrialized proletariat,[88] they witness a dramatic difference from the Black body language they had been obliged to adopt in the South. While in the dining car they are "waited upon by a Black man who did not have

74   AESTHETICS OF EQUALITY

to lace his dignity with a smile."[89] Thereafter the novel finds them having to "negotiate the programmatic spaces of [a] modern city [to achieve] new modes of public citizenship," in a space not designed to accommodate them;[90] "Embracing an intimate relationship with (and within) the city for Morrison's Black characters involves redefining and relocating their interior and exteriors selves, a process that would have been impossible in a Jim Crow South committed to ossified antebellum notions of Black identity."[91] Nevertheless, the adjustment requires vigilance, given all the new "thou shalt nots" (those to which Ralph Ellison refers when he compares Alabama racial oppression to New York's, elaborated below).[92]

As regards the political pedagogy of *Jazz's* plot: simply put, multiple narrators recount Joe and Violet Trace's twenty-year marriage and its disruption. Joe has an affair with eighteen-year-old Dorcas, whom he kills after she drops him. Violet disfigures the dead girl's face with a knife at the funeral and then becomes obsessed with the details of her life and appearance. The novel delivers its telling moments in fragments focused on encounters. They are fragments that construct the staging of the characters duets and solos and treat the various detours into the characters' historical foundations. They locate the city in what Anne-Marie Paquet-Deyris refers to as a "*zero* moment in Black history."[93] A moment that discloses what is to be learned about the Black experience of post–World War I American in which many had to recreate attachments—already under stress in a white-dominant social order—in an unfamiliar urban milieu. However, while the novel's most general social and political revelations are about how the white dominated racial order constrains the possibilities for intimate bonds within America's Black assemblage, it's the novel's egalitarian ethos that is my main focus. Oppressive as a white dominated America has been, they share an aural world that provides a reprieve for all the novel's characters, at least in their part of the city: "Up there, in that part of the City—which is the part they came for—the right tune whistled in a doorway of lifting up from the circles and grooves of a record can change the weather. From freezing to hot to cool."[94]

Ultimately, if not "the right tune" Joe and Violet (and by implication and avowal Morrison) find an agreeable tune, a change from the novel's initiating love-sick blues mood to a more hopeful love-enabling one.

The novel's opening tune in Violet and Joe's apartment, after Dorcas's murder at Joe's hands and the subsequent disfiguring of the corpse at Violet's, is somber. Violet has released her pet birds, and the rooms in their apartment—the stage for their duet—is emotionally empty after the event, haunted as it is by a photograph of Dorcas:

> Up there on Lenox, in Violet and Joe's apartment, the rooms are like the empty birdcages wrapped in cloth. And a dead girl's face has become the necessary thing for their nights. They each take turns to throw off the bedcovers, rise up from their sagging mattress and tiptoe over cold linoleum in the parlor to gaze at what seems like the only living presence in the house: the photograph of a bold, unsmiling girl staring from the mantelpiece.[95]

In contrast and in keeping with Morrison's commitment to exercising the full range of jazz's "intellect, sensuality and anarchy" while recovering her own "I," which throughout the novel had been "playing along with the voice" (of Violet), by the end of the novel the tune emanating from Violet and Joe's apartment has changed. The author who has professed to "know that woman" ("shirt size, what side she sleeps on . . . name of her hair oil, its scent"), and who in some ways reminds her of herself, decides to "mend" Violet and Joe's broken lives and to recognize the freedom to remake her own.

As the song returns to Violet and Joe's fraught lives, repeating yet altering the tune, *Jazz's* underlying blues ontology remains. It's an ontology well captured in Ralph Ellison's famous characterization of the blues:

> The blues is an impulse to keep the painful details and episodes of a brutal experience alive in one's aching consciousness, to finger its jagged grain, and to transcend it, not by the consolation of philosophy but by squeezing from it a near-tragic, near-comic lyricism. As a form, the blues is an autobiographical chronicle of personal catastrophe expressed lyrically.[96]

That such a blues ontology, expressed in a variety of artistic genres belongs distinctively to Black experience is captured by Ma

76 AESTHETICS OF EQUALITY

Rainey's remark (in the August Wilson's play "Ma Rainey's Black Bottom"): "White folks don't understand the blues . . . They hear it come out, but they don't know how it got there . . . They don't understand that that's life's way of talking. You don't sing to feel better, you sing because that's your way of understanding life."[97]

That she is implementing that ontology in her account of her characters' lives become evident as Morrison begins the last chapter with the word, pain, in a riff that echoes Ellison's and Ma Rainey's insights and at the same time figures how she composes her writing:

Pain. I seem to have an affection, a kind of sweettooth for it. Bolts of lightning, little rivulets of thunder. And I the eye of the storm. Mourning the split trees, hens starving on rooftops. Figuring out what can be done to save them since they cannot save themselves without me because—well it's my storm, isn't it? I break lives to prove I can mend them back again. And although the pain is theirs, I share it don't I?[98]

Pain! Those familiar with the blues (those whom Amiri Baraka famously calls "blue people"[99]) appreciate its ontological depth and its "animating paradox," its "compressed yoking of tragedy and comedy."[100] Pain, as a variety of thinkers have noted, is what best testifies to one's being alive. Adam Smith refers to it as a more "pungent sensation" than pleasure (and ought to be avoided insists the sensation-aversive Scotsman), while similarly for the Marquis de Sade, it is the "keenest sensation" (and thus ought to be sought and indulged insists the libertine Frenchman).[101] Certainly Morrison, with a "sweet tooth" for pain, indulges it throughout *Jazz*.

However, while practicing Sadean indulgence rather than Smithian avoidance, Morrison also follows (while reinflecting) Wittgenstein's insight that "to recognize pain or any other 'feeling' . . . is to . . . be able to evoke the appropriate language game at the appropriate time and place."[102] But rather than presuming that there exists a consensual language game, Morrison expresses the pain (and the reprieves from it) in a musically composed "sociolect,"[103] a blues-inflected jazz that is a distinctively Black language game. That it's an embodied game that transcends mere words is reflected in the novel's last jazz riff, in which the main tonic is snapping fingers. Morrison as narrator wonders if Violent and Joe "know they are the sound of snapping fingers"; as their "victrola plays in the parlor . . . The click of dark and snapping fingers" is driving them "into places their fathers have warned them about and their mothers shudder to think of. Both the warning and the shudder come from the snapping fingers, the clicking."[104]

At this point—near the end of the story as Violet and Joe are restoring the bond that had been broken—Morrison's (literary) fingers are also snapping to the tune. She is participating in the text as an active and productive listener to the song she herself has been improvising, singing with what Roland Barthes designates as a "middle voice," a writing voice that carries the tune at the point at which "the distance between *scriptor* and language [jazz-as-language in this case] diminishes asymptotically." Moreover, it's the moment of writing in which the author as "subject is constituted as immediately contemporary with the writing, being effected and affected by it."[105] As Morrison-as-narrator states during the novel's final set, while observing that the restored love between Violet and Joe has made her envious, "I envy them their public love." She follows with an admission that she has "known it in secret shared it in secret and longed, aw longed to show it—to be able to say it out loud."[106] Mirroring the harmony of modal jazz, the novel thus ends with a mood rather than a resolution. It avoids a "teleological conclusion, focusing instead on the present tense of performance and individual voice."[107]

While dramatizing a story of love lost and regained the novel conveys what jazz performances often convey, a combination of pain and inspiration and at the same time a sense that much of Afro-American life remains implicit rather than explicitly sounded. However importantly, her narrative of the sundering and restoration of a bond between two individuals should be read allegorically as a historiographic trope applied to the collective African American experience of "fragmentation and re-assemblage." As she puts it in her comparison of the collage canvasses of Romare Bearden with jazz compositions, "much like jazz music . . . and indeed like the process of reclaiming African American history (or by historiography), African-American culture from the Middle Passage forward is of course broadly characterized by fragmentation and re-assemblage."[108]

78 AESTHETICS OF EQUALITY

At the same time that Morrison is providing that insight, she is asking the readers to snap their fingers to a jazz-like passage that, as earlier in the novel, is structured as repeated "thats." Following her remark about what she'd like "to be able to say out loud," is a reach out—an expression of "public love"—to readers holding the book, a desire to pass on the transformation she has experienced in inventing a version of public love: "*That I have loved only you, surrendered my whole self reckless to you and nobody else, that I want you to love me back and show it to me, That I love the way you hold me, how close you let me be to you. I like your fingers on and on, lifting, turning*" (emphasis in original).[109] "When jazz is played well," Gregory Clarke suggests, "the reach of that transformation extends deep into the audience, where individuals can share a soloist's tension as she anticipates the next improvised phrase."[110] Morrison does play well, comping her characters with keen attention to jazz ensemble interactions. Like the performances of free jazz soloists and ensembles that seek to reach out to and stir their audience, encouraging them to move (dancing, foot tapping, finger snapping, etc.), her *Jazz* is not a score-regimented performance. Improvising to make aspects of a city's Black life present to herself and the reader in a palpable way—a presence unavailable in an urban planner's eagle-eyed view from above—the author herself becomes rhythmically present to those lives, snapping her fingers to their songs, backing them up, reflecting on how her own tune is affected by theirs, showing how the city, performing as "in turn, friend and foe,"[111] both assists and impedes one's ability to compose a Black life, and effectively passing on the feelings associated with the tensions surrounding such lives (which have achieved their most enduring expression in blues-oriented jazz).

In and Out of Tune

As has been often pointed out by many African American writers, much of Black civic expression resides in musical composition. Morrison's musically structured novel tracks and performs that civic expression as it was located in the period before the national print media, provoked by the mid-twentieth-century civil rights movement, became attentive to African American voices. The novel's egalitarian ethos, delivered through close attention to and resonance with the vagaries of Black lives under pressure, operates with what Matthew M. Heard refers to as a "contraband tonality that stretches the way we think about listening and attunement."[112] That version of tonality characterizes the "sonic subjectivity" of Black citizen/subjects, and given the tonal divide it references calls for "an entirely different protocol of ethical attunement," one Heard suggests that "resonates through the tonality of the other."[113] It conveys an ethical obligation (which he derives from Derrida's neo-Kantian riff on "an apocalyptic tone in philosophy"[114]) to "respond to the 'scene' of the other."[115]

As I have been suggesting throughout the analysis, free jazz ensembles are constitutively responsive to the Other (both each other and the audience in their case). The egalitarian ethos of their scenes—what Clark refers to as episodes of "civic jazz"—is a micro version of what an egalitarian ethos implies for the larger scene, the social formation as a whole. Morrison's *Jazz* negotiates that transition of levels through the process with which her characters adapt to the city. Exemplary in that respect is the way Joe becomes attuned to the city—or in terms of *Jazz's* characteristic grammar—adjusts his tune to the city's tune as he moves through the streets. In contrast with Alice, whose fears direct her pathways and self-management, is Joe's more confident demeanor, derived from his hunting savvy. In Morrison's terms, which connect his tracking behavior learned in the South with his developing ability at urban navigation, "he stalks through the City [in search of an estranged Dorcas], and it [the city] does not object or interfere . . . The streets he walks are slick and black . . . [and once he's inside a] train, which stops suddenly, throwing passengers forward [it facilitates his search]. As though it just remembered that this was the stop where Joe needs to get off if he is to find her."[116] At that moment as in many others, the city's design structure is alternatively facilitating and obstructive, permitting and impeding. Morrison's version of the city has it hosting and inflecting events as her characters struggle to become civic subjects. In the process, the characters articulate the novel's historiography as they endeavor to manage the experiential "disjunction between the rural, southern past of historical memory [where Morrison situates them in moments in her nonlinear narrative]

80 AESTHETICS OF EQUALITY

and the immediate urban present" within which they struggle to find themselves and maintain rewarding intimacies within "the programmatic narrative of the built spaces they inhabit."[117]

The Right to the City

To the extent that the characters in Morrison's *Jazz* are to achieve a measure of "public citizenship" they have to negotiate the space of a city that is "programmatic"—alternatively inviting and recalcitrant, controlling and acquiescing.[118] In the case of New York City's most intense center of activity, Times Square provides what two commentators refer to as the "right to the city [as] spectacle," quoting Marshall Berman's description of the enticement:

> Presents the modern city at its most expansive and intense. It gives people ideas about how to look and to move, ideas about being free and being oneself and being with another . . . [Times Square] has enticed and inspired all sorts of men and women to step out of line, to engage actively with the city, merge their subjectivity with it and change the place as they change themselves.[119]

Berman's celebratory look at the city center doesn't apply well to "*all* sorts of men and women." Noting how Morrison's protagonists manage to negotiate public spaces that are racially ordered, Dale Pattison puts it succinctly: "Examining the novel's engagement with architecture, blackness, and eroticism [helps us discern] how Joe and Violet ultimately learn to cultivate an intimate space between the public and private in the modern city."[120] It's not an easy accomplishment, as Ralph Ellison learned when he arrived in New York. His prior management of an effective and acceptable public conduct in the racist milieu of Alabama did not effectively serve his management of his new city. While initially he assumed that New York was more or less the way Berman was to subsequently describe it, "the freest of American cities,"[121] once he commenced to negotiate its distinctive racially marked spatial order, he found that he had to be alert to geographic nuances and learn what he referred to as a set of "arcane rules of New York's racial arrangements."[122] Figuring one of his humiliating encounters musically—his interlocutor laughs at him in "bright major chords, while he (Ellison) responded in "minor sevenths and flatted fifths"—and he concludes, "I doubted that he was attuned to the deeper source of our inharmonic harmony."[123]

As I've noted elsewhere, like Morrison, Ellison discerned that "the development of the blues through jazz musical trajectory is inextricably tied to a dynamic African American experience."[124] Here, I want to frame Ellison's—and accordingly Joe and Violet's—negotiation of New York's "racial arrangements" with resort to Henri Lefebvre's concept of "the right to the city," in which (with notable inattention to the strictures of racial disparities) he figures "the human as *oeuvre*" operating in "urban society."[125] Lefebvre's contemporary urban person-as-*oeuvre* is different from the "old 'social animal' . . . of the ancient city"; it's an "urban animal," a "polyvalent, polysensorial, urban [person] capable of complex and transparent relations with the world (the environment and himself)"; he ponders different eligibilities for those "relations" with resort to an urban eschatology. Concerned ultimately with urban society's implications for a "new humanism" and "new praxis,"[126] Lefebvre asks, "What is important? Who thinks? Who acts? Who still speaks for whom?"[127] and ultimately comes around to the view that a realization of the "*right to urban life*" requires "the working class," which must become "the agent, social carrier or [its] support."[128] Attuned as he was to what he calls "the production of space,"[129] Lefebvre suggests "that architecture and urban governance, planning and design can and should provide opportunities for remaking the city as a more humane, accessible and livable social space by understanding its social production."[130]

As Morrison's construction of the design of city spaces suggests, her Black "city-dwellers found themselves simultaneously participating in future oriented visions of the city and victimized by the modes [of] institutionalized discipline inherent is those designs."[131] As is well known, in the case of New York City's modern urban life, subsequent to the period in *Jazz*, the "social" aspect of urban space to which Lefebvre refers paled in comparison with governmental and bureaucratic initiatives. In particular, the reshaping of urban space overseen during Robert Moses's tenure as a park and public

82 AESTHETICS OF EQUALITY

works commissioner changed New York City's physical environment, altering existing neighborhoods while building parks, highways, bridges, playgrounds, housing, tunnels, beaches, zoos, civic centers, exhibition halls, and configuring the 1964–65 New York World's Fair. He redesigned the city's architecture in ways that tipped the balance toward victimization for the city's Black residents. In his documenting of city history, Robert Caro shows comprehensively the way Moses's projects constituted a racist intervention. As Daniel Kolitz, puts it, "As Parks Commissioner . . . he imported racist building methods to are dense with people of color."[132] He destroyed Black neighborhoods by building highways that cut through them, issued condemnation orders to clear spaces to which he referred to as "blighted," and produced a traffic structure (resulting from his highway and bridge projects) that cut off much of the Black population from public parks and pools.[133] Referring to what is arguably his most racist design project, Caro "reveals that Moses ordered his engineers to build the bridges low over the parkway to keep buses from the city away from Jones Beach— buses presumably filled with the poor Blacks and Puerto Ricans Moses despised."[134]

Moses's architectural legacy abrogated much of the right to the city that Morrison accords to her protagonists' participation in public life in New York. His architectural projects are an exemplary affirmation of Bernard Tschumi's mantra, "There is no architecture without action, no architecture without events, no architecture without program . . . no architecture without violence."[135] The anti-Black architectural barriers Moses designed within New York's urban formation, compromising African Americans' equal access to public space, were paralleled by the architectural barriers afflicting Black musical participation. Notable in that respect was Harlem's Cotton Club, which opened in 1923 and was a virtual plantation annex. Black musicians performed in a space that at first "excluded all but white patrons although the entertainers and most of staff were African American."[136]

Black musicians were destined to take over the jazz music scene nevertheless, many of whom (e.g., the famous Count Basie and his band and Charley "Bird" Parker) relocated from Kansas City where much of modern jazz was incubated. Heeding that connection, I want to conclude the chapter by retreating to the Kansas City music scene in the 1930s, as it is represented in Robert Altman's film *Kansas City*, which like Morrison's novel is a jazz-scored text. The film composes a politics of aesthetics that exemplifies both what Morrison does with New York's architecturally partitioned space—treating bodies entering and learning to manage a complexly designed life world while "bring with them spontaneity and creativity"[137]—and illustrates what Tschumi accords to architectural disjunction, a jazz-like dissonance between what is designed and what is practiced in urban space.

The architectural dissonance that Tschumi theorizes focused on the disjuncture between design and use, and accords with the form disjunctions in Morrison's jazz-structured writing, which features continual breaks in the narrative frame. Formally similar to the way modern jazz performances generate aesthetic breaks within the musical score—as they engage in "participatory discrepancies" to render the music "out of [expected] tune"[138]—is the way marginalized urban residents use space in ways that are disjunctive with official design protocols. Similarly, what Altman's film accomplishes is a dramatization of a disjunctive Kansas City, operating with two separate, criminally manipulated practices. There is a white-dominated electoral politics run by the Democratic assemblyman, Thomas Pendergast, which contrasts with a gambling syndicate run by the Black jazz club-owning crime kingpin, Seldom Seen. Picking up that bifurcated political dynamic during the 1934 presidential election, Altman's *Kansas City* functions conceptually as historiographic metafiction which articulates a historical moment of parallel election and musical politics. Composing a jazz structured cinematic text, Altman sets jazz history and political history paratactically side by side as the film's montage rhythms cut back and forth between the two historical presences. As I have noted elsewhere, "The disjuncture between African American and Euro-American civic expression is nowhere better portrayed than in Robert Altman's feature film *Kansas City*."[139]

Kansas City: Two Political Centers, Two Gangsters

The film's initiating event is a robbery by a white hoodlum, who in blackface with the cooperation of a Black cab driver, robs one of

84 AESTHETICS OF EQUALITY

Seldom Seen's (Harry Belafonte) gamblers as he is headed to Seen's Hey Hey club. Once the robber, Johnny (Dermot Mulroney) is detained by Seen's henchmen and brought to the club, his wife, Blondie (Jennifer Jason-Leigh) kidnaps the wife, Carolyn Stilton (Miranda Richardson) of a prominent politician, Henry Stilton (Michael Murphy), whose political clout she thinks can get Johnny released in exchange for his wife's return. Although many of the film's reviewers complain that the plot is thin, Altman has stated that he was not concerned with composing a cogent narrative structure; his compositional aim was directed more toward the film's musical framing than its animating plot. As is the case with Morrison's *Jazz*, the musical aspect of Altman's *Kansas City* is not mere background. It's essential to how the film is composed. It's structured as "a kind of freewheeling jazz improvisation," as Altman puts it.[140] "The story . . . is just a little song, and it's the way it's played that's important."[141] Reviewing his characterizations of the film's musical voices, he adds, "Harry Belafonte is like a brass instrument—when it's his turn to solo, he does long monologue like riffs—and the discussions of the two women are like reed instruments, maybe saxophones, having duets."[142] Implementing the musical form of his film, Altman makes the sonic rhythms of *Kansas City* articulate a marginalized America whose political sensibility is manifested aurally, whether with musical instruments in hand or not. The voices of *Kansas City's* characters double the voices of the performing jazz musicians.

As I have noted, the historical context of that aurality is crucial to how the film thinks because there is much that is distinctive about the Kansas City of 1934:

As the film narrative develops, the pervasive historical doubleness that Kansas City represents is shown to persist. Missouri contained both sides of the slavery conflict in the nineteenth century, and in the twentieth, its most vibrant city contained a juxtaposition of two exemplary racial orders. It is important to note however that the form of *Kansas City's* film (its cuts, juxtapositions and both tonal and visual homologies) is the primary way in which the film speaks of a politically divided American nation. As was the case in his *Nashville*, Altman's focus in *Kansas City* is on encounters between two systems of meaning-making, two domains of discourse, economy and music,

A RIGHT TO THE CITY 85

which distinguish the white and Black ethnoscapes of an American City.[143]

As for the relevance of turning to Altman's *Kansas* City in this investigation, both architecture and personae stand in opposition in the film. The Black population is mainly represented through their performative and embodied association with music. As LeRoi Jones/Amiri Baraka has pointed out after investigating the historical trajectory of Afro-American music:

> As I began to get into the history of the music, I found that this was impossible without, at the same time, getting deeper into the history of the people. That it was the history of the Afro-American people as text, as tale, as story, as exposition, narrative, or what have you, that the music was the score, the actually expressed creative orchestration, reflection, of Afro-American life, our words the libretto, to those actually lived lives. That the music was an orchestrated, vocalized, hummed, blown, beaten, scatted, corollary confirmation of the history.[144]

Enabling the Kansas City realization of Afro America's expanding musical text is a flow of Black bodies. The film cuts occasionally to the in-migration of Black musicians from the South and Southwest destined to be part of Seen's Hey Hey Club's jazz performances, so that the bodies and the building become intimately associated. The club is not only a hub for Seen's crime syndicate but also a community-creating artistic space. It testifies that "creativity and innovation in the modern cultural economy can be understood as rooted in the production system and its geographic milieu." The film shows that it is in the creative field that one can observe, "the formation of cultural communities."[145] The other hub is Thomas Pendergast's Democratic Party precinct headquarters. A front for crime as well as a political precinct hub, it organizes a flow of illegal voters and manages an illicit exchange of political favors. Yet paradoxically, it also facilitates the flourishing of the Black musical community. Pendergast's rule in the 1930s had allowed jazz to flourish while at the same time enabling the city's red-light district, the largest in the country. Architecture commands

86 AESTHETICS OF EQUALITY

attention throughout the film. The two buildings, the club and precinct, command two separate but nonconflictual enterprises, triangulated with another building that mediates their activities, the central railway station through which the dual flows of bodies pass. Accordingly, the railway station is on screen in much of the film narrative.

Seen's jazz club, as one side of the architectural disjunction, is also at the center of the film's racial disjunction as it portrays what Jennifer Lynn Stoever calls "the sonic color line." As she notes, "sounds, heard and unheard, have histories. If we listen, we can hear resonances with other times and places . . . segregation's hostile soundscapes."[146] By the 1930s, jazz, which had increasingly become an artistic genre within which Black America asserted its cultural/communal presence, was anathema to much of white American, which experienced the music as an "ethnic dissonance" whose growing popularity challenged the hierarchical view of America that had been musically reinforced by the "Centennial" composers, William Mason and Charles Ives. Part of the dominant nineteenth-century Euro-American musical culture, the two identified themselves in racial terms and "believed," as Macdonald Smith Moore points out, "that the true moral community of neighborliness had been born in Old New England."[147] When an increasing number of "white Americans first heard jazz toward the end of World War I," it invited "a crescendo of moralizing . . . and vituperation that peaked in the mid-twenties."[148]

Thanks in part to the subsequent popularity of the African American musical innovations that developed as the Kansas City brand of jazz, by the next decade, such Yankee conceits and hostility were eclipsed, especially after such notable Kansas City jazz musicians as Count Basie and Charlie Parker had brought their talents to New York by the end of the 1930s. In particular, the bebop jazz that Parker initiated is the basis for the jazz structure of Morrison novel. Parker and others involved in spreading African American musical creativity helped fashion a racially shared public sphere, economically enabled once it became apparent to the record companies that African Americans spend money on recordings. For example, after Perry Bradford, a "black show-business entrepreneur [rebuffed by the large labels] . . . convinced a smaller label to let him make 'Crazy Blues' with Mamie [Smith], within a month of its release on Okeh Records 75,000 copies were sold."[149]

Arguably, once African Americans were able to participate in a shared musical culture, they were more enabled as civic participants. Black music, as Morrison's novel implies, was in integral to the way that the modernizing metropolis resisted former patterns of racial separation, and as Pattison suggests, operated in parallel with an architecture of the city that enabled her exemplary characters "Joe and Violet . . . to cultivate an intimate space between the public and the private in the modern city" (i.e., to assert their "right to the city").[150] Nevertheless, as has become increasingly apparent (and well publicized), the assertion of that right remains contested, especially in light of pervasively violent "law enforcement" which renders Black lives precarious while it "protects some [white] people through a safety net of schools, government-backed home loans, and ancestral wealth."[151]

To close this chapter, I want to note that music has been only one of the arts in which Black cultural and ultimately civic assertion has been conducted. In the mid-twentieth century Langston Hughes, addressing the importance of Black literary contributions, pointed to the importance of James Baldwin's *Notes of a Native Son*. In his review of the novel, he begins by figuring "the great artist" as an egalitarian, suggesting that "a great artist is one who projects the biggest dream in terms of the least person" and identifies Baldwin as such an artist. Welcoming him as a writer/civic activist who has crossed the color line, he refers to Baldwin's "pungent commentary" on "Harlem, the protest novel, bigoted religion, the Negro press and the student milieu of Paris," and adds, "When the young man who wrote this book comes to a point where he can look at life purely as himself, and for himself, the color of his skin mattering not at all, when, as in his own words, he finds 'his birthright as a man no less than his birthright as a Black man,' America and the world might as well have a major contemporary commentator."[152]

With respect to African American civic assertion, the city has been the primary space in which struggles for equality have been most visible. As I've emphasized, in the case of New York, it's a space that Morrison figures as an agent, alternatively facilitating and frustrating Black individual and collective self-assertion. Moreover, it has had agency assists, such as those by the infamous Robert Moses, whose

88 AESTHETICS OF EQUALITY

barrier-creating redesign of the city weighed in heavily on the side of frustration. In Chapter 3 my investigation moves from New York to Paris (where for nine years Baldwin resided) and focuses on another struggle for equality by that city's people of color, the bulk of whom are a residue of France's colonial past.

3

Sculpting in Time

Michael Haneke's *Caché*

Urban Interventions: Seizing a Right to the City

Shifting from the aural to the visual, while continuing to emphasize the right to the city, this chapter is an inquiry into the way visual arts intervene and disrupt the inequalities within the metropolitan venues in which immigrant populations from former colonies dwell. In a reflection on a historical context for the hegemonic structures that such interventions seek to disclose and challenge, Edward Portes points out, "The major contemporary migration flows do not follow a blind economic logic, but are commonly patterned by historical bonds of hegemony and the structural imbalance of peripheral societies subjected to the influence of more powerful nations."[1] That structural imbalance follows migrants into their postcolonial status. Addressing an aspect of the hostile political reactions of portions of the host countries' long-term resident populations, Portes notes that anti-immigrant nativist campaigns' "aggressive measures against immigrants do not stop with their arrival"; they "render their process of social and economic incorporation much more difficult."[2]

Seeking to obviate the social level difficulty to which Portes refers, the performance artist, Krzysztof Wodiczko stages interventions that introduce visual and aural dissonance into metropolitan spaces. Turning immigrants from exotic bodies into durational lives, he creates what Theodor Adorno attributes to one of the "invariable traits of [modern] art," a surface-disturbing "explosion" that inheres in the art work's "immanent temporality."[3] Among the "critical vehicles" Wodiczko has invented and distributed throughout urban spaces is the *bâton d'étranger* (alien staff), "a piece of storytelling equipment and a legal and ethical communication instrument and network

Aesthetics of Equality. Michael J. Shapiro, Oxford University Press. © Oxford University Press 2023.
DOI: 10.1093/oso/9780197670347.003.0004

for immigrants,"[4] which he first introduced into public spaces in Barcelona in 1992 and subsequently in several other metropolises. The staff, resembling the rod of a biblical shepherd, is equipped with a mini-video monitor running a short biographical sketch of the wearer. There's also a loudspeaker powered by batteries the wearer carries in a shoulder bag (Figure 3.1). The small size of the image on the screen induces an observer to move closer for a better look with the effect of diminishing the "usual distance between the operator . . . and the passersby."[5] Wodiczko's devices create "an incitement to infringe on

Figure 3.1 Alien staff, a Krysztof Wodiczko urban intervention
Source: Courtesy of Krzyztof Wodiczko

SCULPTING IN TIME 91

the barrier between stranger and non-stranger."[6] As they "disrupt the functionally and aesthetically designed urban environment and open it up to strangers,"[7] they serve as a material "critique of the fixity of forms of political interpellation" while expanding the range of legitimate civic bodies.[8] By repunctuating the pattern of daily interpersonal encounters, Wodiczko's devices encourage wary residents to look more closely at strangers whom they have thought to be too exotic to engage. The political force of his interventions is its impact on the "inequalities and stratification [of] . . . public space [which] is often barricaded and monopolized by the voices of those who are born to speak and prepared to do so."[9]

In Paris there has been another kind of urban intervention that similarly affects the visibility of the city's marginalized immigrant population. Beginning in the 1970s, the Arab-French theater troupes Al Assifa and Kahina "performed sketches on immigrant workers' experiences in France [Al Assifa]" and "gathered a mostly second-generation North African community to address the gender bias that plagued immigration politics [Kahina]."[10] Performing as street theater in Paris, the Al Assifa troupe would have an actor "run down an unspecified street while two others yelled 'stop him, stop him, he stole yogurt, it's an Arab.' The chaos that ensued would eventually be settled with a public conversation on the biases underlying the crowd's reaction." The interventions are aimed at establishing what Ermine Fişek refers to as an "aesthetic citizenship" that challenges the government-sponsored "aesthetic dimension" traditionally assigned to French citizenship.[11]

What follows is an extended focus on another temporality-attuned urban intervention into a city's field of vision, Michael Haneke's film *Caché*, which constitutes a different kind of disruption of a city's visual exchanges. Instead of attempting to attract the gaze of established nonimmigrant bourgeois citizens toward their "foreign" consociates, Haneke's camera trains an anonymous gaze on one of them. He selects for surveillance the life of an exemplary Parisian bourgeois resident, Georges Laurent, and creates a disruption that performs a different kind of ethno-political interpellation, one that targets long-settled white domestic rather than immigrant bodies. What I want to emphasize is the disturbance the film produces. Haneke's *Caché* reverses the

92 AESTHETICS OF EQUALITY

"imperial gaze."[12] It challenges the ethnic hierarchy of a French society in which the identity/difference matrix—a result of France's postcolonial immigration flows—is already disturbed. And crucially with respect to how the film is shot, it produces an unsettling phenomenology of reception by inhibiting the usual identification between viewer and camera focus. Incessantly concerning himself with a scene's effect on the viewer—"the question I ask myself isn't 'how do I show violence?' but rather how do I show the spectator [her/]his position and its representation?"[13]—Haneke's "sustained acts of vision," as David Rhodes puts it, "force us to stand outside its images, to experience the unknown-ness of the world, our own strangeness to ourselves."[14] While making viewers aware of their narrative expectations, the film has them accompanying the protagonists in a search for answers that it never unambiguously delivers.

Racism/Xenophobia as Event

Like Morrison's *Jazz*, featured in Chapter 2, Haneke's *Caché* is an aesthetico-political intervention into the history of a racial-spatial order. His political perspective is immanent in what he refers to as his aesthetic duty: "In all of my films, I try to fuel mistrust in our faith in reality. We know nothing about the world, except the things we have experienced directly. And we can examine these things. But everything else we experience through the media . . . I see it as my aesthetic duty to reflect this." "How do you behave when confronted with something that you should actually admit responsibility for?" he asks. "These are the sort of strategies that interest me, talking yourself out of guilt."[15] While implicating the viewer in the film's problematic by "moving 'the guilt out of the screen and into the auditorium of the arthouse,'"[16] Haneke makes architecture a pervasive protagonist within the film as well. Sharing a crucial aspect of Morrison's *Jazz* is an architectural narrative thread that radiates out from the film's "juxtaposed home and media space,"[17] as its focus moves back and forth between domestic and media-franchised work spaces, taking the viewer on an "architectural itinerary."[18]

SCULPTING IN TIME   93

Much of the film's thinking is delivered by the frequent shots of the exterior and interior of the capacious, fashionably furnished and decorated townhouse in an upscale neighborhood inhabited by Georges and Anne Laurent (Daniel Auteuil and Juliette Binoche), which are contrasted with shots of the exterior and interior of the cramped and barren apartment of an Algerian immigrant, Majid (Maurice Benichou), off a narrow corridor in a much less affluent neighborhood. The other main architectural object of scrutiny is the television studio from which Georges hosts a literary talk show. Television footage, an important medium in the film, intervenes frequently, for example running a news broadcast of occupying forces involved in the first Iraq War, which resonates with aspects of a French colonial history that has all but vanished from official and popular attention. That contemporary moment complements *Caché*'s implicit historiographic narrative, which references without directly witnessing a past historical moment, the French police's use of killing force against peaceful Algerian French protesters. That incident was fueled by a reciprocal historical process. After "the police seep[ed] into army operations in Algeria . . . army activities [had] come to form part of the job description of the policeman in the large cities of metropolitan France." The primary agent of that militarization of domestic policing was Maurice Papon, the head of the Paris police prefecture, who orchestrated the "infiltration of the French Army into the [domestic] police."[19] Having brought back to Paris the military measures he implemented during the Algerian War, Papon employed them to massacre hundreds of Algerians involved in the peaceful protest on October 17, 1961. As the film implies, responsibility for that atrocity has been conjured away in both official and popular media cultures. Black American expatriate writer William Garner Smith's novel *The Stone Face* (1963), which provides "a wrenching account of the police massacre of Algerian protestors on October 17, 1961—[is] the only one that exists in the fiction of the period."[20] The most palpable legacy of the event in Haneke's film is articulated through the character Majid, Georges's would-be foster brother whose parents perished in the massacre.

As the film narrative progresses one learns that Majid's temporary stay in the home of Georges's parents has been repressed by

94 AESTHETICS OF EQUALITY

both Georges and his mother (Annie Girardot), much as the Papon-instigated atrocities were largely ignored by much of the nonimmigrant portion of a French society, which, paradoxically, professed a republicanism that eschewed ethno-racial hierarchies of worthiness. Tzvetan Todorov identifies a "irony" associated with such historical phenomena. He contends that "racism . . . becomes an increasingly influential social phenomenon as societies approach the contemporary ideal of democracy." There's "the possible explanation of that fact." He suggests "that in traditional, hierarchical societies, social differences are acknowledged by the common ideology hence physical differences play a less crucial role . . . in such societies it is more important to know who are masters and who are slaves than whose skin is light and whose dark . . . [whereas] in democratic societies . . . although actual equality does not prevail, the ideal of equality becomes a commonly shared value; differences . . . continue to exist but the social ideology refuses to acknowledge them [as a result] we attribute to race what we no longer have the right to attribute to social difference."[21]

Forty years after the Papon-led massacre, ethno-racial identity achieved intensified attention as a rightist anti-immigrant nationalist political party with growing support among diverse media sponsored a resurgence of anti-Muslim sentiment in reaction to a contemporary event, the beheading of a teacher by a Chechen religious militant on October 16, 2020, who was enraged after the teacher showed his students cartoons of the prophet Muhammad. The episode was akin to dropping a grain of sand into a super saturated solution, a reservoir of ethnic hatred sponsored and influenced by the vociferations of Marine La Penn's National Front party. The growing wave of anti-immigrant sentiments put renewed pressure on France's claim to be living up to its motto, the officially and popularly recognized legacy of the French Revolution: "Liberty, Equality, Fraternity."

As is well known, it is not the first such test of French republicanism. As Adam Gopnik points out in his reprise of the (in)famous Dreyfus affair, "it was the first indication that a new epoch of progress and cosmopolitan optimism would be met by a countervailing wave of hatred that deformed the next half century of European history." And as is the case with the current situation, diverse media rode the wave of anti-immigrant hatred, for example Édouard Drumont's "anti-immigrant manifesto," which "was responding to the waves of Jewish immigrants from Germany and Eastern Europe who had arrived in France during the previous twenty or so years, bringing with them, he argued, values and a faith alien to Christian France."[22]

The current anti-immigrant outburst is inextricably tied to French colonialism, the historical trajectory of which has continually challenged the lived reality of France's republicanism, initially in light of France's violent treatment of the peoples within its colonial possessions and subsequently in its treatment of its domestic immigrant populations. Although the "particular history of the *banlieues* varies from suburb to suburb ... the ethnic segregation [they represent bears witness to] the failure of [the] deep-seated French republican imaginary."[23] The contemporary hostile responses to the migrant Muslim population are, as Gopnik implies, a repeat of what happened during the Dreyfus affair, which was a decisive repudiation of the enlightenment narrative. It "showed that a huge number of Europeans ... liked engaging in raw, animal religious hatred, and only felt fully alive when they did. Hatred and bigotry were not a vestige of the superstitious past but a living fire—just what comes, and burns naturally."[24]

Cinematic Responses

France's cultural/racial schism, articulated with social and economic inequalities, and exacerbated by a smoldering racism that episodically ignites, has been notably played out in Paris. The city harbors a microcosm of the geopolitical rift that separates white French citizens from its migrant nonwhite population, largely from Africa and consigned to heavily policed and surveilled *Banlieue*. That schism is elaborately explored in Mathieu Kassovitz's 1995 film *La Haine*, and is revisited a decade later in a more oblique way in Haneke's *Caché*, which is focused more on visibility within the social field as it bears on the legacy of Papon's 1961 Paris massacre than on the contemporary unequal deployment of violent policing featured in *La Haine*. Haneke had learned the details of the 1961 Paris massacre of more than two hundred French-Algerians, who ended up as bodies floating in the Seine. Taking that 1961 episode into account, and noting the extent to which

96 AESTHETICS OF EQUALITY

it has been largely absent from official and popular versions of French history, Haneke invents Majid and Georges and has Georges's lies about Majid, which gets him expelled from Georges's parent's home, reflect the big lie that Papon employed to attribute terrorist danger to France's Algerian immigrant population.

Georges's parents had employed Majid's parents on their farm as laborers. When they disappeared, presumably victims of the 1961 massacre, the plan was to adopt their son Majid. Jealous of the older boy's share of his parent's affectionate solicitude, Georges uses destructive and dishonest strategies aimed at getting Majid expelled from his home. After convincing Majid to decapitate a chicken, he informs his parents about the attack on the chicken and also claims he has seen Majid coughing up blood. Once Majid is seen as both disruptive and dangerous, he's forced to leave the farm. Instead of obtaining the benefits of a bourgeois existence, he grows up in an orphan's home. Thereafter, Georges represses his complicity in Majid's fate until anonymous tapes and images start appearing at his home and office. He presumes that Majid is the one responsible for the surveillance and its material manifestation, video footage of the Laurent home and his son's school, delivered along with drawn images of a decapitated fowl and of a head seeping blood from its mouth, because the drawings mimic the two blood-related episodes that Georges had ascribed to Majid on his family farm.

Inasmuch as Georges and the viewer are never apprised of the source of the videos and images, Haneke's interpersonal drama, which at a micropolitical level involves the abjection of an Algerian immigrant and at a macropolitical level refers allegorically to French society's treatment of their immigrant population, is carried out in the genre of a whodunit (an unconsummated one in which the viewer is positioned as a co-investigator in a drama in which there is no singular "who" to find). Haneke's cinematic, aesthetico-political intervention reverses the optics of *La Haine's* scenario. Where Kassovitz's film focuses on the policing authority's surveillance of Paris's *banlieue*-residing immigrant population, Haneke's film trains the gaze on a white bourgeois family and, by allegorical implication, contemporary France. It's a destabilizing gaze that disturbs Georges's will-to-forget his treatment of Majid, while it impugns France's collective will-to-forget its treatment of its immigrant population.

SCULPTING IN TIME   97

That collective will-to-forget is energized by France's distinctive form of cultural governance. The history of its violent treatment of immigrants is hidden in part because of its long-standing cultural assimilation policy which has been aimed at effacing ethno-racial difference. Echoing the pre-Enlightenment past, it's a secular version of "Christian efforts to exorcise Medieval Christendom of Jews and Moors."[25] And as Achille Mbembe notes, subsequent to the ending of its imperial hegemony, which had "been so deeply entrenched in French identity, its loss (and especially that of Algeria)," was experienced as "tantamount to a veritable amputation in a national imaginary suddenly deprived of one of its sources of pride."[26] No longer able to hold on to an imperial historical narrative, its "minorities were progressively hidden away, placed in the dark and covered with a veil of prudery that obfuscated their visibility in the nation's political and public life."[27]

In the case of the Algerian immigrant population that Majid represents, that willful obscuring now includes the proscription of cultural emblems. A historical juxtaposition of dress codes provides a perspective on the singularity of the contemporary version of France's assimilation policy: "In 1416, a Jewish woman named Allegra was arrested in Ferrara, Italy for not wearing earrings. The symbolism could not have been clearer. In an era when superfluous adornment was condemned as a sign of sin, Jews were required by law to wear conspicuous jewelry." The distinctive attire "reinforced the idea that Jews were a physically distinct and deviant people."[28] The assimilationist protocols of France's cultural governance reverse that cultural identity policy. Exemplary is the famous 1989 *Affaire du Foulard* (the headscarf affair). When three young Muslim women entered a middle school in Ceil wearing them, they were expelled, an expulsion that was officially validated when the highest judicial body in France ruled that the girls were in violation of the *Laicite* (secularism) law. Rather than being mere religious insignia, the wearing of the headscarves was deemed by the court to be an act of proselytizing.

Thus, while Ferrara's cultural governance applied to their Jewish population required them to show their ethno-religious identity, France's, applied to their Muslim population, required them to hide theirs, rendering their cultural being out of sight and out of mind.

98 AESTHETICS OF EQUALITY

What is at stake for a France that seeks to hide cultural difference? To put it in Jorge Fernandes's apropos terms, "Postcolonial . . . migrants challenge . . . [France's] narrative . . . of negative difference." In France, as elsewhere, their "presence denatures the link between nations and identities."[29] Featuring video long takes of Georges and Anne Laurent's grand urban apartment and Majid's modest one, Haneke's *Caché* takes on France's drive to hide disturbances to its identity narrative by turning to what an individual strives to hide. Concerned with what is "hidden" at individual and collective levels, it thinks with a cinematic technique that is best identified (using Andrei Tarkovsky's expression for his filming style) as "sculpting in time."[30] The political force of that filming style becomes apparent in juxtaposition with Kassovitz's *La Haine*.

To review briefly the different formal approaches of the two films, *La Haine* opens with typical cinematic action footage, television news coverage of the urban riots in the *banlieue* of a commune on the fringe of Paris (in reaction to an episode of police brutality). While *La Haine's* aesthetic approach evokes the MTV pop video style of a John Woo-directed film, *Caché's* aesthetic is more photographic. Seeing-oriented rather than action-oriented, *Caché* begins with a long take of an urban villa in an upper middle-class section of Paris. Referring to such a filming style as transcendental, the filmmaker Paul Schrader describes the effect on the viewer: "By delaying edits, not moving the camera, forswearing musical clues, not employing coverage, and heightening the mundane, transcendental style creates a sense of unease the viewer must resolve."[31]

While in the film's initial scene it appears that the viewer is seeing real-time filming, it turns out to be a video of an earlier filming moment being watched by Georges (Daniel Auteull) and his wife Anne (Juliette Binoche) Laurent, whose urban townhouse is the object of the camera's gaze. Their unease upon receiving an anonymous video of their home is shared by the viewer. Style-wise, rather than inviting the viewer to keep up with a rapid unfolding of action captured in the tracking and panning shots featured in *La Haine*, Haneke's filming style is akin to that of Michelangelo Antonioni's "cinema of poetry," which, as Pier Paulo Pasolini puts it, "allow[s] the camera to be felt."[32] Moreover, as is also the case with Antonioni's films, Haneke's *Caché*, is more an "*optical drama*" than a traditional one.[33] Crucially for purposes of the egalitarian impetus of *Caché's* optical drama, the film's scopic field has no commanding center. No character has a privileged perspective because as in Antonioni's films, in which the camera's perspective is "semi subjective,"[34] scenes are composed from points of view that do not coincide with the characters' perceptions. And while the film engages the viewer's "attentive perception,"[35] there are never unambiguous clues within the frame to provide a clear point of view. There is always a sense that something off screen is impacting on what can be seen, a sense from which consummation is withheld. In cinema, "the '*champ visual*' (field of vision)," as Pascal Bonitzer notes, "is always doubled by a '*champ aveugle*' (field of blindness),"[36] which in the case of *Caché* is "a site of historical trauma."[37] As a result, the diremption between *Caché's* camera consciousness and that of the perplexed protagonists whose home is under surveillance affects the viewer as well, whom Haneke endeavors to unsettle in order to encourage "thinking" rather than (secure) "knowledge."[38] As he remarks, "I attempt to stir up the viewer's distrust in the value of mediated images . . . when a film wants to be an art form, it has an aesthetic-moral obligation to reflect the questionability and dangers of its means of manipulation."[39]

Caché's form resonates with another aspect of Antonioni's cinematic poesis. In his criticism of what he regards as Alfred Hitchcock's suspense narratives, Antonioni remarks, "Life is also made up of pauses." In contrast with Hitchcock, he "aspires to discharge suspense" and organize his camera work to create ambiguity as to whose point of view shapes the scene.[40] Effectively in accord with that cinematic style, Haneke's *Caché* is composed as an Antonioni-like sequence of pauses. However, as Lisa Coulthard suggests, the film is also a listening text. The soundtrack is punctuated by long silences, soundless pauses in the film narrative in those moments when the camera is aimed at the Laurent villa for several minutes. That aspect of the film's style, to which Coulthard refers as an "acoustic minimalism,"[41] renders *Caché* as an aurally as well as an optically oriented drama. I want to note however that the film's punctuated silences frequently give way to a contrasting aspect of its aural composition. In the midst of dialogues among its characters there are media voices that intervene and scramble the soundtrack, such as a moment in which the television in the Laurent

100 AESTHETICS OF EQUALITY

home is broadcasting a noisy intervention in the couple's conversation, the above-noted *Euronews* report covering a gubernatorial appointment of an Italian diplomat to an Iraqi province during the Iraqi occupation. That broadcasted reference to a place of France's former colonial occupation is one among many instances of the film's cluttered "aural canvass."[42]

Coming to Terms with the Ethnoscape

In a commentary on Haneke's film, Eon Flannery refers to the complex choices involved in conceptualizing France's postcolonial population: "Cultural hybridity, liminality, diasporic consciousness, nomadism, migrancy, exile," are all possibilities, and "each has become differentially privileged in recent theoretical, schools."[43] Certainly the choice will inflect the conceptual home of the analysis. For purposes of the direction toward which this chapter points, a critical sense of the politics of equality, I am sorting two levels of interpellation. One is in accord with Flannery's emphasis on the conceptual framing's demands on viewer reception, the need to compose an identity matrix with historical depth. The other operates at a different level; it involves the specific identities ascribed to the film's protagonists. With respect to that level of interpellation, our attention is drawn to an ethos, a commitment to civic recognition for marginalized bodies on their own terms— "enunciations of self," in Ermine Fişek's apropos expression[44]—and a historical accounting of those who have deprived them of their own terms (a deprivation with significant material consequences). Such an ethos is reciprocal. As Edouard Glissant suggests, "Sometimes, by taking up the problem of the Other, it is possible to find oneself."[45]

In the case of France's relationship to the immigrant Other, self-assertion rather than self-discovery has been the dominant mode. Translating that situation for the field of visibility, the moving and still images that accompany the discursive agon within which postcolonial bodies have had to struggle in a state and society that has been *un*reciprocal, what is involved is control over how one can look at oneself. The film deconstructs what has historically been a hierarchically controlled scopic field. As it does so, we witness the main protagonist, Georges Laurent, becoming increasingly agitated as he tries to cope with his loss of control of that field. That personal experience constitutes the film's micropolitical level as it tracks the process by which a frantic Georges seeks to reassert control over how he is looked at, an attempt to be able once again to look at himself in the way he imagines himself seen (as the television talk show host mediating literary conversations). He identifies with a generalized social gaze that accords with how he locates himself in the present, while his retrospective gaze supports the normalizing autobiographical narrative with which he prefers to remember himself, enabling him to tell a story to himself and others that exonerates him from the violence he perpetrated on Majid.

The Gaze

As others have discerned, the film's rendering of a scopic field that destabilizes Georges's domestic and biographical self yields itself to interpretation through a Lacanian lens, an attention to what Jacques Lacan refers to as "the split between the eye and the gaze." The latter, as Lacan identifies it, is something unsettling for subjects, a sense of being seen that disrupts subjects' assumed positions in the scopic field, undermining their confidence in being in control of perceptions. Allocating the gaze to a level below one's conscious grasp, it is in his words "that which performs like a phantom force . . . In our relation to things, in so far as this relation is constituted by the way of vision, and ordered in the figures of representation, something slips, passes, is transmitted, from stage to stage, and is always to some degree eluded in it—that is what we call the gaze."[46] Hugh Manon captures the relevance to *Caché* of the eye-gaze split that Lacan conceives: "By depicting the protagonists' responses to an unseen (and ostensibly unseeable) video camera, repeatedly reminds us that the gaze is not the look."[47] Within a scopic field in which one is no longer in control, a sense of a returned gaze that does not coincide with the place from which the subject sees results in trauma for the subject that must cope with the suspicion that it is not an autonomous agent.[48] For Georges that trauma, associated with his loss of control over the scopic field, is especially disconcerting

102 AESTHETICS OF EQUALITY

because he has been comfortably viewing himself as a popular commentator/interviewer on television, managing dialogues among well-known authors and critics. Given his frequent programmed media exposure, he has become used to being a figure that is valorized by a substantial viewing public. As the film progresses, we watch Georges's personality disintegrate as he is haunted by a past that threatens his comfortable social and professional statuses. By implication, we observe the disclosure of a colonial past as the film deconstructs the egalitarian pretenses of France's republican heritage. Crucial to what *Caché* states is the way it shows the past in both Georges's and France's present.

Haneke's Sculpting in Time

While much of the promotional material surrounding the release of *Caché* nominates it as a "psychological thriller,"[49] it yields to political interpretation if conceived instead as "historiographic metafiction."[50] Haneke's film cuts back and forth between a present drama and what is a troubling (repressed) past for its protagonists. In a nonlinear cinematic narrative that embeds the biographical times of its protagonists within portions of France's historical time, it proceeds with "flashbacks and reverse-rewind shots [that] disrupt linear narratives of time, and by implication, linear models of history."[51] To appreciate the temporal confrontation that structures the film's aesthetico-political contribution, we have to recover the key historical changes that have reformatted the city of Paris's media ecology. As Friedrich Kittler points out, cities are media, among which are its architecture. Moreover, the "architectural media" represent a durational trajectory revealed by what Kittler identifies as the optical result of the city's structural changes: "Since cities no longer lie within the panopticon of the cathedral or castle, and can no longer be enclosed by walls or fortifications, a network made up of intersecting networks dissects and connects the city—in particular its fringes, peripheries and tangents."[52] Accordingly, while in her reading of Haneke's film, Brianne Gallagher's compelling focus on "policing Paris" concerns itself with contemporary coercive practices, I want to expand the temporality of that policing to note that the contemporary structure of Paris that Haneke's camera explores contains an immanent temporality that results from earlier police initiatives concerning the city's accessibility. In particular, "It was the police prefects of absolutism (such as La Reynie in Paris) who saw to it that the hand painted guild signs on the older houses conformed to the same standard and ultimately made them independent from the location of the house number."[53] Consequently, one aspect of the encounter of temporalities involved in the way *Caché's* story reveals itself is the ease with which Georges, after watching a video that reveals street signs on a filmed drive to Majid's apartment, finds his way there after having decided that Majid must be responsible for the videos and drawings arriving at his home and office.

Along with signage and other locational technologies (city maps, address and telephone catalogues) is another crucial technology on which Haneke's camera is frequently focused: the inclusion of Paris in modern automobility (at least for the resident bourgeois portion of the population). The shots of the Laurent's street location, with its long rows of late-model passenger cars, tells much of the contemporary story. However, if we imagine the sedimented history within the shot, we have to begin the story earlier. Automobility in France was spurred by an acceleration of production that was encouraged when France's car manufacturers embraced the American production model: "Production managers at Citroen, Peugeot, and Renault . . . aware of the methods of Henry Ford and Frederick W. Taylor, adapted them to specific situations within the French industry and within their own companies."[54] Unlike the history of automobility in the United States, automobility in France developed abruptly (after World War II).[55] However, as regards effects of that consumption, the relationship between class and automobility functioned in France the way it did in the United States. Car ownership rapidly became an "identity marker" as well as a means of transportation.[56] Among other things, it became an item of "glamour . . . a kind of daily apparel."[57] However unlike the consumption demographic in the United States, where people of color, especially African Americans, achieved a high level of car ownership after the automobile had begun dominating American transportation, the film shows that Paris's marginalized people of color, primarily its Africa-origin *banlieue* residents, had not been largely incorporated into France's automobility.

104   AESTHETICS OF EQUALITY

A seemingly incidental moment in the film registers the class and racial rift in Paris's automobility. It's a moment when Georges and Anne are about to enter their parked car after leaving a police station where they have reported the reception of the anonymous video tapes and drawings. Failing to see an Afro-French bicyclist, Georges opens the street-side car door, steps out, and narrowly misses being hit by the cyclist, who swerves to avoid colliding with him. A hostile confrontation ensues. After Georges shouts an insult, "watch where you're going, dickhead," the cyclist returns to confront Georges, demanding that he repeat what he said. Intimidated, Georges shrinks from his earlier belligerent posture and is told to by the cyclist to keep his mouth shut as he departs. It's an encounter that distils several relevant aspects of what the film is thinking about. As regards Paris's unequally distributed automobility, what is telling is that the Afro-Frenchman is on a bicycle. That aspect of the event accords with what is shown when Georges makes his way to Majid's neighborhood, which is not as densely filled with late-model parked cars. And most significantly, while Georges uses his car to move about freely, driving around the city, out to the countryside to visit his mother, and thence beyond his old family residence to a business meeting, the only times Majid is in a car is as a result of coercion.

Two remarks during the encounter speak to how the film structures the equality–inequality thematic. Georges's shout of "look where you're going dickhead" raises the issue of the normative reciprocities of the gaze, that is, on whom falls the responsibility to look (at what, at whom, when and how). It doesn't seem to occur to a self-righteous, privilege-assuming Georges that taking care to look for possible collisions is his responsibility. When the cyclist tells him to shut his mouth, he is referring to a speech organ that plays a crucial, continually referenced role throughout the film narrative. In terms of the allegorical connection between Georges and French colonial history, his mouth—hardly ever shut but ever unreliable—is crucial to how the film thinks about what it thinks. Georges continually dissembles, misleading himself and others during his frantic attempt to cope with the mystery of the tapes and drawn images. It is with respect to the disconnect between what is the case and what comes out of Georges's mouth that a scene in which he visits his mother is telling.

Madam Laurent, an Attendant

The figure of the attendant is conceived in Gilles Deleuze's analysis of some of Francis Bacon's paintings in which he observes the presence of a figure or figures that have no narrative relationship to what is happening with the central figure. In his words, the attendant is "a constant or point of reference," a "spectator," but not in the ordinary sense. The attendant is a "kind of spectator" who "seems to subsist, distinct from the figure."[58] Deleuze's attendant, a guide to what is taking place in the scene, "is robust enough to apply to other visual media," as I have noted; it adapts well to cinema in which many characters play such a role.[59] In *Caché* Georges's mother functions as an attendant who helps disclose what is the case, both immediately with respect to Georges's penchant for denial and historically with respect of France's denial of a historical atrocity.

Georges's denials precede his conversation with his mother. It is shortly after a scene at a dinner party at his home that Georges drives out to his birth home to visit his mother. The party had been interrupted by another tape delivery, which Georges, coming back to the guests at his dining table from his front porch, where he picks up the tape and stuffs it in a coat pocket, initially denies; "there was nothing," he says. But when Anne then tells the guests about getting tapes and images, Georges confesses to the delivery while evoking the film's title, saying, "I won't hide it." Nevertheless, his hiding persists. After he arrives at the family farm where his aging mother is now bedridden and attended by a nurse, a conversation ensues in which his mother exposes the egregious gap between what is the case and what Georges says. As George sits by her bed, she begins by asking after the well-being of the family. Lying, Georges says everything is fine. She avers to the contrary, saying he looks troubled. Thereafter, she continually challenges his utterances, which are consistently at variance with reality. When he refers to her being unwell, she corrects him, saying she's not unwell, she has gotten old; "for my age I'm very well," she says. When he wonders whether she's lonely in her isolation, she points out that loneliness is a perspective, not a condition, asking if *he's* lonely when he's at home and when he's at work. When he finally brings up what's on his mind, telling her he has dreamed about

106 AESTHETICS OF EQUALITY

Majid, she asks, "Who's Majid?," having repressed the memory of his stay on their farm. After he reminds her about him: ("Majid, Hashem's son. The kid you planned to adopt . . . do you ever think about him?"), she replies, "It was a long time ago; it's not a happy memory." Although she too is part of the repression of Majid's abjection from their home, she is also a voice that points out what is the case with Georges's incessant reality denials. Transcending her role in Georges's past family life, she's a figure who gestures toward the film's allegorical, macropolitical theme, France's willful "colonial amnesia,"[60] in which its repression of the 1961 Papon-led atrocity participates. What mother and son repress stands in for a pervasive institutionalized forgetting. Government media control has been so effective that a 2001 opinion poll "revealed that most French citizens had never heard of the massacre."[61]

The conversation between Georges and his mother—redolent with repressions—barely touches on one of the film's primal scenes. Later in the film we witness the return of the repressed as an episode at the family farm returns during one of Georges's dreams. In the dream sequence, the camera observes from a substantial distance (thereby conveying the scene as obscured history) the moment when Majid is forcibly packed into a car belonging to the orphanage to which he has been consigned. What Georges strives to repress stages an oneiric return, showing the viewer a past that has been hidden, generated by a memory that Georges would rather neither recall nor share. Georges repeats his subterfuge in a conversation with Anne, claiming after his first visit to Majid that he could not find him. After he and Anne watch the tape that is delivered with a recording of his visit to Majid's apartment, he apologizes to Anne for lying. However, he is wholly unapologetic about why he had the hunch that Majid was responsible for the tapes (a hunch he had refused to share). Pressed by Anne, he admits lying about Majid to his parents in order to get him sent away but claims he cannot recall the actual lies, and adds that it was only a trivial "interlude" in his family's life. "I don't feel responsible," he says. Once again, what comes out of his mouth is contrary to what is the case, a profound sense of responsibility and guilt, evident in his dream sequences, which in his waking life he will not acknowledge, even to himself.

SCULPTING IN TIME 107

While focusing extensively on what Georges is reluctant to admit, the film reflects allegorically on what France has been reluctant to admit. "Sixty-four years passed before French President Emmanuel Macron admitted (in 2021) that Ali Boumendjel, a prominent wartime defender of Algerians imprisoned by the French [in 1957] did not commit suicide [but rather] . . . was tortured and assassinated."[62] As for who or what are responsible for recording the video sequences and drawing the images that afflict Georges, who never apologizes and never ultimately extracts an admission from his suspect, Majid, the viewer shares the enigma. We are never certain about the agency for what we are seeing. Rather than moralizing, Haneke's film withholds consummation and demands reflection. At a symbolic level that exceeds the specific drama in which its characters are involved, the film places the same ethico-political burden on the viewer that it places on France.

Caché as a Cinema of Seeing

In his analysis of the difference between a cinema of action and a cinema of seeing, Gilles Deleuze focuses on what it implies for viewer reception. In the former, "the viewer's problem becomes 'What are we going to see in the next image?'" while in the latter, it is "What is there to see in the image?" because in the cinema of seeing, there is "no longer a sensory motor situation, but a purely optical and sound situation."[63] That optical and sound situation emerges in *Caché's* opening scene. The viewer, confronted with an almost two-minute-long take of the Laurent's urban apartment from across the street, has no context for what she is seeing until rewinds and dialogue intrudes. Then it becomes evident that the shot is a video being watched and then rewound by the Laurents, who are in conversation about why the video was delivered and what it implies. Before the couple is introduced, what is heard is a male voice, "*Alors?*" (well), followed by a female voice, "*Rien*" (nothing), then "*C'etait ou*" (where was it), followed by "*Dans un sac plastique dans la porte*" (in a plastic bag inside the entryway). Moreover, and revealingly, in a remark that characterizes both the characters and viewers of Haneke films, Georges says, "I don't know what to say." It's the kind of experience that is pervasive in Haneke films. In his *Code Unknown* (2000), for example, he uses a title that makes not knowing what to say explicit. It's a film in which we are not sure what we're seeing, what's important (as the film takes us back and forth in time), or *what to say about it*.

What is most confounding in Haneke's *Caché* is the source of the shots. After the opening sequence, which reveals no apparent agent doing the filming, the viewer and the Laurents are faced with a mystery, sending both on a search for signs. What immediately ensues onscreen is a domestic disturbance as Georges and Anne Laurent express their anxiety in irritable exchanges. While in the immediate foreground of the filming at that point we see an agitated couple bickering as they lay the table in preparation for their evening meal, in the background are objects with more temporal depth. There's a large collection of books in floor to ceiling bookcases that dominate the room (Figure 3.2). While the couple is oblivious to what is simply a familiar background containing what they have accumulated during the span of

Figure 3.2 Laurent home bookcase in Michael Haneke's *Caché*
Source: France 3 Cinema + Boudrian Film Vega

SCULPTING IN TIME 109

their domestic life, the viewer is enjoined to read it as a sign that is best read retrospectively, after the film shows Majid's humble apartment, which is a cramped space with virtually bare walls. On the one hand, the books speak to George and Anne's class, educational backgrounds, and employment—the viewer sees in subsequent scenes that Georges is a moderator and host of a television literary talk show and that Anne is an employee in a book publishing company—and on the other, they reflect a crucial aspect France's political economy. A substantial personal library speaks less to the practice of reading than to the unequal distribution of capital, a process of accumulation that the French bourgeoisie's inherited wealth and associated educational capital makes possible. Inasmuch as no one is seen reading throughout the film narrative, the latter is the more important sign. The books serve as props whose content is irrelevant to the story's drama, only to its setting and implications. A reading of the book collection as a sign of class becomes especially compelling in a later scene when Majid's son confronts Georges in his workplace and accuses him of having deprived his father of an education.

Once Georges and Anne have begun their evening meal, their son Pierrot (Lester Makedonsky) shows up a bit late and seems at that point to be a relatively inconsequential character, a typically laconic adolescent who delivers minimal responses to his parents' questions about his day. However, he subsequently becomes an important figure in the film narrative. Early in the film his role is simply that of being a child of a bourgeois family. Thus, shortly after seeing him at dinner, he is a subject in another education-relevant sign, which surfaces when there's a cut from the scene at the family table to a pool where Pierrot is at swimming practice. There he becomes part of a revelatory process, one which typifies a preoccupation of the French bourgeoisie, an intense focus on inducting their children into meritocracy. Rather than a space of leisure, the pool is an intensively surveilled classroom where a swimming coach is micromanaging the students' form, continually shouting corrections to their strokes, breathing, depth, and turns. The class-shaping pressures to which Pierrot is subjected are reaffirmed when his parents come to witness his performance at a swim meet later in the film (in which fortunately for him, he wins his heat). Revealingly as well, it's the only scene in which Georges and Anne appear emotionally in accord, seated paratactically (side by side), in contrast with their usual face-to-face bickering—it's Anne *and* Georges rather than Anne *against* Georges (and vice versa)—as they cheer for their son's achievement.

After a cut from Pierrot's swimming practice, the camera is again still. There's an even longer take of the Laurent residence, taking between four and five minutes, this time in the evening. In the midst of that long take are two shots of Georges, one that has him returning home while his residence is being filmed, another that takes us to his television studio as his interview program is signing off. Visible in the studio's background is another floor-to-ceiling display of books. However, in this case there are no actual books. What is visible is a mural of shelves full of books without titles, implying once again that the film's shots of books are meant to mark the class of those for whom they are signs of status (Figure 3.3). The scene speaks (in Jean Baudrillard's terms) to a book's "sign function value" rather than to what may be available in its distillation of thinking. As Baudrillard puts

Figure 3.3 TV studio books in Michael Haneke's *Caché*
Source: France 3 Cinema + Boudrian Film Vega

it, sign function value inheres in a "practice of objects," a class's engagement in a process of "sign exchange" that signals its status within a social hierarchy.[64] The book images in Georges's television studio are participating in "social pretention."[65]

Immediately after Georges's interview program finishes signing off, ending with a close-up of Georges mouthing his program's usual closing remarks (about when to expect the next episode), he's summoned by a TV station employee who hands him an image of a mouth spewing blood that has been delivered to his workplace. Shortly thereafter, Haneke gives the viewer a clue about the significance of mouths. Within a few moments after the film has cut back to the evening's video surveillance of the Laurent residence, there's a break in the scene. The camera reverses and aims at a widow opposite *chez* Laurent, where an "ethnic," an Algerian immigrant-looking adolescent, is framed with red fluid dripping from his mouth and running down his chin. Although an initial look suggests that his mouth is mimicking the bloody mouth in the image delivered to Georges (doubtless an aspect of what is being conveyed), a closer inspection suggests that it's likely juice from a piece of fruit he's been eating while peering across the street toward the Laurent home. The image of the youth supports two of the film's emphases. One is the increasing focus on mouths; another is a preview of an emerging theme, children distributed across the ethno-racial divide as witnesses. To provide a framing for that second aspect of the film I want to suggest that what emerges as the film reaches its conclusion is a Bergmanesque narrative thread; children play the role of witnesses in many of Ingmar Bergman's films, pervasively in two of them: *The Silence* (1963) and *Fanny and Alexander* (1982). Crucially however, Haneke resists an "idealization of children." His "child figures," as Alexandra Lloyd points out, are "caught between victimhood and perpetratorship, innocence and guilt, and innocence and experience."[66]

Childhood looms large by the end of the film but is already seeded in earlier. Picking up the sequence: although the next cut is to the inside of the Laurent's home, where Georges and Anne are discussing the latest delivery of a video and image, the viewer is already left to ponder the increased complexity of a scopic field to which an anonymous child-as-witness has been added. The importance of that aspect

112   AESTHETICS OF EQUALITY

of the drama is to be subsequently reinforced. As the flow of symbolic assaults on the Laurents increases—a pair of anonymous phone calls asking for an absent Georges that Anne receives, and more deliveries of drawings with bloody images (from a mouth and from the neck of a chicken)—we witness a Georges who continually refuses to share what he suspects as the source. After he first lies to Anne about what he knows and is pursuing, it drives her in despair to a tearful meeting with a male confidante, her work colleague with whom she has been involved in a mild flirtation. His warm, affectionate physical reaction as he hugs her is witnessed by Pierrot, who sees them through the window of the café where they're meeting. Disturbed, Pierrot disappears for a while, making his parents frantic and leading them to suspect that Majid has kidnapped him. When Pierrot finally shows up, having stayed overnight at a friend's house, he angrily pushes his mother away when she greets him emotionally, accusing her of an illicit romance.

With that latter act, a consequence of Pierrot's role as a witness, the film has elevated his significance as an agent in the drama, which is consummated in the last scene (an analysis of which I will defer for the chapter's conclusion). What I suggest at this point is that as the film turns Pierrot into a protagonist, Haneke's drama has begun mimicking the family stories in many of Ingmar Bergman's films. For example, in an analysis of Bergman's film *The Silence* (1963), in which a child, Johan, a preadolescent staying in a hotel with his mother and aunt, becomes the witness through whom the relationship between the sisters and between his mother and a lover is played out, I've put it his way:

> While the fraught relationship between the sisters drives much of the film drama, as is the case with much of his film corpus, in Bergman's *The Silence* a child is the film's main witnessing protagonist. The film turns the hotel where most of the film drama takes place into a series of cameras managed by Johan and aimed both within and without. Within the hotel, Johan looks from room to room as the tense relationship between Anna and Ester proceeds; he peers around the empty hotel corridors; he looks into the hotel porter's room, and he peers into other rooms.[67]

SCULPTING IN TIME   113

Policing Paris

By the end of the film, it has become clear that Pierrot is fed up with the neurotic antics of his parents. His mood registers itself in his temporary disappearance, his failure to come home one evening. Panicked about Pierrot's failure to return home, his parents involve the police, who, acceding to Georges's suspicion of Majid's role in his son's disappearance, accompany Georges to Majid's apartment, arrest him and his son, and hold them temporarily until it becomes clear that they're not involved in Pierrot's absence. That form of coercive policing, visited disproportionately on the immigrant population of Paris, speaks to their lack of equality before the law (as it's implemented) by the actual police. However, in contrast to policing as carried out by Paris's uniformed police personnel is a more abstract form of policing Paris. Gallagher provides a critical intervention into that aspect of policing, changing it from its usual reference to the coercive tactics of official, uniformed police forces to a Deleuzean structural perspective, to what Deleuze refers to as contemporary "societies of control."[68] Translating that perspective to illustrate what Haneke's *Caché* discloses, Gallagher emphasizes the way the urban grid, and its related coding of habitation and movement within it, exercises a generalized form of control. She points out that Haneke maps and provides historical depth for "the plan of Paris's urban infrastructure . . . specifically, mapping the privacy of the [Laurent's] home onto France's historical and *ongoing* colonial practices."[69] Heeding Gallagher's translation, I want to emphasize the way the film treats the subjectivities assigned to alternative kinds of bodies and their differential access to space, an aspect of policing that Jacques Rancière has famously theorized (in a way that comports well with a film that emphasizes what is willfully hidden). For Rancière

> The police . . . is first an order of bodies that defines the allocation of ways of doing, ways of being, and ways of saying, and sees that those bodies are assigned by name to particular place and task; it's an order of the visible and the sayable that sees that a particular activity is visible and another is not.[70]

114   AESTHETICS OF EQUALITY

A New York City episode that Rosalyn Deutsche reports and analyzes provides an exemplary illustration of Rancière's conception of policing. A group of neighborhood residents took it upon themselves to police a park in Greenwich Village, locking it in the evening in order to prevent its use as a place to sleep by a homeless group. While a feature in the *New York Times* supported the initiative, bannering it "The Public's Right to Padlock a Public Space," and the City Parks Department "welcomed [public collaboration,] 'public' help in achieving its aim, the eviction of homeless people from the park," Deutsche has a reaction that accords well with Rancière's version of policing:

> Is it possible, to speak with assurance of a public space where social groups, even when physically present are systemically denied a voice? Does anyone hold a key to public space? What does it mean to relegate groups to a sphere outside the public, to bar admission to the discursive construction of the public, and in this way prohibit participation in the space of public communication?[71]

Similarly, Majid's voice went unheeded as he was evicted from the Laurent family farm. The policing in his case "assigned his body by name to a particular place," an orphanage. A late scene, represented as Georges's dream, reviews a collaboration involved in his eviction. It's one between the family and the agents of the orphanage, as Majid's odyssey from private space to a public institution is forcibly imposed; he's dragged kicking and screaming by orphanage personnel into their vehicle (one of his earlier noted experiences of coercive automobility).

How *Caché* Thinks Ethico-Politically

In a critical review of Haneke's *Caché*, Paul Gilroy, noting Haneke's oblique, allegorical treatment of the Papon-instigated massacre, refers to it as "an overly casual citation of the 1961 anti-Arab pogrom by Papon's police," and concludes, "the dead deserve better than that passing acknowledgement."[72] As an approach to aesthetics, Gilroy's critique of *Caché* adheres to what Rancière call the "ethical regime

SCULPTING IN TIME **115**

of images," which requires a work to point toward an ethico-political telos. Gilroy puts his sense of the film's failure to do so this way:

> Many people involved in building a habitable multicultural Europe will feel there are pressing issues of morality and responsibility involved in raising that history only to reduce it to nothing more than a piece of tragic machinery in the fatal antagonism that undoes *Caché's* protagonists.[73]

Resisting Gilroy's critique, I suggest that the film's protagonists are functioning as aesthetic subjects whose experiences and actions transcend the level of the individual and serve to animate the provocation of a whodunit narrative that challenges the viewer to think about France's historical responsibility for the 1961 atrocity. *Caché* is a feature film, not a documentary. Its allegorical structure delivers the indictment of the episode that Gilroy wanted to have directly addressed. While Gilroy refers to the "aestheticism" of the film's "misplaced tactic," its "whodunit narrative structure," it's better conceived as a politics of aesthetics that discloses a particular historical atrocity and the persistent violation of France's egalitarian pretensions. In his *Caché*, as in his other work, Haneke resists moralizing. The role of the arts, as the novelist and screen writer Thornton Wilder puts it (while pondering the undecidability between necessity and contingency that catastrophic events evoke) "is not to answer questions, but to state them fairly."[74]

Haneke states the questions visually, leaving the viewer to ponder fairness. As Nancy Virtue puts it, "He is less interested in representing a consumable version of the historical 'truth' of 17 October 1961 than in creating for the viewers a film that requires interpretive work."[75] To demand that a moral treatise be embedded in *Caché* is to miss the subtle ways that its form encourages critical ethico-political thinking rather than "reassuring or instructing its viewers."[76] For example, although we observe a "bifurcated past" in which Georges and Majid occupy vastly different circumstances[77]—the former a successful media personality with an accumulation of material and cultural capital and the latter relatively impoverished in both senses—we also see them achieving an equivalence in two scenes that we should be able to connect, for they are clearly meant to refer to each other (one of

116 AESTHETICS OF EQUALITY

the films many referential montages). Each scene shows one of them weeping. The first takes place after Georges's first visit to Majid. The camera returns to Majid's apartment where he is seen breaking into tears because the sight of Georges has brought back a painful recollection (he had told Georges that catching sight of him on television had made him feel ill). In the second, Georges is shown weeping after returning home, dissolving in tears of anxiety and frustration because his encounters with Majid have not yielded satisfaction with respect to the enigma of the tapes. Despite what divides the two in terms of the enormous differential in their possession of capital, they are shown to be equally human and thus equally vulnerable to despair. Although many of the film's montage sequences articulate "the various rifts that exist between its characters,"[78] the weeping scenes respond to a question about what persons who are so divided fundamentally share. The juxtaposition of the scenes suggests that whether possessed of wealth and position or not, no one is immune from being emotionally ambushed when an encounter with signs unleashes the hauntings of one's past. For both Georges and Majid, their encounters overcome a disjunction between "the calendar of facts" and "the calendar of feelings."[79]

The film's allegorical structure shows as I've suggested that Georges's lies about Majid constitute a micro-level evil that gestures toward the France's lies about their colonial and postcolonial atrocities. The micro level registers itself in the two weeping scenes. As Haneke states (in an interview about the film), "there's such a thing as emotional memory for evil deeds."[80] As for the macro (allegorical) level, what the film delivers is not an explicitly stated indictment of the excesses of France's colonial and postcolonial violence (much to the disappointment of reviewers who lament its lack of an explicit moral stance).[81] Instead it is a nuanced treatment of what Haneke refers to as "the primal legacy of colonialism,"[82] expressed through a cinematic form that looks at the way the past registers itself in psyches that have closed themselves off from that legacy. At the same time, the film's implicit allegorical level creates an uneasy articulation between the characters' "emotional memory" and French history. It opens a thinking space to reflect on a (hi)story that official French cultural policy has sought to silence. Among the significant political questions pertaining to the

SCULPTING IN TIME 117

memory-history relation is about whose memories become recognized as history, an issue that Pierre Nora has addressed extensively.

Identifying that issue in a way that pertains to Haneke's Majid and the like, Nora refers to "a process of interior colonization [which] has affected ethnic minorities, families and groups that until now [the late twentieth century] have possessed reserves of memory but little or no historical capital."[83] Nora's analysis of that memory-history divide effectively captures the politico-epistemological dynamic underway in *Caché's* Paris. The Georges-Majid struggle is about memory, which involves a "dialectic of remembering and forgetting, unconscious of its successive deformations, vulnerable to manipulation and appropriation, susceptible to being dormant and periodically revived."[84] In contrast, "history," as Nora juxtaposes it, "is the reconstruction, always problematic and incomplete, of what is no longer."[85] And crucially with regard to what Haneke's film discloses, official history constitutes a "conquest and eradication of memory;"[86] "its true mission," as Nora puts it, "is to suppress and destroy it."[87]

In response to that suppression, Haneke's video camera, in particular the anonymous surveillance long takes, interarticulate memory with history to provide a cinematically delivered combination of countermemory and counterhistory. To situate the implications of the agency of Haneke's camera we can heed what Nora refers to as "the most tangible sign of the split between history and memory," which has been "the emergence of a history of history . . . in France . . . a historiographical consciousness."[88] That historiographic consciousness takes the form of what Michel Foucault famously calls counterhistory. Referring in one of his lectures to a history of race struggle as a counterhistory to the one preferred by the modern state, a consensual, self-congratulatory sovereignty-oriented history, he states:

> Not only does counterhistory break up the unity of the sovereign law that imposes obligations, it also breaks up the continuity of glory . . . it reveals the light—the famous dazzling effect of power . . . a divisive light that illuminates one side of the social body but leaves the other side in shadow or casts it into darkness. And [a] . . . counterhistory . . . will of course speak from the side . . . of those . . . who now find themselves . . . in darkness and silence.[89]

118 AESTHETICS OF EQUALITY

Foucault's light/shadow imagery provides a propitious language for translating the "image facts" that Haneke's camera illuminates.[90] As it shines its light on the George–Majid relationship, it draws a shameful episode of French history out of the France's officially and popularly imposed shadow. Cinema's suitability for a counterhistorical sensibility is effectively demonstrated in Gilles Deleuze's work on cinema's time image, a direct image of time in which rather than basing temporality on the movement of characters (an indirect time image), time is a function of the director's sequence of shots. Interpreting the time image's functioning in a "counterhistorical film," as noted in Deleuze's cinema analysis, Marcia Landy writes, "Refusing to monumentalize, reinforce national identity, and elevate heroic action, [the] counterhistorical film destabilizes revered styles of militarism and patriotism derived from popular history, photography, and cinema."[91]

I want to suggest, by way of confronting the enigma of the tapes and images, that Haneke's *Caché* both uses and thematizes time. Dominated by time—rather than movement—images, the film lends agency to time. Sculpting in time, Haneke directs his surveillance videos (with their accompanying drawings) and assembles other video filmed scenes in a way that lends agency to a counterhistorical temporality. The camera evokes and shows obscured biographical memories that articulate with an obscured historical event. As exemplary historiographic metafiction, *Caché* makes use of cinematic flashbacks that insinuate the past in the present while it *hides* a compelling ethico-political challenge to France's egalitarian pretentions within a whodunit. Rather than providing a banal moral lesson, the film provokes the viewer to find that challenge. And importantly, its ethico-political sensibility gestures toward a future as well: an aspect to which I turn in the next section.

Liberty, Equality, Fraternity

As I suggested, Georges and Anne's son Pierrot ultimately becomes a major protagonist. By the end of the film he is joined in that role by Majid's unnamed son (Walid Afkir), whose presence, while confronting Georges in his workplace, helps to move the film narrative

SCULPTING IN TIME   119

from a drama involving two families to a collective national drama. However, what is immediately evident as the conversation begins is how Majid's son has inherited his father's emotional maturity, "in stark contrast with Georges's emotional immaturity," as Joy Schaefer observes.[92] As she points out, during his first conversation with Georges, after Majid says, "Why do you talk as if we're strangers," we see that "Majid has analyzed their *fraternal* affective economy" (my emphasis). He recognizes the combination of cultivation and aggressiveness of an assertive white bourgeois male. However, because Georges is unreflectively certain about his accusations, Majid's "words are wasted on the deaf ears of Georges (and allegorically, the French government)."[93] So Majid ultimately selects a more dramatic statement, summoning Georges and then slitting his own throat in front of him, after saying, "I wanted you to be present for this." Majid's last words imply that he wanted Georges to be both present for the end of a life he has ruined—a decisive sundering of a relationship that *could have been* fraternal—and present to himself, finally confronting what he has been responsible for destroying (and allegorically confronting what France has been responsible for).

Paradoxically, the bloody end of Majid, which actualizes the virtuality of the drawing of a head George received with blood flowing from its mouth, is carried out with remarkable *sangfroid*. When Majid's son visits Georges in his workplace he maintains the same *sangfroid*, which contrasts with his agitated interlocutor. After he has chided Georges for having deprived his father of an education, an irritable and defensive Georges, still masking his anxiety with the outward sense of certainty about his conduct (which he has maintained with his "friends, colleagues and his wife"),[94] asks if he's expected to apologize. To that Majid's son replies, "To whom would you apologize, me?" To situate the sense of that reply I want to report an analogous situation in the United States, reported by the Associated Press on August 6, 2005.

SAN FRANCISCO—Giants [baseball] manager Felipe Alou called a one-week suspension given to a radio host for making racial remarks about the team's Latino players "a slap on the hand" and said he wouldn't accept an apology from Larry Krueger. "He came to apologize to me? You have to be kidding me," Alou said Saturday, one day

120   AESTHETICS OF EQUALITY

after the suspension ... he wasn't in position [he added] to accept an apology on behalf of the "hundreds of millions" of people offended earlier this week when Krueger went on the Giants' flagship station, KNBR, and went off about the struggling club and its "brain-dead Caribbean hitters hacking at slop nightly."[95]

Majid's son's similar question gestures toward the film's allegorical level. He is implying that he is in no position to accept an apology for the treatment not only of his father but also of upward of two million immigrants (counting first- and second-generation French Algerians). Just as Georges and Majid are aesthetic subjects whose roles transcend the sundering of their personal potential brotherhood, so are their sons. As the last scene approaches, we observe how through them, the next generation, the film gestures toward a restoration of a fraternal bond.

The film ends with a scene in front of Pierrot's school. As the credits are run the viewer can catch a glimpse of the two sons, Georges's and Majid's, standing amiably side by side (posed paratactically, with neither subordinate to other). There's a barely audible conversation in the background. A female voice says, "*Elle est ou*?" (She is where?) to which a reply is given by a girl wearing a purple backpack, "*Elle nique ton père*" (She is fucking your dad).[96] That remark has two resonances. First, as an obscenity it accords with Haneke's challenge to the bourgeois habitus: "In my definition," he says, "anything that could be termed obscene departs from the bourgeois norm. Whether concerned with sexuality of violence or another taboo issue, anything that breaks with the norm is obscene."[97] Second, and crucial to the last part of Haneke's sculpting in time, it's a gesture toward a future carried out by the next generation. I suggest that rather than referring to a sexual encounter, the remark "fucking your dad" is meant to say "fuck the dad"; he and his generation are unable to transcend their xenophobia and live up to France's republican motto, *Liberté, égalité, fraternité*. As the film closes, Haneke's sculpting in time is reflected in imagery that articulates a grammatical shift, the subjunctive (fraternity as something that might yet be) and the future anterior (fraternity as a possibility that always will have been). The Rancière assertion quoted in Chapter 1 applies here as well and provides a fitting conclusion: "Fraternal community is won," he writes, "in the combat against the paternal community . . . By destroying the portrayal of the father [the burden of much of the film narrative], which is at the heart of the representative system, it opens the future of a fraternal humanity."[98]

4

An Egalitarian Istanbul

Ethos's Cinematic Portraiture

Preface: Image Capital

The prologue of Kazuo Ishiguro's novel *The Remains of the Day* testifies to the historical depth of the relationship between portraiture and privilege. Stevens, a butler at work in Darlington Hall, Mr. Farraday's English manor, has been offered a driving journey away from his daily employment "in the comfort of Mr. Farraday's Ford." Recounting the circumstances in which the offer is made, Stevens says:

> The idea of such a journey came about, I should point out, from a most kind suggestion put to me by Mr. Farraday himself one afternoon almost a fortnight ago, when I had been dusting the portraits in the library. In fact, as I recall, I was up on the step-ladder dusting the portrait of Viscount Wetherby when my employer had entered carrying a few volumes which he presumably wished returned to the shelves.[1]

The political sensibility of that portrait scenario is concisely glossed in a 2022 gallery exhibition preview: "For centuries, portraits . . . were reserved for capturing images of the elite, leaving a distorted historical record largely limited to the wealthy, the pale and the male."[2] It is similarly captured in a curational accompaniment to an earlier 2016 gallery exhibition, "The Politics of Portraiture":

> Portraiture is a political act. Who gets to be represented and revered, passed through the channels of history and power long after they have left the earth? Who gets to have wall panels written in their

Aesthetics of Equality. Michael J. Shapiro, Oxford University Press. © Oxford University Press 2023.
DOI: 10.1093/oso/9780197670347.003.0005

AN EGALITARIAN ISTANBUL   123

name, their lives detailed while their likenesses become a commodity available for purchase and view, and mass reproduction?[3]

As the commentary on the exhibition proceeds, it engages the issue of technological change, noting how contemporary widely available technologies and venues for producing and circulating images have resulted in the democratization of "image capital." As is well known, the technological narrative that the exhibition enters begins much earlier. It was the invention of photography that created the possibility for economically and ethnically diverse individuals to rise above the threshold of public recognition. Photographers challenged the power- and privilege-invested representational practices that had limited image capital to political leaders and "the individual propertied male,"[4] posing difficulties for those political and economic elites seeking to perpetuate and manage hierarchies of human worthiness. For example, at a crucial historical moment the photographer August Sander's famous photographic collections *Man in the Twentieth Century*, "a meticulous examination of human appearance, personality, and social standing . . . each fitting into a sweeping scheme of categories and subcategories,"[5] and his *Citizens of the Twentieth Century: The Nazi and the Jew*, challenged the Nazi regime's politics of representation, predicated on a moral anthropology that designated some lives as unworthy: *Lebensunwertes Leben* (lives unworthy of life).[6]

Providing another politically attuned perspective nearly a century later—in an era that has become increasingly cognizant of the historical and contemporary precariousness of Black lives—the photographer Dawoud Bey issues a similar challenge (with considerable temporal depth) to the circulation of image capital. He "draws a direct line [with work exhibited at New York's Whitney Museum] between the treatment of Black people in the 19th century, and now."[7] His photographic portraiture has a historiographic sensibility that "visualizes [Black] communities that have been underrepresented" and conveys "the power and possibility of bearing witness."[8] Prior to the invention of photography, when portrait painting was the primary technology with which image capital was actualized, the circulation of likenesses was restricted to a powerful few. With that observation as

124 AESTHETICS OF EQUALITY

preface, I turn to an example of one of the powerful few whose portrait achieved international circulation.

From Paris to Istanbul

The portrait to which I am referring belongs to a spatial story that connects two cities, Paris (featured in Chapter 3) and Istanbul, featured in this one. From October 3, 2006 to February 18, 2007 a Bellini portrait of the Ottoman ruler Sultan Mehmet II was on display in Paris's *Institute du Monde Arabe*, while posters of the portrait "adorned every Paris metro station during the five months of the exhibition."[9] The occasion for the execution of the painting in 1479 was precipitated by Sultan Mehmet II's request for "a good artist" to render his image in the "Western fashion" to which he had become enamored. As Jacqueline Karp points out, Mehmet II's "fascination" with Western portraiture was "the beginning of a tempestuous Turkish love affair with European culture."[10]

The vicissitudes of that love affair have been elaborately addressed by the writer Orhan Pamuk, whose fiction and nonfiction elucidate the tensions between Turkey's aspirational Eurocentrism, articulated as a desire to represent itself as a modern Western nation, and its Ottoman Islamic legacy to which much of its population retains an allegiance. In an observation about his grandmother's sitting room, Pamuk captures the secular Eurocentrism that the room was designed to reflect:

> If she thought we weren't sitting properly on her silver-threaded chairs, our grandmother would bring us to attention. "Sit up straight!" Sitting rooms were not meant to be places where you could lounge comfortably; they were little museums designed to demonstrate to a hypothetical visitor that the householders were westernized.[11]

At the same time, Pamuk observes "the melancholy of a dying [Ottoman] culture . . . bitter memories of the fallen empire" whose vestiges were also present in his grandmother's comportment, the way she "tapped her slippered feet to '*alaturka*' [traditional Turkish] music."[12] Pamuk treats that same tension in his *My Name is Red*, a novelistic commentary on the theologico-political gulf between the paintings of Islamic miniaturists and western perspectival portraiture.[13] The novel explores the historical origins of an artistic cleavage that still speaks to a cultural identity struggle in a Turkey divided between nostalgia for its Ottoman faded glory and its occidental aspirations.

The contemporary Kemalist-fundamentalist tensions on which Pamuk's writing has been focused (most notably in his 2004 novel *Snow*) are played out in the series *Ethos* (broadcast as a Netflix series in 2020), whose main protagonist Meryem (Öykü Karayel) is a religious headscarf-wearing cleaner working in a bourgeois man's apartment when we first see her in Episode 1. The episode's opening tracking her on a long commute that requires both walking and public transportation, an excursion in which the singularity of her head covering stands out as she approaches the posh neighborhood where she works. What also stands out is her role in introducing the city (in particular the class differences observable when one traverses different neighborhoods). Rather than a mere named abstraction, Istanbul emerges through the way she, along with "myriad individuals generate the meaning of urban space by moving through it."[14] Arriving at her destination from her working class, peripheral part of the city, Meryem enters a fashionable apartment in a modern high-rise building in the urban center and begins going about her cleaning chores. Barely underway with her cleaning, she faints after seeing her employer, Mr. Sinan (Alican Yücesoy) naked in his shower. The film then rewinds to a year earlier and cuts to a counseling session to which Meryem had been referred to deal with her fainting spells. The camera with portrait-like framing shots alternates between long takes of Meryem's face and that of Peri's (Defne Kayalar), her analyst seated across from her. Deferring the details of the session for later in my analysis, I want to stress that with its focus on an apartment cleaner's face (repeatedly an object of *Ethos*'s cinematic gaze), the series articulates an aesthetics of equality that links its political sensibility with similar artistic practices that have lent recognition to cleaners. In diverse textual genres portraits of cleaners have given them image capital, providing public recognition for an underclass of working bodies that facilitate the work venues and leisure lifestyles of economically privileged classes.

126   AESTHETICS OF EQUALITY

Cleaners

To amplify the egalitarian implications of *Ethos*'s selection of a woman working as a cleaner as its main protagonist, I review three textual explorations of the social fault lines that afflict women in that occupation, beginning with an ethnography that explores the way Istanbul's culture-economy interface levies restrictions on the right to the city. A house cleaner whose employment is necessitated by her disabled husband's inability to work is among those the investigator interviews. An object of moral obloquy, she is beaten by her father-in-law and shunned by her neighbors because they regard her work "as signaling lax sexual morality." Her experience is one among many that reveal the gender-related strictures that limit Turkey's "range of [respected] identity performances."[15] In *Ethos*, there's a softened version of the obloquy that afflicts Istanbul's cleaners. In Episode 6, without explanation, Peri mistakenly calls Meryem by another name, Hazal, before quickly apologizing and correcting herself. It's a mistake that imperils the rapport between them at a crucial moment in which Meryem is seeking solace for her stressful situation. She is struggling to cope in her brother Yasin (Fatih Artman) and sister-in-law Ruhiye's (Funda Eryiğit') emotionally chaotic household, which features a suicidal Ruhiye, a hyper-controlling Yasin, and two fearful children to whose care she contributes. This visit with Peri is in secret because Yasin, who attributes her lack of docility to secular influences, has forbidden her from continuing with the therapy. Defying Yasin's edict, Meryem has asserted a right to a more expansive city than one permitted by an angry controlling male. As for the name Peri has mistakenly given her, it isn't until midway through Episode 7 that we learn why Peri came up with it.

After Episode 7 opens with a panning shot of the iconic sections of Istanbul (featuring its famous mosques), there's a cut to an unhappy-looking Peri in her office. The camera then returns to the cityscape, zooms in toward a fashionable neighborhood and enters the lavishly appointed townhouse of Peri's parents, which is filled with orientalist paintings and designer furniture. The first body we see inside is a young headscarf-wearing woman working as a cleaner. After vigorously vacuuming and dusting, she approaches Peri's mother to inquire if she should change the sheets in the guest room. Peri's mother looks up from a photo album she's exploring and corrects her employee, explaining that it's her daughter's room rather than a guest room. Having been looking at Peri's childhood photos, she impulsively picks up the phone and calls Peri to press her about whether she is meeting eligible marriage partners, and while on the phone calls to the cleaner by name, "Hazal!" We thus finally learn the basis of Peri's naming parapraxis. She had lumped together the two women, based on their shared occupation and religious adherence. It's evident that for Peri, Meryem's identity is almost exhausted by her subject position as a religious, headscarf-wearing cleaner. It's a form of class bigotry to which Peri confesses in an earlier episode that covers her own therapy session. I address that moment along with the other therapeutic encounters that pervade the series after developing a context for the conversations by pursuing a comparative reading of artistic genres that treat cleaner portraits, followed by a reflection on the ontological difference between still and cinematic portraits, before turning my attention to the translation of psychiatric discourse within Turkish culture.

Another City, Other Genres

Washington, DC shares its primary ethno-cultural schism with many other cities:

> Every day, in every urban center of the world, thousands of black and brown women, invisible, are "opening" the city. They clean the spaces necessary for neo-patriarchy, and neoliberal and finance capitalism to function. They are doing dangerous work: they inhale toxic chemical products and push or carry heavy loads. They have usually travelled long hours in the early morning or late at night, and their work is underpaid and considered to be unskilled. They are usually in their forties or fifties.[16]

To appreciate the historical background of the racially inflected hierarchical structuring of DC, we have to heed an urban plan—originally implemented by slave labor (euphemistically referred to as "Negro hires")[17]—that has always been inhospitable to the daily life of its residents. What is now recognizably an iconic DC, which despite the way it has been "modified, extended [and] built again,"[18] remains very much a realization of Peter Charles L'Enfant's plan: "a cityscape designed for absolutism, regularity and display . . . [making] no allowance for the organic life of a city."[19] In particular, the city's African American residents' right to the city has always been tenuous. Lydia Walsh, a Black character in one of Edward P. Jones's contemporary Washington DC stories, experiences the city as alien territory. While she's in a taxi passing by DC's iconic buildings, "the city's white world floods her consciousness." She recalls that "white men had allowed her father to make a living pushing a broom."[20]

What Jones's literary portrait of Lydia conveys was expressed visually decades earlier by the photographer Gordon Parks as a parody of Americana, a Black versioning on the famous 1930 Grant Wood portrait *American Gothic* (figure 4.1). Growing up among Black Kansas sharecroppers, Parks arrived in DC in 1942 with a fellowship at the

Figure 4.1 Grant Wood, *American Gothic*
Source: Art Resource

Figure 4.2 Gordon Parks, *American Gothic*
Source: Gordon Parks Foundation

Farm Security Administration. Reporting his experience of DC's racial segregation, he says, "White restaurants made me enter through the back door; White theaters wouldn't even let me in the door." Using his camera to "document the African American population's attempt to manage daily indignities," he posed Ella May Watson, a cleaner whose father was murdered by a lynch mob and whose husband had been shot to death (Figure 4.2).[21] His parody of Wood's famous portrait elevates an assemblage that was largely invisible in a city known for its iconic government buildings and iconic portraits of elected officials featured in many of them, most notably in the National Portrait Gallery. It took seven decades for African Americans to achieve significant image capital in DC (with the 2003 founding of the National Museum of African American History and Culture). By way of transition, I want to note that while *Ethos* is a portrait-oriented text that also distributes image capital to nonelites, its characters are durational; they are cinematic subjects who emerge within a different image ontology.

130   AESTHETICS OF EQUALITY

From Still to Moving Images

Addressing the divide between photography and film, Jessie Green states, "No still photographer can capture an eye roll in one shot."[22] Andrei Bazin's famous discussion of the differing ontologies of photography and cinema provides a more elaborate reflection on the difference between the two visual technologies. Whereas as he puts it, "photography . . . embalms time,"[23] cinema, "no longer content to reserve the object, enshrouded as it were in an instant . . . delivers baroque art from its convulsive catalepsy . . . [so that] . . . the image of things is likewise the image of their duration."[24] Although there are durational effects in photographic portraits, duration is more recognizable in cinematic portraits because they record changing facial expressions. As Deleuze points out in his treatment of Bergsonian temporality, "the body *is* something other than a mathematical point."[25] Image-wise it wears its temporal experience on its face, even in seemingly timeless paintings. For example, as I have suggested elsewhere, Albrecht Dürer's 1497 portrait of his father at seventy, executed with what we now would regard as photographic realism, locates him at a crucial stage in his emotional life while at the same time gesturing toward a transindividual narrative. "The face is a veritable megaphone," as Deleuze and Guattari put it.[26] Looking at this face (Figure 4.3), composed by an artist capable of "granular realism,"[27] one is able to read the emotion. Because duration also plays an important role in reception— as social animals who have a "bulwark against the contingencies of nature,"[28] we have the luxury of being able to train our gaze on individual objects—"a quick look suggests that what is being broadcast is anger," while a longer look yields a different impression. With a longer look, as I've suggested, we see fear "and the related querulous suspicion behind the anger of a man who is losing his grip and likely his moral authority as well."[29]

Literary facial portraits are also capable of disclosing emotional dynamics. For that there is no better practitioner than Leo Tolstoy, "the great novelist of physical involuntariness," as James Wood puts it,[30] and accordingly a master at describing what a face is saying despite itself. In *Anna Karenina* Tolstoy constructs the developing expression on Anna Karenina's face as she converses with the man who would

Figure 4.3 Albrect Dürer's portrait of his father
Source: National Gallery London

become her paramour, Count Vronsky: "Every time he spoke to Anna the joyful light kindled in her eyes and a smile of pleasure curved her rosy lips. She seemed to make efforts to restrain these signs of joy, but they appeared on her face of their own accord."[31] In the case of cinematic face close-ups, we can observe an actual dynamic. A durational portrait unfolds, greeting the viewer as it records a face in real time. A commentary on Chantal Akerman's famous cinematic portraiture addresses that durational effect: the long takes of her faces portray them "in the fragile persistence of an emotion."[32]

Durational Portraits

Cinematic portraiture offers perspectives that transcend the particular characters that are the objects of the camera's gaze; it condenses them into what Wieslaw Godzic calls a "culturological synthesis."[33] Deleuze provides a similar insight. Referring to the transindividuality of cinematic

132   AESTHETICS OF EQUALITY

portraits, he identifies a paradox that he explicates in reference to Ingmar Bergman's close-up shots of faces. In Bergman, "The facial close-up is both the face and its effacement"; it "extinguishes the face."[34] What Deleuze implies is that rather than merely representing a person's psychological disposition, the "external effect of an interior cause,"[35] Bergman's close-ups signify a collective potential, "possible confrontations, expectations, creations."[36] Like the photographic portrait, "the [cinematic] face is bursting with meaning, but what that particular meaning is" depends on both the durational situation of the subject and, as Andreja Zevnik puts it, on "the scopic field in which the face is made to appear."[37]

Bergman's *Persona* (1966) dramatically actualizes Deleuze's observation about the displacement of individual subjectivity in his cinematic face close-ups. As his camera elaborately explores the faces of two women protagonists—one, Elisabet Vogler (Liv Ullmann) the patient who has suffered a nervous breakdown, the other, Alma (Bibi Anderson) her caretaking nurse—the healing topology becomes mobile; it moves from hypotaxis (with the patient subordinate to the caretaking nurse) toward parataxis, consummated when the women's faces merge. Two side-by-side faces slowly become a single one, shortly after the two women become intertwined and the boundaries of their individualities begin to blur (Figure 4.4).

The portraiture dynamic in *Persona* cancels the hierarchical relationship between patient and health practitioner. Similarly, the two women in *Ethos* begin their first session in a hypotactic configuration before the relationship of dominance is slowly cancelled. At the outset Meryem is under interrogation as the conversation begins with the camera alternating between close-ups of each face. Peri initially controls the conversation as she tries to solicit the concerns that led to Meryem's referral for psychiatric counseling, while Meryem becomes increasingly evasive yet subtly assertive as the session progresses. Although unlike what transpires in *Persona*, the women remain facing each other, Meryem slowly deconstructs the hierarchical structure of the psychoanalytic encounter as the sessions progress, becoming contentious in their first session and taking over in moments as an interpreter of Peri's strategy in the second (even going so far as to interrogate Peri about her life). However, there's a significant difference in the deconstructive consequences in the series' portraits. Whereas in Bergman's *Persona* the

Figure 4.4 Elisabet and Alma in Bergman's *Persona*
Source: Cinemagraph AB

dynamic portrait effect deconstructs personhood, generating a challenge to reception and judgment with respect to the stability of subjectivity, what transpires in *Ethos*'s mobile configuration is the disclosure of a cultural schism. Psychoanalysis's famous talking cure requires a patient to be responsive. Meryem's evasiveness registers her reluctance to respond to questions that probe what is culturally as well as psychologically repressed. *Ethos*'s counseling conversations are constrained by the cultural context in which they are situated. Conversation partners in Turkey, especially those who speak across the Fundamentalist-Kemalist divide, operate under different strictures from the ones that have governed the therapeutic practice initiated in Freud's Judeo-Christian-dominant Western European venue.

Situating the Psychiatric Conversation

The practice of psychoanalysis in Turkey faces the kind of situation it experiences in the other middle eastern countries that share its part

134   AESTHETICS OF EQUALITY

of the "psychoanalytic world."[38] It's a world in which psychoanalysis must compete with a theological authority that prescribes divinely sanctioned healing.[39] Moreover, the famous "family romance" that was a predicate for Freud's cases, shaped by the patriarchal structure of the Judeo-Christian biblical text to which Freud was famously attentive, is not operative in Islam. Because the Koran does not figure Allah as a patriarch, there is a significant translation problem for the functioning of psychoanalysis in Turkey and other countries where Islam flourishes. As Nathan Gorelick points out, "Islamicate thought and theology . . . begins with a repudiation of the doctrine of divine parentage, Allah, in other words, is not a father."[40] Moreover, spiritual counseling within an Islamic assemblage is highly politicized; it often takes on a form of critique in which the spiritual and political are entangled as Stefania Pandolfo points out.[41] A soft version of that insight emerges in *Ethos* as the tension between psychiatric and spiritual counseling is dramatized in Meryem's session with her Hodja (religious school educator), which follows a session with her psychiatric counselor Peri.

The Counseling Sessions

The first shot of Meryem, seated in preparation for her conversation with Peri, is a long take of the face of a person who would rather be elsewhere (Figure 4.5). It takes several seconds before Meryem looks straight ahead at Peri. The camera stays on her face as it slowly changes from an evasive to a grudgingly congenial expression, registering only *her* face for a matter of minutes, while Peri is initially present solely as a voice offscreen. Peri tries to put an obviously anxious Meryem at ease, telling her that they have a half-hour to chat, that she can talk about whatever is on her mind, and that Meryem is a beautiful name. As Meryem begins responding it becomes evident that she is withholding more that she's disclosing. While she admits that she has been referred to Peri because her fainting episodes seem unconnected to anything physical (she mentions fainting at a wedding), she does not initially disclose her feelings about working in Mr. Sinan's apartment.

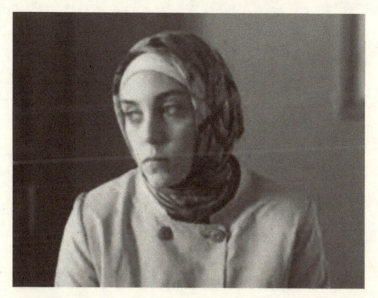

Figure 4.5 Meryem
Source: Netflix, Inc

When the camera switches to Peri and concentrates for a while on *her* face, what we see initially and subsequently throughout the conversation is a stern and distant expression. She too gives the impression of discomfort. The shot sequence thus equates the counselor and her client; both are finding the encounter trying. Struggling to remain cordial, Peri manages to evince occasional half-smiles (we see subtle, constrained movements of her lips as she tries patiently to elicit what is on Meryem's mind). It's not evident as yet whether Peri's sternness is a result of her strict professionalism, the need to maintain emotional distance, or personal distaste (Figure 4.6). For whatever reason, the half-smiles are coming from a face that shows affective ambivalence. The reason becomes evident subsequently when we observe what Bertolt Brecht famously calls the "fable," the "delimited total event," which "gives . . . the actor the opportunity to put the contradictions into context." It's a context that emerges slowly in *Ethos*.[42]

As the episodes progress, it becomes apparent that Meryem and Peri transcend their roles as individuals in a psychiatric session. They are types that represent women on the two sides of the fundamentalist–Kemalist

Figure 4.6 Peri
Source: Netflix, Inc

(and largely class-based) divide. Instead of merely watching Meryem and Peri, we are seeing a headscarf-wearing part time cleaner from an emotionally struggling family, living on the periphery of the city and trying to manage moral quandaries, in conversation with a foreign-trained, cosmopolitan upper bourgeois professional from a prosperous section of Istanbul, who harbors serious (unprofessional) prejudices against those who practice religion. Peri finds their public visibility especially anathema. In a session with *her* analyst, we learn that she is disturbed by believers' coverings and their speech practices, such as the way they punctuate their observations about their plans with "inshallah" (Allah willing). She also fears Islam's pervasive surveilling presence, which makes her feel as if she's living in an "aquarium," as she puts it.

In the first counseling session with Meryem, after Peri tries to elicit relevant information about what is concerning her, Meryem eventually becomes talkative but initially only about her immediate concern. Seeking comfort by imagining herself in a postsession moment, she asks about whether the number 24 bus stops nearby. When she finally brings up something relevant to the session, she mentions that a neighbor had recommended counseling and that she asked her Hodja if such a thing is O.K. with Islam. And when she finally mentions Mr. Sinan after Peri presses her about who he is, she at first only refers to the way she makes his coffee. That the camera comes back more than once to the coffee-maker—to which Meryem pays extravagant attention during each visit to Sinan's apartment—reflects an obvious displacement. To put in in psychiatric language, "Desire, thwarted by prohibition, transfers itself by metonymy to a nearby object."[43] It's a mechanism to which Peri is attuned, given her psychoanalytic training. However, when she tries to pursue Meryem's feelings about her employer, Meryem becomes agitated and complains about "those women" (Sinan's romantic partners): "I wash, I iron, I clean, even wash his briefs [while] those women do nothing." They leave their underwear about; "What kind of woman is that?" As Peri again tries to elicit more about her feelings toward Sinan, Meryem becomes aggressive and challenging: "I didn't come to gossip; don't keep asking me about it . . . you seem to have a bee in your bonnet about it." The session ends with both women unsettled, leaving uncertain the plan for future sessions. Meryem leaves, headed toward a bus to pick up her niece and bring her home while Peri leaves in a taxi, headed to her own therapy session.

Tableau and Montage

As the camera cuts back and forth between Meryem's and Peri's postsession journeys, it reveals *Ethos*'s dual cinematic temporality. While the long takes of faces record the dynamics of emotion in each of the characters, another temporality in the form of montage sequences connects the facial tableaus with events of encounter. What results is a "tableau aesthetic" familiar to theatrical productions that embed "the frame-like closure of each element," in the "flow of events."[44] It's an aesthetic that is especially adaptable to cinema. In particular, the montage sequences in *Ethos* have a legacy that David Bordwell attributes to "scene dissection in Danish cinema . . . editing-based techniques [which film] historians argued, replaced the purportedly heavy tableau

138 AESTHETICS OF EQUALITY

of 'theatrical cinema.' "[45] That editing practice produces what Deleuze was later to refer to as "direct" images of time, time resulting from the editing structure rather than emerging indirectly from following movements.[46] In *Ethos* what that aspect of temporality with its cuts back and forth between the experiences of the different characters discloses initially is an equality of unhappiness: "Everyone is struggling with their own troubles, shadows and demons."[47] In what is doubtless an oblique reference to Tolstoy's opening lines in *Anna Karenina*—"All happy families resemble one another, each unhappy family is unhappy in its own way"[48]—a commentary on *Ethos* points out that "Each character is unhappy in their own way."[49] To put it yet another relevant way, "pain is democratic,"[50] says a character in a John le Carré spy novel.

Before the segment cuts to Peri's session with her analyst Gülbin (Tülin Özen), there's a cut to a long take of the *most* unhappy character. The camera does an extended portrait of Meryem's sister-in-law, a traumatized (and suicidal) Ruhiye, at home. Once that is followed by Peri's session with Gülbin—in a scene prior to Meryem's conversation with her Hodja—we have been introduced to what is arguably the primary "normative mentality" of the series,[51] a feminine matrix consisting of women who all suffer in their own way, in large part we learn because of constraining cultural strictures that are maintained by the policing practices of Turkish men.

Throughout the drama, the women interact both directly and vicariously in alternatively conflictual and supportive ways as they seek reprieves from the constraints men impose. As a result, the drama of *Ethos*, focused mainly on the female characters, reveals a city that rather than a static object is a "perpetually [re]organizing field of forces in movement."[52] Accordingly, *Ethos* exhibits yet another Bergman-like dynamic. In several Bergman films, supportive interactions within a "feminine matrix" undermine male dominance.[53] For example in his *Fanny and Alexander* (1982), a matriarch, Helena, along with her daughter-in-law Emily, rescue Maj, a former maid (arranging her escape to Stockholm at her request) from the coercive lust and generosity of Helena's son Gustav Adolf, who has arranged a café position for Maj in Uppsala in order to keep her close by as an extramarital sex partner. It's a collaboration typical in Bergman films in which "it is women who cut through the intellectual posturings and dishonesty of the men."[54]

AN EGALITARIAN ISTANBUL   139

In *Ethos*, in which the "posturings and dishonesty of men" are exemplified by Sinan, it is Gülbin who exposes his in a scene in which she shares her observations with female friends. Sinan is privy to the humiliating scene, which takes place at his workout club. Out of sight on the other side of a partition, he overhears Gülbin mimicking his seduction moves for a group of the women who are laughing knowingly at her parody.

The controlling forms of masculinity in *Ethos* operate didactically as well as coercively, the former exemplified by the Hodja and the latter by Sinan and Yasin. Before we see Meryem's session with the Hodja, he is mentioned in Peri's session with Gülbin. As is the case with the Meryem–Peri session, the two are seated facing each other while the camera alternates between long takes of their faces. Peri, still struggling for composure, admits "having a hard time" and confesses her prejudice toward religious conservatives. Asked what troubled her most in her session with Meryem, she refers to "the bit about the Hodja" and mentions that she "feels a strange agitation inside whenever a covered woman comes and sits across from her." She adds that the feeling is a family legacy; "a covered woman was a monster for my mother," she says. However, aside from sharing parental attitudes, it emerges that Peri's family also has its own inner conflicts, as does Sinan's, Meryem's, Gülbin's, and the Hodja's. For each unhappy protagonist, their families *all* fulfill Tolstoy's above-noted observation that each unhappy family is unhappy in its own way.

Before Peri's session with Gülbin ends it reveals itself as a referential montage, because that session begins to resemble the one Peri had with Meryem. Like her own client, Peri tries to deconstruct the counseling session by diverting its focus. She proposes a postsession social outing with Gülbin (who politely resists). Later we learn that Gülbin, who seemed stoic and composed throughout the session, had been struggling to maintain her calm demeanor because she has a conservative headscarf-wearing sister, one with whom she is continually fighting (even to the point of physical confrontation). When Peri leaves their session, Gülbin breathes an audible sigh of relief. The long takes of her face have shown her having to hold herself aloof during a session that opened a very familiar and personal wound (Figure 4.7).

Figure 4.7 Gülbin
Source: Netflix, Inc

In between sequences of the Peri–Gülbin session, the camera follows Meryem to her counseling session with her Hodja. As she arrives at the Hodja's mosque, the series' architectural narrative thread becomes strikingly evident. Whereas Meryem's approach to her session with Peri shows her walking through a generic office building with long impersonal corridors to knock on a door that looked like all the others, the mosque she approaches is architecturally distinctive. Awe-inspiring rather than alienating, it contrasts dramatically with anonymous-looking office buildings as well as with the cluttered yard and cramped household Meryem shares with the Yasin-Ruhiye family. When she arrives at the mosque, there's an iconic architectural moment. The camera frames Meryem in front of the mosque's façade with its distinctive window showing above her head (Figure 4.8). As was the case with Gordon Park's cleaner portrait discussed earlier, the shot (more indirectly in this case) evokes the Grant Wood *American Gothic* painting, this time for a different feature. Wood's inspiration was not the couple he chose to pose in front of the building, but the building itself. As Wanda Corn, points out, "The immediate genesis of

Figure 4.8 Meryem at the mosque
Source: Netflix, Inc

the painting occurred when Wood saw a Gothic Revival wooden farmhouse ... What caught his eye" was the building's design, "its prominent, oversized neo-Gothic window and its vertical board-and-batten siding."[55] However, whereas what caught Wood's eye was architectural revival, what summons the gaze in *Ethos* is architectural persistence. The modern cityscape remains punctuated by iconic religious buildings, which continue to attract allegiance and which as "event spaces" (structures made to house spiritual healing) operate in competition with secular healing practices.[56]

As Meryem's session with the Hodja proceeds we observe an oblique reference to the Peri-Gülbin encounter. Like Peri, who while making sense of her difficulty with Meryem retreats to formulaic psychoanalytic terms, referring for example to the mechanism of countertransference, the Hodja, to make sense of a different kind of struggle (Turkey's ongoing culture war) rehearses God talk with an allegory. Handing Meryem an artificial (what he calls a "fake") flower, he likens it to the fake versions of life on television with which he contrasts the "reality" of God's work. It's an allegorical liturgy he repeats in a later encounter

142 AESTHETICS OF EQUALITY

with Yasin. In the midst of that Meryem–Hodja conversation, there's yet another significant architectural punctuation. The camera pulls back and shows the two partly visible through openings in a latticework that serves as a wall dividing sections within the building. That shot participates in one of the series' drama's main concerns: its exploration of a social order in which a cultural divide imposes a complex rhythm of revealing and concealing. The series continually explores prohibitions on what can be seen and said. Crucially, the constraints fall more on the women than on the men. The men are portrayed in various restriction-enforcing roles vis-à-vis the series' women.

Men: The Good, the Bad, and the Ugly

I Begin with the Good

In all that meets the eye, the Hodja, Ali Sadi Hoca (Settar Tanrıöğen) appears to be a good man throughout his presence in all eight episodes of the series (his spiritual didacticism notwithstanding). Despite his suspicion that psychoanalysis is a foreign import that is anathema to theological observance, he doesn't discourage Meryem's therapy. And although he suspects that his daughter Hayrunnisa's (Bige Önal) enthusiasm for what he calls "foreign" (and what his deceased wife Mesude had called "evil") music is estranging her from fundamentalist Turkish culture, he issues no edicts forbidding it. In his home, a humble architectural space, he exhibits a humbler personality than he does in his mosque, a grand building that enhances his authority. When he enters his daughter's room, he is on her turf. As he sees her dancing to music with her headphones on, he is evidently upset by her distraction. However, rather than remonstrating, once he gets her attention he raises a different subject, sharing his feelings of grief for his deceased wife. He mentions how she visits him in his dreams and laughs with his daughter about how he has to manage his grief by hanging out in a "dream world." And finally, when he faces the ultimate test of his theological/parental authority—his daughter heads off to her university without wearing a headscarf—he resigns himself to the new reality. It's a reality that ambushes him suddenly as they prepare for him to drive

Figure 4.9 The Hodja
Source: Netflix, Inc

her to her bus, having exited the house with her baggage. Unaware of the transformation at that point, when he sees that she has not yet put on her headscarf, he tells her she must get ready so they can get to the bus on time. After she replies that she *is* ready, the camera does an extended close-up of his face. What unfolds is a cinematic portrait that initially shows a face registering shocked surprise and then slowly changing to one that registers resignation (Figure 4.9). Although forlorn about his daughter's departure from piety—he says at one point, "are you leaving your father behind"—he tolerates her entry into a modernity he has striven to resist.

The Bad

Reflective acceptance also comes slowly for *Ethos*'s "bad" men, Sinan and Yasin. Before Episode 1 ends we see Sinan, a serial seducer, in his apartment involved in a seduction routine on his couch with an initially reluctant Gülbin. Moving closer to touch and kiss her, he tries to

144 AESTHETICS OF EQUALITY

get her into his bed while smiling in a way that he thinks is appealing (the moves she later parodies for her women friends). Although it succeeds this time, it does not in a subsequent encounter in which she decides to leave and not return. Because for Sinan sex seems to be a form of recreational consumption rather than intimacy, when Gülbin departs he gets on his cell phone and without leaving his couch calls a replacement. It turns out to be Melisa (Nesrin Cavadzade), a popular soap opera star who is familiar to all the other characters who watch television (which the Hodja has disparaged as a fake form of life).

As the swap of Melisa for Gülbin progresses, the series picks up another important part of the architectural narrative thread. Sinan's bathroom turns out to be an important event space in the encounters among some of the women. Before leaving Sinan's apartment building, Gülbin does an about-face and rushes back to his apartment in order to consummate her permanent absence by retrieving her toothbrush from the toothbrush holder on the bathroom sink. By the time she gets there, Melisa had arrived and is sitting on the toilet. Their encounter is brief; they give each other startled stares, whereupon Gülbin rushes out of the bathroom and confronts an embarrassed Sinan. She claps her hands in mock applause, says "bravo," and leaves. Later, while Melisa is still there bare-legged and looking obviously postcoital (wearing one of Sinan's shirts), Meryem arrives to do her cleaning. Having seen Melisa on television, Meryem also stares, in her case with wide-eyed wonder upon seeing a celebrity in person. Star power seems to obviate the moralistic (and doubtless symptomatic) disapproval Meryem had levied on Sinan's other women. The characters Meryem, Gülbin, and Melisa all have Sinan bathroom events. While Gülbin had marked her place with her toothbrush, Meryem marks it with one of her head wraps, which she keeps in in a bathroom drawer to retrieve and wear while cleaning. On the bathroom sink counter is a visual prop that testifies to Sinan's masculinity aspirations, a muscle magazine. Upon seeing it, Meryem covers it with the headwear while checking herself in the mirror. For her the magazine belongs among the things to be unseen. In contrast, when Gülbin sees it, rather than covering it she looks at it with disgust, seeing it as evidence of Sinan's pretentiousness, and when Melisa enters the bathroom and sees it, she picks it up and looks through it briefly. By the end of the series, Sinan has been abandoned by his paramours. By Episode 8, Meryem is the only woman entering the apartment. Moreover, he faces yet another woman-administered abjection. When he visits his mother on a visit to his childhood home, she criticizes him in a scene that evokes the earlier one with Peri's mother on her phone with the same concern. Sinan's mother tells him she wants him to meet "a nice decent girl and have a family." By the time we see him in Episode 8, his self-confident smirk has faded. In his very last onscreen appearance, he's weeping.

Episode 2, which begins with our first glimpse of Yasin in his role as bouncer in a music club, is followed by another bathroom scene, which involves a different relationship with women. After Yasin is shown, looking intimidating in a full-body pose that emphasizes his brute physicality, there's a noisy disturbance in a bathroom where women are swearing and shouting. Trying to cool them down, Yasin gets into a violent physical confrontation with them. As is the case with many of *Ethos*'s scenes, we are treated to a referential montage; the nightclub bathroom scene is a reinflected repetition of the Sinan apartment bathroom scene. There are also related scenes that differentiate the men with respect to the same aspect of physicality, muscles. We see that they both work out, Sinan at an upscale workout club and the less affluent Yasin with a weight bench in his front yard. It's clear that given both his club membership and the magazine to which he subscribes, for the softer-looking Sinan, muscles are aspirational. As with his sexual behavior, his exercise is a form of consumption. He has succumbed to the masculinity-semiotics of images of muscles, while Yasin uses his not only in his work but also in other encounters, as it turns out. Among other things, Yasin's bouncing migrates out of the club and is actualized at home. There's a scene in which he grabs his children and his wife while they're all in their front yard, lifts each of them one at a time, and bounces them in his arms vigorously. He is as physically intimidating while playing as he is while policing behavior at his workplace and elsewhere. However, by the end of the series, right after he tells his wife Ruhiya that weeping is forbidden, Yasin himself breaks down, weeping in relief while she is massaging his back at a moment when their marital harmony seems restored. It's yet another scene connecting the two "bad" men; Yasin's weeping in relief is a moment that anticipates the last Sinan sighting, as he weeps in despair.

146 AESTHETICS OF EQUALITY

The Ugly

When Hilmi (Gokhan Yikilkan), who has a menial teaching assistant position in the Hodja's mosque/school, first sees Meryem his eyes light up; it's love at first sight (although he is too shy and awkward to confess his feelings). That emotion is not to be reciprocated. At one point, after being in his presence a few times, Meryem says to herself, "he can't admit he likes me, the ugly little guy." *Ethos* doubles down on Hilmi's alleged ugliness. There's a scene in which he's face-to-face with a turkey, imitating the turkey's gobbling. However, Hilmi's role in the series transcends his lack of masculine charisma and his hopeless, lovesick condition. He turns out to be a thinker who at one point while in conversation with Meryem tells her about Carl Jung's version of religion. That, along with another speech he makes about ontologies of life (which I reserve for the chapter's conclusion), suggests that he is serving as a "conceptual persona,"[57] one who delivers the ethos of *Ethos*, an ethico-political perspective writer and director Berkun Oya achieves with his cinematic composition as well as with dialogue.

Hilmi's Jung soliloquy bridges the divide between the religious and psychoanalytic counseling sessions because Jung's version of psychoanalysis integrates the two thought systems. In Jungian psychotherapy the therapist views the counseling process from a spiritual as well as a clinical perspective. Unlike Freud and some of his other followers, Jungians are hospitable to religious beliefs, striving to develop psychological referents for the traditional religious terms: soul, transcendence, the sacred. As a result, the Jungian interpretation of religion has been and continues to be influential among theists as well as psychologists. Significantly, Hilmi holds forth on Jungian thinking while standing outside the mosque (most of his encounters with Meryem take place outdoors). He tells Meryem that according to Jung the second part of one's life is no longer about proving oneself, and that the repressed parts are to linger as part of one's destiny. That claim turns out to be prophetic because at the very end of the series while Meryem is cleaning Sinan's apartment in Episode 8, there's a return of the repressed. While Sinan is in the shower, Meryem avoids the bathroom and instead begins straightening the apartment. She then pauses to look at the gift she had gotten from Hilmi, sees that it is a ring rather

AN EGALITARIAN ISTANBUL   147

than a piece of candy, and faints (seemingly because yet again she is reminded of a wedding where she had fainted before).

When she regains consciousness she opens the gift, sees the ring more clearly, and smiles as the last episode ends. Among other things, we are reminded of her last encounter with Hilmi in which she reciprocates a gift of candy he has given her with a gift a new pair of socks (having seen that there's a hole in one of his usual pairs). It's a moment of reciprocity that also contrasts with other key encounters in the counseling sessions, which are clearly nonreciprocal. Meryem's reciprocal moments constitute a significant aspect of the series' egalitarian sensibility, to which I return in the conclusion after reviewing the aspect of the tableau montage involving the series' women.

The Women: The Aesthetic, the Lonely, the Fugitive, the Traumatized, the Protagonist, and the Secular

The TV actress Melisa is an aesthetic subject and is the only significant female character who seems to have no issues to resolve and no dysfunctional family with which to cope. Like Hilmi, but in her own way, she transcends the cultural fault lines that operate within social life and, consequently, in family life. The Melisa character is not furnished with a family that judges her lifestyle and she does not feel obliged to deal delicately with a coercive male. Although she occasionally chooses to have sex with Sinan, she is wholly self-possessed. While in his apartment she makes herself at home and evinces a gently mocking attitude to her paramour host. Making clear that as far as their relationship is concerned she can take it or leave it as her mood dictates, at one point she chides Sinan, "Don't give that phony look whenever you have sex on your mind." While Hilmi, as I've noted, is a conceptual persona, a character whose essayistic commentary accompanies the plot, helping to convey the series' ideational, ontological, and political thinking, Melisa is what I have elsewhere called an "aesthetic subject," one who helps animate the plot's interactional matrix. As I've noted elsewhere, aesthetic subjects' "movements and actions (both purposive and nonpurposive) map and often alter experiential, politically relevant terrains."[58] As an aesthetic subject Melisa's role is

148   AESTHETICS OF EQUALITY

more significant for what it reveals about the world in which she moves than about the singularity of her personality.

During her first appearance Melisa is at a typical bourgeois venue, a yoga studio where she meets the lonely and unhappy Peri and invites her for a postsession coffee. While a friendship slowly builds between them—like Gülbin, Melisa urges Peri to confront her discomfort with religious conservatives—the most notable thing their friendship discloses is Peri's extreme degree of isolation from both face-to-face and virtual engagement. Her rigid stoicism, accompanied by an almost permanent expression of distaste for what she sees around her in public places (e.g., in a happy hour bar, one of the "awful places [she goes] to meet a guy and then come home alone") keeps possibilities for intimacy at bay. No one except the series' universal emotional solvent, Melisa, comes near her. And unlike what seems to be the case for most of Istanbul's residents, until she becomes Melisa's friend, she had never seen her soap opera (Meryem registers surprise on learning that Peri doesn't know its name when she mentions it during a counseling session). Peri's loneliness, and interpersonal isolation, is doubled by her media isolation. Until late in the series, she is uninitiated in an aspect of popular culture that shapes one of the few ways diverse types in the city have something in common. Before succumbing to watching Melisa's soap opera she has told her, "I won't watch an entire Turkish TV show."

Television enters many homes, even religious ones, as a secular guest (there's a moment in the Hodja's household where the family is watching a home improvement program). Moreover, television affects the organization of domestic space. Among the ways the egalitarian aspect of the Melisa effect is articulated is through the way her viewers bodies are deployed to watch her. For example, in the Yasin-Ruhiye-Meryem home, the relationship among the characters is reconfigured while watching Melisa's soap opera. A TV console affects "the distribution of the living room furniture," which is "dictated by where the TV is placed."[59] In most of the encounters in their home Yasin confronts Meryem in a dominating (hypotactic) face-to-face posture. However, when they are both watching the soap opera their bodies are arranged on furniture that has them (paratactically) side-by-side, both turned toward the TV. The equalizing effect Melisa's virtual self has *within* a

AN EGALITARIAN ISTANBUL 149

household carries over to the relationship *between* households. As the episodes of *Ethos* survey the diverse households, we see several of the characters watching her soap opera. Sinan is watching it right before he calls her in Episode 2; Meryem and Yasin are watching it together in Episode 3; Peri and her parents are watching it in Episode 5. And finally in Episode 8, Peri, having joined Melisa for a drink, admits that watching her on TV has made her feel more connected to the city. No longer sharing her mother's hierarchical view of culture (expressed as contempt for those she sees on TV), Peri expresses relief that she has been able to be part of a common world.

The Fugitive

Throughout her appearance in *Ethos* the Hodja's daughter, Hayrunnisa, seeks to escape both from her strict Islamic upbringing and from a heavily policed heteronormativity. When we first see her, she's walking outside. As she negotiates Istanbul's gender-policed public space she appears furtive and uncomfortable, a discomfort that is exacerbated when she's accosted by Yasin, who chases away a dog that has bitten her. He leaves for a moment, then circles back and overattentively tries to help her find treatment for her leg wound, first at a pharmacy and then at a hospital. Clearly obsessed by Hayrunnisa's attractiveness as much as by the heroic rescue he is staging, he lingers in the hospital waiting area before reluctantly leaving. Before the series is over, Hayrunnisa, still uncomfortable in public space, has to manage Yasin's presence yet again, this time during a more frightening encounter in which he is belligerent rather than merely overly attentive (upon seeing her with her same-sex lover).

In the confines of her room, Hayrunnisa is exuberant rather than furtive. In two scenes she is shown dancing in a happy reverie with her headphones on, listening to emotionally stimulating music that originates outside of Turkish culture, while using "the interior as a space of marked privacy, of sonic-socio-spatial insulation."[60] However, the liberation she achieves with her home-protected listening is only part of her ultimate escape from religious orthodoxy and gender policing. Her acoustical escape is ultimately accompanied by a physical

150   AESTHETICS OF EQUALITY

one, achieved with the help of her same-sex lover, who assaults Yasin by stabbing him with a knife in the leg when in that second encounter he accosts them in the street, aggressively disapproving of their amorous relationship. As in much of the series' composition in which one scene refers to another, Yasin's wound, which requires hospitalization, is a reinflected repetition of Hayrunnisa's earlier, dog bite-inflicted leg wound, for which she visits a hospital.

Hayrunnisa's lover performs an important role within the supportive feminine matrix. After having rescued Hayrunnisa from Yasin's obsession—a combination of intimidating policing and overattentiveness—she joins her in her final escape, accompanying her on her journey out of the city toward her university education. However, Oya's camera had already anticipated Hayrunnisa's transition from her conservative religious upbringing to her entry into a polycentric version of modernity. At a moment in which she's applying makeup in her bathroom at home, the camera zooms in for an extended close-up shot of her lipstick container on the shelf below the mirror. It is shaped like a small minaret.

The Traumatized

The discursive context applied to Ruhiye's suicide attempts (three in all) is contentious. While it seems a clear case of depression to the analyst Peri, Meryem, while describing the attempts, treats the behavior in ethical rather than psychological terms. She refers to Ruhiye as "ungrateful," that is, nonreciprocal, an observation that fits with the way Meryem treats interpersonal encounters in general. As I've suggested, she practices an ethos of reciprocity. For example, uncomfortable with having her counseling sessions merely a matter of consuming a service, she presses Peri to accept a gift of baked goods she wants to prepare for her. However, one might describe Ruhiye's condition—she's sleeping much of the day, chain-smoking while awake, hardly able to leave her house, and disoriented when she tries to pray (on returning home at one point, Yasin finds her kneeling and faced in the wrong direction, not toward Mecca)—she is clearly not functioning well as a wife, mother, or Muslim.

AN EGALITARIAN ISTANBUL 151

Neither her husband Yasin, who races around with desperate perplexity, nor her calmer sister-in-law Meryem, with her moral crotchets and perceptiveness, are able to affect Ruhiye's condition. Yasin continually exacerbates the situation by exploding in anger and trying to force her to behave as one would expect from an obedient wife. He complains, "You'll ruin us all, is that what you want?" He attempts to control her every moment: "Where are you going?" he shouts when she gets out of bed at one point; "to the toilet," she responds. In search of solace, Yasin seeks spiritual counseling. He goes to see the Hodja, who repeats the same artificial versus real flower formula he used with Meryem. After Yasin comes home with a prop central to the Hodja's spiritual pedagogy (a small vase of flowers that he places on a window sill next the one with which Meryem came home), a subsequent camera shot reflects on Yasin's dominating behavior in the household. A close-up of the two vases of flowers shows that Yasin's is considerably taller than Meryem's.

After her unsuccessful suicide attempts Ruhiye contrives to solve her condition another way, telling Yasin that she wants to return to her village but refusing to disclose the reason. She wants to return to the scene of her traumatic experience (to "spit on the grave" of the man who raped her, she says *sotto voce* when Yasin demands her reason for returning). Yasin capitulates to her request but insists on coming along *en famille*. The trip is ultimately aborted because Ruhiye becomes self-destructive in response to Yasin's constant recriminations during the drive. After she beats her head repeatedly against her passenger-side window, Meryem tries unsuccessfully to alter the mood by getting everyone to join her in a dance outside the car. Yasin angrily turns the car around to return home. Realizing that she must solve the issue on her own, Ruhiye slips out of the house early one morning. Taking her son Ismail (Göktuğ Yildirim) with her, she heads to the village on public transportation. The most dramatic scene during her stop in the village is her discovery that her erstwhile rapist, Ramazan (Aziz Çapkurt)—reported to be dead by Yasin, who had returned to the village and beaten him—is alive and living with her sister. It's during an emotionally fraught visit at her sister's home that Ruhiye finds out that Ramazan is alive.

152 AESTHETICS OF EQUALITY

After encountering Ramazan on the hillside where the rape had occurred, Ruhiye has an epiphany. She learns that the beating he had gotten from Yasin, in a public square for all in the village to observe, has left him humiliated and physically disabled. After saying that he was young and confused at the time and cannot identify with the person he was when he engaged in the act, he hands Ruhiye a gun, telling her he would gladly have his miserable life of humiliation, constant pain, and limited mobility end. Although she doesn't take him up on the offer, she is seemingly restored to equanimity, not it seems because she sees that he has suffered more than her but because she now has a sense of closure after he has assisted in bringing into present scrutiny what had been for her a trauma that had remained an "unclaimed experience."[61]

Although Ruhiye's recovery features a remarkable change of disposition—upon her return home she is able to take over management of her household and both nurture and humor her sullen husband Yasin (her man problem now behind her)—a change in her son Ismail's disposition is even more significant for what *Ethos* conveys about the Turkish life world. Ismail, who has been silent to the point of seeming to be autistic up until the village episode, starts talking, initially issuing the simple query, "Are we going home, Mommy?" That he is heard for the first time is a reflection of the role his name assigns to him in the series. In Arabic Ismail translates as "God hears" or "God will hear." Hence a bit of noninstitutionalized theology shows up at an important moment in a narrative that addresses what should and should not be heard.

I want to lend Ismail's role a conceptual amplification by suggesting that all along Ismail has been an attendant. Like Georges Laurent's mother, to whom I ascribed that role in Chapter 3's analysis of the film *Caché*, I refer to Ismail as another example of what Deleuze designates as the kind of aesthetic figure he sees in the canvasses of the painter Francis Bacon, one peripheral to the main theme but a provider of facticity of the scene, "the relation of the Figure to its isolating place."[62] In *Ethos*, Ismail's silence conveys the way the series thinks about prohibitions on what can be said. Once he is speaking—much to the relief of both Ruhiye and Yasin—his talking reflects a thaw in their relationship that Ruhiye initiates. After she returns from her village, at her prompting she and Yasin are able to discuss their early courtship in

AN EGALITARIAN ISTANBUL   153

the context of the event back in their village. Yasin confesses that he had lied about Ramazan's death because he thought that it was best to silence the past in order to put it to rest.

The Protagonist

While the role of the Ismail character is about the strictures that shape the said versus unsaid, the Meryem character continually discloses what is supposed to be unseen as well as unsaid. While her fainting constitutes a silent testimony to the impropriety of a religious woman seeing and being attracted to a naked man to whom she is not married (thereby threatening her assiduous attempts at hiding her erotic feelings from herself), her voice is also important. On several occasions she refers to what is not supposed to be seen. For example, when Yasin tells her about witnessing Hayrunnisa's dog encounter, from which she ends up at a hospital with a badly injured leg, Meryem wonders out loud about how she could have gotten there on her own without Yasin's assistance. She suspects that Yasin has broken a taboo about being seen walking with a single woman who is not his wife (Yasin's reaction to her suspicion is to shut her up). And in a later scene, when many of the characters are attending the burial ceremony for the Hodja's wife, she notices that Yasin keeps staring at Hayrunnisa. When she's alone with Yasin at home later she asks, "Why did you keep looking at that girl?" When instead of replying he rushes away, she says to herself, "I saw how you looked at the Hodja's daughter; I'm not an idiot."

Meryem's pointed exposure of Yasin's behavior is deployed on others as well, in particular Peri. She cultivates her ("You put it beautifully, sister"), interrogates her about her practice and life ("How many patients do you see?"; "Are you married?"), and finding her discursive tactics transparent, turns her attempts at analytic practice into her own meta-analysis ("You're very good at leading the conversation where you want it to go"). As noted, she also has Hilmi's number: "I'm not a fool; I can see his real intentions." Although not well attuned to her own desires—Episode 1 ends with a Ferdi Özbeğen song from the 1980s that registers hidden desire, "I hid your love like a secret, I muttered your name in my dreams at night," heard at a moment when

154 AESTHETICS OF EQUALITY

Meryem is watching a kettle boil—Meryem is a critic while observing others. Continually questioning the behavior of her intimates as well as others, she exemplifies what Michel Foucault famously refers to as a "critical attitude"; "critique," he asserts, "is the movement by which the subject gives [itself] the right to question truth on its effects of power and question power on its discourses of truth."[63] Nevertheless, while she is attuned to everyone else's desires and subterfuges, her own remain hidden. However, what is hidden from her personally, I suggest, is meant to be taken culturally rather than as something merely symptomatic of personal inhibitions. Transcending her particular malady, her fainting reflects a complex cultural inhibition rather than an individual psychologically driven reflex.

The Secular

At her first appearance, Gülbin seems calm and centered as she guides the counseling session with her visibly upset client Peri, who mentions having a hard time at the outset (trying to manage her negative feelings toward her fundamentalist client). When Peri leaves the session she passes a headscarf-wearing woman in Gülbin's waiting room, whom we later learn is Gülbin's fundamentalist twin sister Gülan. As the episodes progress, we see that the Kemalist–fundamentalist schism in Turkish political culture sits in the midst of Gülbin's dysfunctional Kurdish family. That it's often a violence-provoking schism becomes evident when the second time Peri comes to Gülbin's office, her sister Gülan is trashing it (while Gülbin is away). A subsequent angry encounter between them takes place in their parent's living room, where we see their parents and their quadriplegic brother whose condition is a source of their conflict. Gülan blames Gülbin's anti-spiritual foreign-acquired psychiatric practice for bringing evil into their home, victimizing a brother who might otherwise respond to spiritual healing. Tellingly, when Gülan charges her twin with a lack of piety, Gülbin responds by saying that she (Gülan) is pious enough for both of them.

Meanwhile, Oya's camera is saying something that connects Gülbin's family scene with those that take place in Peri's family home. His camera explores the still portraits that have preexisted the cinematic

AN EGALITARIAN ISTANBUL   155

ones in his drama. A panning shot of their family home makes old family photos the main objects of the camera's gaze. Paradoxically, in a room in which the violent intrafamilial conflict—angry accusations and physical attacks between Gülbin and Gülan have turned family space into a virtual war zone—there are many family photos, a medium which, as Pierre Bourdieu suggests, "serves principally to represent the family's 'image of its own integration.' "[64] Locating that function within Euro-modernity, Bourdieu points out that "as the family became progressively dispossessed of most of its traditional functions, economic as well as social," a semiotic function became dominant. The family began asserting itself by "accumulating the signs of its affective unity, its intimacy," the primary role he accords to family photos, a "practice," he says, that "only exists and subsists for most of the time by virtue of its family function."[65]

Photography is not an incidental medium in the *Ethos* series. There is for example a contrast between its paradoxical role in the Gülbin/Gülan household and how it shows up in Peri's home. There the photo album is aspirational rather than solidarity-implying; Peri's mother awaits the fulfillment of wedding pictures. However, Peri's parental home hosts its own media paradox. In a conversation in which Peri's parents are disparaging a contemporary generation—complaining about how the baby boomers are not getting the lesson of being frugal and are only looking for what they can get and not give—their outlook is being affected by a medium that shapes that generation: they're on their iPads reading about generation Z on Facebook. Unlike Gülbin, who tries to manage her secularism within a secular/religious divide *within* her family, Peri's family regards themselves as besieged from the outside. For them, their home is haven in a society capitulating to religious orthodoxy. Peri's mother complains about the pervasiveness of "covered girls." Every TV show "now needs one," she says in disgust (while paradoxically, *she* seems to need one to clean her home). Her lack of self-reflection is an exemplary aspect of the series' normative mentality. Through its explorations of diverse unhappy characters, *Ethos* reflects on an egregious lack of attunement both within and between them. Consequently, the democratic ethos within which all the lives are equally present to the camera's gaze carries the implication that only through an attunement to oneself can one be ethically attuned to an Other.

The Ethos of *Ethos*

The Ferdi Özbeğen song segment sung at the fadeout at the end of Episode 1 refers to a lack of attunement; it reflects on what the characters hide from themselves. As one commentator suggests, it's a song that Oya picked because it's "lodged/suppressed in [one's] unconscious" (to repeat): "I hid your love like a secret, I muttered your name in my dreams at night."[66] How then can one figure an ethos of attunement? In pursuit such an ethos—one that resonates well with the interpersonal engagements in *Ethos*—Matthew Heard suggests that attunement to an Other requires embracing an "ethos that prolongs our engagement with the other's marks and noises."[67] What that implies is allowing the other to disrupt one's usual way of coming to terms with oneself. It's a practice of other-assisted self-reflection that articulates with the management of interpersonal engagements. By the end of the series, which traverses a negative egalitarian narrative (in which everyone is initially unhappy in their own way), the characters have changed sufficiently to permit themselves to be unsettled. They have become vulnerable enough to themselves to be able to experience the vulnerability of others.

How then does Oya map the encounters through which that comes about? Recalling the genre form I referred to as a tableau aesthetic, which embeds the frame-like closure of each element in the flow of events, I suggest that the ethos of *Ethos* that Oya composes emerges most clearly in the juxtapositions in Episode 8. Ultimately, it seems, the attunement to themselves and others that the characters achieve (at least for those who do achieve it) occur in moments of reciprocity outside of their households. They happen during moments when they're free from their family's affective matrices. As I noted, Meryem's reciprocity with Hilmi is exemplary in that respect (where Meryem reciprocates the gift of candy from Hilmi with a gift of socks—in exchanges that occurred outside). Those forms of reciprocity, which Claude Levi-Strauss famously refers to as "games of exchange," provide a "stabilizing function in the always unpredictable and in principle insecure interaction with other human beings."[68] Importantly, the effect is egalitarian. It contrasts with the hierarchical relationships operating in counseling sessions, for example the one leading to the strategic

AN EGALITARIAN ISTANBUL 157

struggle in Meryem's last session with Peri. While Peri, seeking to impose an interpretation, refers to Ruhiye's visit to her village as "brave," Meryem refers to it as "foolhardy." Without privileging either interpretation, I suggest that what Meryem does in the sessions is find a voice that enables her to resist the weight of the psychoanalytic discourse that Peri wields over her. While counseling sessions, despite the insights on which they're based, are hierarchical and disempowering, the accidental encounters are edifying and reciprocal.

Before Episode 8 ends with Meryem's fainting (followed by the epiphany she experiences while looking at the gift of a ring), another encounter takes place while the Hodja is on a solitary trip in his camper. It's the last and perhaps most telling encounter that articulates the ethos of reciprocity toward which *Ethos* points. While at home in family space, the Hodja is locked into the struggle against a secular modernity that has overtaken his daughter's life. And while in his mosque/school, he's locked into the protocols of spiritual counseling. However, once on the road in his camper, away from family and work space, he's nomadic. He is outside the spaces that house the institutionalized parental and religious protocols he has felt obliged to administer in his home and school respectively. He is temporarily away from what Mark Twain's Huckleberry Finn calls "cramped up and smothery" places.[69]

The encounter occurs as the Hodja sits in front of his van parked by a lake. A car pulls up and a man of his generation calls out seeking directions to a nearby park. After telling him how to find it, the Hodja invites him to linger and share a meal. Claiming to be too full to eat, the man decides to join him for some tea. Once their conversation is underway something much more important is shared. After the Hodja mentions having recently lost his wife, his new acquaintance mentions a similar loss; his first wife died from an embolism after a vein operation. In the midst of exchanges of religious talk—may she rest in peace; yes, I have a daughter may Allah bless her—the visitor, on seeing a picture of the Hodja's daughter with his late wife, says "she has your wife's eyes." The Hodja is then moved to break a long-maintained silence by disclosing a secret he had locked away. He and his wife had actually adopted their daughter. There's a mother-daughter resemblance, he says, because they were advised to make a selection in which the eyes matched. He then admits that although they contemplated telling her

158   AESTHETICS OF EQUALITY

when she reached the age of eighteen, they had decided not to. A combination of his nomadic departure from his usual spaces, along with the reciprocity of sharing past losses in a chance encounter, opens the Hodja to reflect on and utter what has hitherto been unsaid.

Earlier in the episode it had already become clear that sharing what has hitherto been unsaid is the condition of possibility for Ruhiye and Yasin to restore the emotional basis of their marriage bond. Restoring to dialogue the hitherto unsaid also affects many of *Ethos*'s other characters. The disclosures of what had been unsaid reinflects several of the series interpersonal relations. Along with the (mostly) felicitous changes that occur when the unsaid is uttered is an important observation supplied by the character Hilmi, who leaves very little unsaid (as Meryem notes sarcastically at one point). Hilmi delivers a discursive supplement to what Oya's cinematic portraits and montage sequences implicitly say about overcoming cultural constraints. In a soliloquy during a conversation with Meryem in Episode 6, he makes an observation that delivers the underlying ethos of *Ethos*: Hilmi says in effect that to live well one should free oneself from various intensively surveilled institutionalized norms for how to manage intra- and interpersonal relationships. One should regard life, he says, as a "festival."

5
Latinx Visibility
Architecture and Public History

Blue Blobs

My inquiry into the architectural articulation of Latinx presence in public history begins with a look at one of Los Angeles County's most visible architectural features: swimming pools. Flying into Los Angeles International Airport affords one a view of the acres of swimming pools that reflect what Laura Bliss refers to as "chlorinated class politics," which registers class stratification:

> Peering out from an airplane window, it's hard to miss the swimming pools. Hundreds of thousands of sparkling blue blobs patch the county's landscape—though not evenly. In Southern California where space and water are getting rarer by the day.[1]

What accounts for the proliferation of those blue blobs? While currently they register income disparity, historically they are part of an ethnic segregation story that begins in the mid-twentieth century. Municipal swimming pools were desegregated in the 1950s, and by "the 1970s and 1980s tens of millions of mostly white middle class Americans swam in their back yards or at suburban club pools, while mostly African and Latino Americans swam at inner city municipal pools."[2]

The class profile of private swimming pool owners is well-captured in John Cheever's 1964 East Coast–situated story "The Swimmer." As his protagonist "Neddy Merrill sat by the green water [of his own private backyard pool], one hand in it, one around a glass of gin . . . he saw, with a cartographer's eye, a string of swimming pools, a quasi-subterranean stream that curved across the county. He had made a

Aesthetics of Equality. Michael J. Shapiro, Oxford University Press. © Oxford University Press 2023.
DOI: 10.1093/oso/9780197670347.003.0006

160 AESTHETICS OF EQUALITY

discovery, a contribution to modern geography; he would name the stream Lucinda, after his wife." On an impulse he decides to take a swim along the "Lucinda stream," which requires making his way through the path of pools in his segregated white bourgeois enclave. His encounter when he reaches "the Bunkers' pool" (where a poolside cocktail party is underway) is exemplary: "Prosperous men and women gathered by the sapphire-colored waters while caterer's men in white coats passed them cold gin."[3] Given the permission that his whiteness affords along with his being known socially by all his pool-owning neighbors, the only impediments to Neddy Merrill's long swim are drink invitations that slow his progress.

The Los Angeles version of the ethnic segregation story is in part zoning-related, a result of "redlining and other restrictive practices to keep out Black people and immigrants." As "single-family zoning became the norm . . . by 2010," LA's shrunken "zoning envelope" resulted in a metropolitan "region that has the fewest homes per capita of any metro area in the country." As an investigator of a "housing crisis" points out, "Los Angeles County fell a million homes behind, relative to its population growth, after becoming a single-family mecca, thanks to federal freeway subsidies, subsidized home mortgages, some ingenious modern architecture and the mythology of the pool, the garden and the individual—in essence, a vision of paradise that ended up being primarily for white people."[4]

The pervasive presence of private pools in Los Angeles County attracted two very differently motivated artists to LA's single-family mecca. One is the English artist David Hockney, who executed a series of "splash" paintings featuring shimmering water and the bodies of male bathers. A gay man arriving in LA from the gray, often sunless cityscape of London in 1963, he was inspired by the pools' brightness, colors, and male bodies using them. The substantial corpus of pool images he executed has "done more than any artist to fashion LA's visual identity," as one critic puts it.[5] Noting the irony "of a Yorkshire man becoming the person to reveal California to itself," another critic refers to his pool imaginaries as "utopian spaces of blissful gay domesticity in which it will be afternoon forever."[6]

Inspired by Hockney's pool paintings, another gay man, the Latino artist Ramiro Gomez, imitated and reinflected them. He too

LATINX VISIBILITY 161

composed pools and bodies, most notably a versioning on Hockney's splash paintings. However, rather than objects of desire, the bodies in his pools are class codes; they're Latino pool cleaners at work rather than at leisure, inserted in his Hockney-like pool compositions. Having viewed luxurious homes with their private pools from the perspective of his former work as a nanny, Gomez decided to riff on David Hockney's iconic work *A Bigger Splash*, shifting "the focus from the splash to the worker."[7] In focus for both Hockney and Gomez is what California offers to the eye. Attracted by architecture and bodies, Hockney was especially struck not only by brightness and colors but also by the horizontal style of upscale LA homes.[8] Articulating architecture with eros, Hockney's attention to California backyard swimming pools was both aesthetic and erotic; he was drawn to a setting that afforded views naked or semi-naked male bodies.

In contrast, Gomez, whose paintings are a form of politically attuned productive reception, has been concerned with the bodies that have been invisible. Striving "to bring to the foreground the [Latina/o] laborers who make possible the comfortable lives of the more affluent Angelinos," often "illegal" people who perforce "strive not to be seen,"[9] his riffs on Hockney's pool painting are exemplified in his version of Hockney's *A Bigger Splash* in which he substitutes a pool cleaner and a housekeeper, and titles it *No Splash*.[10]

Gomez mimicked other Hockney domestic style paintings as well, substituting *Woman Cleaning Shower* in Beverly Hills for Hockney's *Man Taking a Shower in Beverly Hills* and replacing Frederick and Marcia Weisman standing in front of their Modern home, in Hockney's *The Collectors*, with their gardeners. His politics of aesthetics—image-articulated interpretations of a Latina/o presence in white domestic space—reflects a major aspect of the "Latinx urban condition." In LA, as in other parts of California, much of the post–Guadalupe-Hidalgo story witnesses "the Chicano community . . . integrated and subordinated into a colonial labor system."[11] While Hockney's "highly selective vision of Los Angeles" was trained on the city's distracting visual presentness, which obscures its ethnohistory,[12] Gomez's politically inflected Hockney homages restore what LA's visual sublime obscures, a pastness. He recovers an ethnohistory sedimented in a contemporary domestic labor force.

162   AESTHETICS OF EQUALITY

Ethnohistory

The backyard swimming pool-owning ethnoscape is a small part of LA County's architecturally archived segregation story. As Mike Davis points out, the pervasiveness of "physical security systems [along] . . . with the architectural policing of social boundaries," has created an urbanism in which "the defense of luxury lifestyles is translated into the proliferation of new repressions in space and movement."[13] Using a figure from Renaissance security practices, Edward Soja offers a similar observation. He refers to LA's civic center zone as a "'citadel' where the architecture articulates a bunkered mentality with a surveillant enactment of official power/knowledge."[14] What Davis figures as "fortress L.A.,"[15] and Soja similarly as "bunkered," represents a historical reversal. Whereas a contemporary securitized LA restricts the right to the city of the Latinx assemblage, in the nineteenth century when California was under Mexican sovereignty and the church's control over land had been abrogated by secularization, a landholding Mexican elite emerged. Wealthy Californios, among whom was the military leader Mariano Guadalupe Vallejo, had accumulated large landholdings (e.g., Vallejo's "Casa Grande in the new pueblo of Sonoma").[16] They lived on large ranchos run with a coerced workforce consisting mainly of Native American's laboring in a virtual serfdom. Those subalterns were part of an earlier ethnohistory that preceded the Latinos who were later coercively integrated into a colonial labor system.

To summarize the subsequent ethnohistory: in the aftermath of the Mexican War the formerly wealthy Californios were displaced by the conquering Anglos under General Fremont. Vallejo, once the Commandant of the San Francisco Presidio and subsequently the military governor of Sonoma, had hoped to broker a Californios-Anglo shared sovereignty. Instead, he joined the others in the formerly Spanish America who "found themselves inside the United States [as] foreigners on [what had been] their own land."[17] Unlike the prosperous Californios, the contemporary Latina/o "foreigners"—part of a several decade "reLatinization" of the American Southwest—are a demographic underclass living in barrios rather than in pueblos or on ranchos. Once part of a hegemonic Spanish America that secured

LATINX VISIBILITY   163

its control with presidios ("fortified settlements with an assigned military contingent"),[18] Mexican Americans, along with other Latinx peoples, are collectively a group against whom Anglo California protects itself. What Davis calls fortress LA is effectively one sizable, disarticulated presidio that impedes the Latinx right to the city with design deterrents—"elevated pedways" and other architectural strategies—that are "rebukes [to] any affinity or sympathy between different architectural or human orders . . . [for example] Otis's fortress Times building [which is part of] . . . the archisemiotics of class war."[19] However, those Latinx-containment strategies pale in comparison with the public projects that have displaced barrio enclaves, for example the building of Dodger Stadium in Chavez Ravine (completed in 1962), for which a Chicana/o neighborhood was evacuated and cleared, and the redlining-engendered forms of privatization that have absorbed much of the available housing space. But doubtless the most notable assault on Latinx urban life in LA country began with the construction of the freeway system in the 1960s, which bisected their neighborhoods. LA County's built structure speaks to a historical trajectory of ethnic repression.

Splintering Automobility

As Henri Lefebvre notes, "The totalizing system that has been constructed around the automobile seems ready to sacrifice all of society to its dominion."[20] Referring in particular to highways, he states, "A motorway brutalizes the countryside and the land, slicing through space."[21] In a similar reflection on the consequences of that spatial intrusion, Ivan Illich addresses the splintering effects of technology-assisted urban design, which he says "isolates people from each other and locks them into a man-made shell." Regarding the development of automobility as the primary assault on conviviality, he writes:

> Cars are machines that call for highways, and highways pretend to be public utilities while in fact they are discriminatory devices . . . Cars . . . shape a city into their image—practically ruling out locomotion on foot or by bicycle in Los Angeles . . . What cars

do to people by virtue of this radical monopoly is quite distinct from and independent of what they do by burning gasoline that could be transformed into food in a crowded world . . . Cars create distance. Speedy vehicles of all kinds render space scarce. They drive wedges of highways into populated areas, and then extort tolls on the bridge over the remoteness between people that was manufactured for their sake.[22]

Along with its impact on conviviality is automobility's differential assault on health. In his inquiry into the health consequences of LA's freeway system, Stephen Graham references research showing that the "largely Hispanic, Asian and African American neighborhoods bisected by freeways . . . carrying the cars of largely white commuters between suburban neighborhoods and downtown breathe by far the highest concentrations of deeply poisonous and carcinogenic substances."[23] The stark consequences of automobility doubtless apply more to Los Angeles than to any other urban area. As Anne Friedberg puts it, "The metropolitan logic of Los Angeles can only be understood through its requisite automotive mobility."[24]

Helena María Viramontes's novel *Their Dogs Came with Them* (hereafter *Dogs*) and Joel Schumacher's film *Falling Down* turn Illich's insightful abstractions, Graham's focused inquiry, and Friedberg's characterization into dramas that illustrate the impact of LA's highway construction on diverse forms of local life. The intrepid journeys through LA on foot of Viramontes's exhausted Latina/o protagonists and Schumacher's rampaging Anglo protagonist provide contrasting ethno-temporalities. With characters fashioned as urban walkers— what Michel de Certeau refers to as "*Wandermanner*, whose bodies follow the thicks and thins of the urban 'text' "[25]—both the novel and the film interarticulate "textual and urban space."[26]

The title of Viramontes's *Dogs* signals its historiographic metafictional framing. The novel begins with an epigraph drawn from Miguel Leon-Portilla's *The Broken Spears: The Aztec Account of the Conquest of Mexico*:

They came in battle array, as conquerors . . . Their dogs came with them, running ahead of the column. They raised their muzzles high;

they lifted their muzzles to the wind. The raced on before with saliva dripping from their jaws.[27]

Linking the present Anglo conquest of Latinx space with the Spanish conquest of "America," the novel features a temporal multiplicity, some of which resides in one of its four protagonists, Turtle, whose name is a temporal trope (she moves slowly on foot, in contrast with the rapid movement of cars on freeways). While the novel's main compositional strategy consists in its pursuit of its human protagonists, freeways, whose configurations metaphorically structure interpersonal as well as urban space, are also main characters. The intersections among the novel's four main characters are homologous with the structure of the East LA freeway interchange. As Viramontes attests, "I realized that the structure of the novel began to resemble the freeway intersections . . . And like the freeways upheld by pillars, I realized I had four pillars in four characters of which most other characters orbited around."[28]

"Disconnect[ing] East L.A. from the rest of the city,"[29] the freeway-fragmenting of the city inspires the novel's "decentered narrative" structure. Viramontes uses the LA freeway system as a model for the disjunctive narrative threads that follow her characters. Living in a city that splinters the urban formation and impedes "productive social exchange,"[30] LA's "layers of premium . . . spaces [are] constructed for socio-economically affluent and corporate users,"[31] while the novel's protagonists are displaced from their already marginal East LA barrio after the construction of the 710 and 60 freeway interchange. The violent destruction of the Latino neighborhood is perpetrated by "earthmovers [described as] . . . invading engines of a Quarantine Authority," an invasion that leaves Viramontes's characters with stories as "their only private property."[32] Facing a heavily policed public space and an increasingly restrictive residential space; Viramontes's Latinx protagonists represent a more general experience of the evacuation of LA's Latinx population's right to the city. Susan Bickford's reflection on the political interarticulation of the two spaces is apropos:

> The issue of policed and segregated public space may seem separable from the issue of controlled residential space . . . is the character of

residential choices . . . a private matter? Infringing on the right to choose where and among whom one loves would seem . . . an unbearable imposition on privacy and freedom. To examine the issue of residential choice as a private matter is to consider two dimensions of "privacy-related liberty"—as a right to limit access and exclude others and as a right to decisional autonomy.[33]

The effect of such an infringement on the right to choose to which Bickford refers is conveyed in the novel through the experiences of Viramontes's diverse characters. Rather than providing all the details of the different narrative threads conveying those experiences, I briefly follow one, Turtle, whose name, as one commentator suggests, "references the slowdown or *space-time expansion* that freeways imposed on inner-city residents who lacked automobiles."[34] Her walks through various neighborhoods map the consequences of the freeway system's evacuation of what had once been a convivial communal enclave. As the novel tracks Turtle's peregrinations through urban space, the narrative focuses on "physical sites that link her to history."[35] What she sees as she visits her old neighborhood is an "endless field of construction [with] . . . houses disappearing inch by inch."[36]

Falling Down

The fragmented LA that Viramontes's novel maps through the eyes and itineraries of her characters, who struggle to recover what they have lost, is represented similarly in Schumacher's film *Falling Down*, which begins on one of LA's freeways. However, the cinematic protagonist we first meet, William Foster, known as "D-Fens" (Michael Douglas)—stuck in traffic on the vehicle-clogged freeway—has a personal history of using a freeway rather than being victimized by it. Nevertheless, he shares something with Viramontes's characters; he's lost his home (and his work as well). He's been let go from his job in the defense industry, has been divorced by his wife, and has been barred from his former home by a restraining order. Moreover, he's delusional; no longer employed by a defense contractor, he has retained his vocational identification on his car license plate (D-Fens), and in

LATINX VISIBILITY   167

defiance of the restraining order, he's on the freeway headed "home"; "I'm going home" is a mantra he repeats throughout his encounters in the city. Although it features a very different kind of protagonist—a white Anglo male, dedicated to the mythology of "the American dream"—the film shares an important aspect of the novel. There's an egregious gap between language and the urban reality that accompanies LA's socioethnic apartheid in both texts. At one point in *Dogs*, the character Ben, while searching for words adequate to his situation, finds his sister Ana's "faith-based discourse" inadequate: "Nothing but the wrong words came out of her lips."[37] Similarly, in *Falling Down* "the physical barriers separating the ethnic groups that represent LA's cultural and economic diversity are complemented by discursive boundaries that operate as much within as between ethnic and occupational assemblages."[38]

In the opening scene as D-Fens is sitting in traffic on a freeway, the camera pans a jumble of diverse phrases on the vehicles stalled in front of him—bumper stickers with a variety of discursive genres, such as a religious slogan, "he died for your sins," and a parodic one, "How am I driving, call 1-800 Eat Shit." And when the film's other main protagonist, detective Martin Prendergast (Robert Duvall), who is also stuck in traffic on the freeway, gets out of his car to help a highway patrolman move the car D-Fens has abandoned to the road's shoulder (he has left the freeway on foot in frustration), a yawning gap between language and reality becomes apparent. While what is visible is a line of immobilized cars, buses, and trucks, the patrolmen cautions him about the precarity of where they're standing: "We got a lot of glass and steel rushing by us at high speeds." That language-reality gap subsequently asserts itself in D-Fens's encounters in LA's inner city.

Although the film proceeds with a "forking-path plot" in which the protagonists are given equal coverage and ultimately meet after both D-Fens and Prendergast show up in proximity on the freeway,[39] and proceed to head in separate directions—shown as the film cuts back and forth between their itineraries (D-Fen's odyssey toward home and Prendergast's last investigative day in his police precinct before he is supposed to clean out his desk and go home)—my attention is on D-Fens's walking tour. Once he abandons his immobilized car, leaves the freeway, and heads into the city, his encounters indicate how far ethnic LA is from his city

168 AESTHETICS OF EQUALITY

imaginary. Throughout his odyssey through inner-city neighborhoods his experiences of ethnic others are filtered through the regulative ideals that have governed a self-understanding based on having lived within the confines of the spaces of white privilege as well as within the ideational confines of a narrow moral economy that attributes economic success to personal striving (even though, paradoxically, the ideals have not served him well). Nevertheless, he keeps as tight a grip on those ideals as he does on the briefcase he's carrying, which serves as a self-deceptive prop for a man no longer employed (all it contains is a lunch he had packed).

It becomes clear as D-Fens's encounters proceed that his inability to be intelligible to himself shapes and extends to his interpersonal encounters throughout the inner city, as all the people he meets deliver challenges to his sense-making. During his first encounter in a Korean convenience store he enters to get change to phone his ex-wife, he's put off by the proprietor's accent as well as by the store's prices (his product price imaginary is as anachronistic as his ethnic imaginary). Rather than accepting the store owner's commercial sovereignty in his own establishment, he rampages through the store with a baseball bat he's grabbed from the owner and smashes all the shelves holding things he regards as overpriced. His assault combines two venerable American pastimes, baseball and violence against ethnic minorities.

The next and most telling encounter takes place when D-Fens, seeking respite from his agitation, walks up on a hill overlooking a Latinx barrio, sits by a rock formation filled with graffiti, takes off his shoes, and mops his brow. Approached by two young Latino men who tell him that he's trespassing on private property, he responds that he doesn't see any signs. One of them points to the writing on the rocks and says, "What do you think that is?" When D-Fens asks if he means the graffiti, the Latino says "That's not fuckin' graffiti; it's a sign. This is fuckin' private property." The confrontation escalates, threatening to transcend a clash of signs. For the young Latino men, the graffiti represent their claim to their barrio space, a claim that D-Fens rejects as anathema to his sense-making. They respond by threatening him with a knife demanding that he hand over his briefcase. Rather than complying, D-Fen's begins beating them with the briefcase and the bat he has retained from his prior encounter. His fiery temper-driven rampage has been reignited.

LATINX VISIBILITY   169

After the two men flee D-Fens begins the rest of his descent into an LA city- and people-scape that has hitherto been terra incognita for a man who had never departed from his usual route between home and work and is impervious to all but his own story. As his city tour progresses, we see a man who is ill equipped ideationally and discursively to make LA's ethnic neighborhoods intelligible. As Elena Zilberg summarizes it, he lacks a "frame of reference with which to make sense of the changed grammar of urban life . . . and temporarily loses his capacity to organize his immediate surroundings perceptually and to map his position in relation to the external world."[40] However, it's Schumacher's camera work rather than D-Fens's perceptions that shape the way the film thinks. As the camera follows what D-Fens can see but not effectively assimilate into an effective sociopolitical imaginary, it affirms Deleuze's insight that "cinema does not have natural subjective perception as its model . . . because the mobility of its centers and the variability of its framings always lead it to restore vast acentered and deframed zones."[41] The film's sense making is owed instead to Schumacher's cuts and juxtapositions, which situate D-Fens's immediate surroundings to disclose the extent to LA's degree of inequality.

Rather than going into an extensive shot-by-shot elaboration, I want to note a juxtaposition delivered with a panning shot and one statement delivered with a framing shot. As for the former, early in D-Fens's walking tour, as the camera pans a group of buildings, it moves past a swap meet store, which serves an underclass and moves on to a bank from which a white guy in a suit and tie is emerging. Reinforcing what that panning shot says, the camera proceeds to follow an African American man holding a sign that says "not economically viable," specifically not eligible for a bank loan, which he underscores verbally by approaching the man leaving the bank and asks him for a loan. Later in his city tour, as D-Fens approaches a downtown golf course that takes up a large piece of real estate in the inner city, the camera zooms in on a sign on the front gate that reads (unambiguously) "No Trespassing." After D-Fens climbs a fence to enter, the golfers he harasses (to a point that one collapses with a heart attack) are elderly white men wearing expensive golfing outfits and traveling between holes in a golf cart. The shot of the golf club sign is one among many moments in the film's referential montage; it contrasts with D-Fen's graffiti moment, where

170 AESTHETICS OF EQUALITY

the young Latino men tell him that the squiggles on the rocks say no trespassing. However, those signs lack the official sanction of the one at the golf club gate, which has the backing of the city's legal codes and policing enforcement.

In Michel de Certeau's apropos terms, the young Latinos' attempt to assert proprietary control over the hill on which D-Fens sat was a "tactic . . . an art of the weak." In an observation that characterizes well much of Latinx LA's precarious hold on space, he goes on to assert that "The space of the tactic is the space of the other," who must "play on and with the terrain imposed on it and organized by the law of a foreign power."[42] In contrast, what de Certeau refers to as "strategies" are capacities of those who have structures of authority on their side. Strategies represent "*a triumph of space over time*" for those who have institutionally supported control over space, which "allows one to capitalize acquired advantages, to prepare future expansions and thus to give oneself a certain independence with respect to the variability of circumstances."[43]

To the extent that there has been Latino place-making in LA, precarious though it has often been, it has developed as an incommensurate mode of urbanism, a style of place-making that has been imperiled by structures imposed by Anglo LA's officially sanctioned design practices. The privileging of automobility that had fractured Latinx space with freeway construction has also operated off the highway and insinuated itself into residential space. Telling that story brings us back to the East LA featured in Viramontes's novel *Dogs*, which treats the Boyle Heights Latinx neighborhood that was assaulted by city planning, yet also served as a center of Latino political activism from the late 1960s to the present. It's a place continually cited in critical scholarship that focuses on automobility's and gentrification's impact on LA's Latinx assemblage.[44]

The Political Aesthetics of Latinx Urbanism

David Diaz provides a succinct description of how Latinx communities were fractured by freeway plans developed for the benefit of well-off Anglo LA residents:

LATINX VISIBILITY   171

Barrios were effectively attacked by state transportation departments, who had the support from the federal highway administration. East Los Angeles (East LA) would suffer the worst from the bureaucratic logic. The barrio had numerous vibrant and cohesive neighborhoods that were either eradiated or radically reconstructed with the imposition of five distinct freeway routes.[45]

In response to the freeway plan, Latinx activists made a documentary film, *East LA Interchange*, which narratives the emergence of a neighbor political voice in a fight against the plan for "the largest freeway interchange system in the nation."[46] And in response to gentrification, an "Alliance Against Artwashing and Displacement" staged demonstrations and called for a named a boycott of a plan for a Boyle Heights arts district.[47] Although the episodic assertion of Latinx presence in Boyle Heights and other barrios (in LA and elsewhere)—marches, boycotts, murals, graffiti, installations, and documentaries—has been a significant aspect of Latinx political activity, I want to emphasize an assertion of Latinx presence that operates with a more extended temporality, a historically developed mode of Latinx domesticity. Latinx sociopolitical presence is articulated through an exoteric lifestyle, an outward-oriented architectural expressivity. With vivid colors and exterior design elements, Latinx houses communicate with their social milieu. While stating their presence with colorful exteriors and garden statuary, their exterior-oriented architectural presence contrasts with the Anglo LA's tendency toward a backyard, secluded lifestyle, exemplified in the above noted pool culture and by an obsessive attention to interior decorating. Privileging the exterior aspect of domesticity, the Latinx domestic habitus has been a practice of front and side yard sociability. James Rojas, a Latino from East LA's Boyle Heights, describes the side yard use of his family home on a corner lot as the place "where life happened . . . The side yard became the center of family life—a multigenerational and multicultural plaza, seemingly abuzz with celebrations and birthday parties."[48] In addition to the intrafamily sociability for which the yard functioned was its facilitation of extrafamilial relationships. Fronting the street, his family's side yard made "private space closer to public space to promote sociability . . . Like a plaza." As Rojas puts it, "the street acted as a focus in

172   AESTHETICS OF EQUALITY

our everyday life where we would gather daily because we were part of something big and dynamic that allowed us to forget our problems of home and school."[49] When urban redevelopment took away the Rojas house they lost their interpersonal life world, a typical experience for the quotidian presence of underclasses. Michael Rios generalizes Rojas's experience and responds to it with an egalitarian political ethos. "For marginal communities, the use of urban space defines much of their economic, cultural, and political well-being." Presuming that "all citizens have a right to the spaces of the city," he refers to the importance of "negative rights, for example the right against displacement discrimination in zoning, or dependence on the automobile."[50]

The Latinx "quotidian presence" that Rojas describes and Rios theorizes has been anathema to the "white spatial imaginary in central Los Angeles [where] redevelopment efforts [have] displaced communities of color." The Anglo bourgeois architectural imaginary—what Henri Lefebvre refers to as a "dogmatized ensemble of [functional] significations . . . [not] the significations lived by those who inhabit" urban space[51]—is contrary to the Latinx practice of everyday life. Their urban imaginary is a "mapping from below" that challenges the Anglo (and accordingly officially sanctioned) image of urban space. As Jorge Leal puts it, "Through their visual or written mappings, Latinos assert themselves and their presence as [a] visible and dynamic part of American metropolis' urban space."[52] That assertion of presence has encountered significant obstacles, the primary one being urban redevelopment planning. When the side yard–equipped home in which Rojas grew up "disappeared," a casualty of the expansion of the local high school which "required paving over Rojas' family home, displacing his immediate family,"[53] their new family home was in a space designed for automobility rather than sociability. As Rojas notes, "overlook[ing] benefits in Latino neighborhoods, like walkability and social cohesion . . . planners focused on streets to move and store vehicles rather than on streets to move and connect people."[54] Noting what has been at stake, the communal aspects of the urban street, the architectural theorist Anthony Vidler refers to "the street as a site of interaction, encounter and the support of strangers for each other; the square as a place of gathering and vigil; the corner store a communicator of information and interchange. These spaces, without romanticism or nostalgia, still define an urban culture, one that resists all efforts to 'secure' it out of existence."[55] With respect to the specifics of a supportive sociability in a Latinx-populated neighborhood, Karla Cornejo Villavicencio states the matter lyrically:

> We needed each other to make life worth living for ourselves ... We warn each other about encroaching dangers, and reach for the same piece of the sky ... the goal, I think. Is to stand strong and reliable, to stay alive ourselves and keep it alive. And above all, send sweetness and strength to those who do not yet reach the sun themselves.[56]

Anglo cultural crotchets reinforce policy planning assaults on Latinx sociability and visible presence. Decades ago, I heard a public radio interview with an Anglo Californian complaining that the way Latinos flaunt their visibility by hanging out in front and side yard is unseemly. He asserted as well that they lack a "pride of place" with respect to their interiors (giving as an example a Latino family that places a TV set on top of their refrigerator). The complaining Anglo Californian has institutionalized support. As Johanna Londoño points out, "Municipal ordinances may seem innocuous, but in shaping the aesthetics of urban space they may also shape the social ordering of space, a process that is deeply political." Such ordinances operate along with "private covenants and home associations that limit cultural expression."[57] Exemplary in this respect was the reaction of the San Antonio Historic Preservation Society to Sandra Cisneros's purple house. Because it violated local historical preservation codes, it had to be repainted. For Cisneros, as is the case collectively for many Latinx enclaves (e.g., Mexican barrios), "color is an important component of an ensemble of cues that lend an ethnic identity to the landscape."[58]

The color component of Latinx landscape has achieved artistic notice. It is featured in the photography of Camillo Jose Vergara, who as I have noted elsewhere documents "the Latino contribution to ... architecturally-inscribed public history." Describing the aim of his documentation, he refers to his "hope to rescue from oblivion a part of this nation's history and to capture the world that survivors are shaping."[59] Among his subjects are the Mexican American house and store's distinctive "design presence" with a "preference for exoteric,

174 AESTHETICS OF EQUALITY

colorful display" that captures a building's "persona—a sense of that place."[60] As Sandra Cisneros noted during her struggle to hold onto her colorful design choice, which was "suspect for straying from historically segregated maps that codify the barrio as a place for people of color and bright colors," Latino design preferences are "a part of American diversity; they [have been] 'another way of being American.'"[61] However, for many official and unofficial Anglo Texans, "bright colors are considered bad taste and [are] unwelcome when they don't fit a dominant notion of architectural history; when they threaten white, elite, or propertied claims to urban space; when they portend barrioization; and when they go beyond the confines of the intimate—the interior décor of middle-class homes or individual fashion tastes."[62]

As Cisneros's experience suggests, taste is among other things a class weapon. Adrian Nathan West makes that case:

> Taste, above all, is an epiphenomenon of privilege, of economic and social inequality, and the establishment of canons of taste in the nineteenth century cannot be understood in isolation from the rise of the bourgeoisie and the substitution of various purchasable status markers for heredity and theoretically inviolate mobility. These gave rise to what Klaus Theweleit terms *a war on two fronts*: the struggle, on the part of the socially ascendant, to distinguish themselves from their inferiors while also trying to infiltrate a higher cultural stratum constantly battling to fend off intruders.[63]

Nevertheless, the symbolic, class-distinction war on Latinx urban presence (which adds an ethnic dimension to the battle) pales in comparison with policy assaults. As a history lesson, the demise of the Latinx Boyle Heights neighborhood featured in Viramontes's novel is best rendered as Los Angeles's Latinx Alamo, which succumbed to an urban planning attack. It's one venue among many throughout the American Southwest that has "long been a contentious battleground, both literally and figuratively, for Mexican American's [and other Latinx groups'] resistance to Anglo-American–led subjugation."[64]

However, unlike the actual Alamo, the scene of the famous 1836 battle (currently an object of contentious historical interpretation), there is no one building left in Boyles Heights to serve an architecture-centered narrative. Moving the analysis from California to Texas provides a definitive architectural site with which to reflect on Latinx public history, because the struggle for Latino historical recognition is distilled in a contemporary contention over how to configure and curate a redesigned Alamo Museum. Among the more compelling commentaries in a variety of textual genres are those that urge us to forget the Alamo. As three writers who have exposed how Alamo history has been officially controlled (with much help from popular culture texts) conclude, "the Heroic Anglo narrative endures [because] those who disagree with it, especially Texas Latinos, have rarely captured public attention."[65] "Maybe," they suggest, "it's time to forget the Alamo, or at least the whitewashed story, and start telling the history that includes everyone."[66]

Remembering/Forgetting the Alamo

In their experience of the destruction of their Latinx Boyles Heights neighborhood, the characters in Viramontes's novel *Dogs*, who want to remember their collective history, have to rely on stories because what remains visible are ruins, for example "rows of vacant houses missing things [left without] hinged doors [and] shattered windows [that] had been used as targets."[67] In an apropos analysis of the forces producing ruins and erasing their significance from memory, Tim Edensor asserts, "modern capitalism proceeds by forgetting the scale of devastation wrecked upon the physical and social world."[68] Noting as well what ruins say about history, he adds, "the objects, space, and traces found in ruins highlight the radical undecidability of the past . . . but they simultaneously invoke a need to tell stories about it."[69]

Viramontes's novel pursues that need. To situate the role of the stories on which Viramontes's characters rely is to reflect on the relationship of memory to history toward which Edensor gestures, I want to recur to a crucial part of the analysis in my Chapter 3's treatment of the officially buried history of the assault on Algerian immigrants, the October 17, 1961 Battle of Paris, where I invoke Pierre Nora's approach to that binary in which he addresses the issue of whose memories

176   AESTHETICS OF EQUALITY

become recognized as "history." To apply Nora's insights to Anglo control over what constitutes the official history of the Alamo, we have to heed his remark about "a process of interior colonization [which] has affected ethnic minorities, families and groups that until now [the late twentieth century] have possessed reserves of memory but little or no historical capital."[70] For Nora, memory is a "dialectic of remembering and forgetting, unconscious of its successive deformations, vulnerable to manipulation and appropriation, susceptible to being dormant and periodically revived,"[71] while history is "the reconstruction, always problematic and incomplete, of what is no longer."[72] And crucially for purposes of approaching the suppression of an ethnic group's claim to a share of what is to become official history, that history involves the "conquest and eradication of memory;"[73] its "mission [is] to suppress and destroy it."[74]

In 2020, such an eradication was underway in Texas by Republican lawmakers who blocked alternative narratives of the Alamo battle. They strove to "obscure the State's history of slavery and racism . . . with a flurry of proposed measures [that] . . . would promote even greater loyalty to [the Anglo version of] Texas in the state's classrooms."[75] In response to an attempt to provide other than a heroic narrative—part of a $450 million "reimagine the Alamo" renovation project that would change it from a shrine to Anglo Texan sacrifice to a complex historical site with a new museum component—state officials blocked the plan.[76] The still ongoing battle for locating the Alamo in an altered ethnohistorical context has been between a coalition of Texas Tejanos and educators seeking to replace myth with history and Republican officials. A potential re-curational moment is a propitious time to look at the future of the Alamo's past. At stake for the state officials is the endurance of a white supremacy narrative, while for others it's about locating themselves in public history. If we heed a future anterior grammar, the outcome of the current Alamo battle will bear on how the Alamo *will have been.*[77]

With respect to the mythic Anglo narrative, most Texans have learned about the Alamo from an officially controlled school curriculum that renders the Alamo battle as a scene of heroic sacrifice by virtuous and intrepid white men, while a broader swath of Americans have learned that narrative from films, the first of which was D. W.

Griffith's 1915 *Martyrs of the Alamo* (rendered also as *The Birth of Texas*). Griffiths's film represents the Mexican invaders much the way he represented emancipated Blacks in his (in)famous *Birth of a Nation* (also 1915) as not only cruelly violent predators, but also as sexual threats to white women. A history of slavery underlies the Griffith racial aesthetic, providing the political context for both the aftermath of the Civil War and a key battle in the Mexican war. Slavery, as Bryan Burroughs (one of the authors of *Forget the Alamo*) notes, is what actually unites the two wars. The Texas war for independence from Mexico "was waged in part to ensure slavery would be preserved" and "was the undeniable linchpin . . . it was the thing the two sides had been arguing about and shooting about for going on 15 years."[78]

Among the most viewed film versions of the heroic Anglo narrative is the Disney version *The Alamo* (1960), directed by John Wayne who stars as Davy Crockett. The *Forget the Alamo* investigation debunks the heroism of Crockett and the other well-known protagonists, Bowie and Travis (the former a "murderer, slaver, and con man," and the latter a "pompous racist agitator").[79] As for Crockett, the historical record shows that he surrendered and was executed rather what the Disney film portrays, his fighting until mortally wounded. In what follows, I turn to another text that urges a forgetting of the Alamo: John Sayles's film *Lone Star* (1996), which takes place in the fictitious Texas border town of Frontera rather than San Antonio. In Sayles's film one of its most important architectural sites, the ruins of a drive-in movie, obliquely states what is shown as the film closes: "Forget the Alamo" is bannered onscreen.

Throughout the film, the actual Alamo has only a spectral presence. Its mythic story haunts Frontera, the fictional Texas border town. With the ethnic lines of demarcation fueling a continual cultural battle over the way the Alamo is to be remembered in mind, Sayles wanted to both recognize and displace that battle. As he puts it, "One of the reasons I was interested in setting the movie on the border is that there is an artificial line."[80] Within the film drama that line, as it is realized in the characters' relationships, is transgressed. Assembling a diverse ethnoscape in Frontera, the film challenges "the symbolic work accomplished through 'remembering the Alamo' with a mythic Anglo story that produces a stigmatized [Mexican] identity."[81] Echoing Pierre

178 AESTHETICS OF EQUALITY

Nora's treatment of the memory-history entanglement, Sayles remarks, "as in many places, the dominant culture gets to write history."[82] His challenge to that lexical dominance is to dramatize a "'history [that] increasingly became the discipline of memory' and the burier of secrets."[83] As Neil Campbell succinctly puts it, "every relationship in the film is steeped in the entanglements of history and memory."[84]

Lone Star

A dramatic genre shift takes place in the film's opening scene. While Cliff and Mikey, two soldiers from the local army base, are engaged in a botanical survey of a desert-scape on the periphery of the town, they discover a sheriff's badge, a bullet casing, and a human skull. When the newly appointed local sheriff, Sam Deeds (Chris Cooper), is summoned and sees the rest of the body, the space of the investigation shifts from forensic botany to forensic police work. It becomes evident that the desert-scape has been harboring a murder victim ("Scene of the crime," says Mikey, holding up the badge). As is the case in Haneke's *Cache* featured in Chapter 3, much of *Lone Star* is organized by a whodunit narrative. However, as is also the case with *Cache's* rendering of Paris's ethnic encounters, in Sayles's film, while the whodunit narrative thread creates the choreography for the interpersonal encounters, the outcome of that narrative, solving the crime, is less important than how the film's moving images speak to the interethnic memory and history conflicts in a town that serves as a microcosm of a larger interethnic conflict throughout America's Southwest. Using sound as well as images to orchestrate the way the past resides in Frontera's present, Sayles infuses his soundtrack with traditional Mexican music from the very beginning of the film. Right after Sam arrives to observe Cliff and Mikey's discovery of a murder scene in the desert and the film cuts to the running of the credits, *Mi Unico Camino* (My Only Way), a conjunto style ballad (a precursor to modern Tejano music) is playing. It's a long lament by an abandoned lover, hoping that his lover will return and "forget old resentment." As Sayles testifies, he was looking for "songs that could take you back . . . songs to bridge transitions from present to past."[85]

Once the camera leaves the desert-scape and begins moving through the border town, it mainly follows Sheriff Sam Deeds, whose late father Buddy Deeds (Matthew McConaughey), a former sheriff, is regarded as a local legend (and is soon to be posthumously honored with a plaque erected in his memory in front of the town hall). The film's most important revelations are connected to the career of the "heroic" Buddy Deeds, whose law enforcement style, represented both in flashbacks and testimony, articulates a local as well as a personal history, both of which emerge in the film's architectural narrative thread. Sam's investigatory movement trajectory traces much of that architectural narrative, as he visits a Mexican restaurant, a home in "dark town," two bars (one Black-owned and one run by an obstreperous "redneck"), a Native American tourist shop, a tire store on "the other side" (i.e., in Mexico), and finally a last scene in the ruin of a drive-in movie theater.

Unlike his father, who carefully maintained the ethnic lines of demarcation, Sam's movements weave a tapestry of interconnections among the various sites, in which forms of intimacy that cross the lines defy his father's former management of them. Sam's murder investigation ultimately becomes less significant for what it discovers about a crime than what it discovers about the personal and interpersonal histories of the town's main protagonists, his own among others. At a micropolitical level Buddy Deed's legendary career haunts Sam's truth-seeking encounters aimed at solving the murder whose victim turns out to be a corrupt former sheriff, Charlie Wade (with many deaths resulting from his law enforcement), who was last seen in a confrontation with his then deputy, Deeds. And apart from his familial, romantic, and career interpersonal relations, the Buddy Deeds character is an aesthetic subject who represents both the alleged heroism attributed to the Alamo's iconic defenders and the Anglo control of the town. At a macropolitical level, the film's exploration of Anglo political dominance in the town and the levels of ethnic estrangements it entails is an allegory for divisive Anglo dominance in the state of Texas as a whole. Texas's ethnic estrangements are summarily expressed by one of the film's characters, the proprietor of an Anglo redneck bar, who refers approvingly to the "lines of demarcation."

180 AESTHETICS OF EQUALITY

As Sam's investigation proceeds, radically entangled personal memories and local histories become objects of interethnic and intergeneration contention and revelation. Just as the recent Alamo investigation turns mythic heroes into ordinary, flawed men by replacing myth with assiduous historiography, Sam's investigation turns his legendary father Buddy into a complex and very ordinary, flawed man, who as sheriff had traded protection for political support and who as a father, husband, and paramour had covered up the history of his interpersonal relations. By the end of the film, we learn that the man who had managed "the lines of demarcation" had crossed them. Reserving the details of his transgressions for later in the inquiry, I want to follow the key parts of the architectural narrative (what Friedberg refers to as "the filmic representation of architectural space"[86]) that lead to it.

The nonlinear architectural narrative that contains the characters' encounters in Sayles's screenplay operates as a dialectic of estrangement and intimacy. The main venues for those encounters are rooms whose function is akin to what Roberto Calasso ascribes to Franz Kafka's affective architectural moments. "For Kafka," he writes, "a room can be as charged as a continent."[87] The fit of that observation to *Lone Star* becomes apparent once the camera moves into town. The scene immediately following the discovery of the corpse in the desert-scape is a very charged space. One of the film's main protagonists, the Mexican American schoolteacher, Pilar Cruz (Elizabeth Peña), is standing in front of a Texas map in a high-school classroom while in conversation with a teacher colleague, saying "Hey, public education these days is a bit of a battleground." It's an observation actualized subsequently in a later scene in one of the school's classrooms where there's a contentious curriculum fight at parent-teachers meeting, a fight that persists in many counties in contemporary Texas.

Although throughout much of the film, Sam and Pilar are on separate trajectories—Pilar managing her school's history curriculum (for a multicultural local population with different kinds of investment in how it is represented) and Sam pursuing the murder investigation—their stories ultimately converge with a mutual discovery about a shared past that had been hidden from them by their parents. Shortly after the first scene in Pilar's school—there's a brief interlude involving her son and his Latino friends in an encounter with the police (her son

LATINX VISIBILITY   181

is charged with having stolen property and is brought to the jail)—the film cuts to one of the film's most important architectural sites, Café Santa Barbara, a Mexican restaurant run by Pilar's mother, Mercedes Cruz (Miriam Colon). In this first of several scenes in the restaurant, the image sequence joins with the music background (another Latino traditional song) to create a transition from present to past with a flashback to a moment when Buddy Deeds, then a deputy Sheriff, recently returned from the Korean War, defies Sheriff Wade's order to pick up the restaurant's monthly protection payments.

The flashback is preceded by a request. Sam enters the restaurant and walks over to a table where the town's mayor Hollis (Clifton James), in conversation with his cronies, is referring to the moment in the restaurant when Buddy Deeds challenged Charlie Wade (with the young Hollis, then also a deputy, present). When Sam asks to hear Hollis's version of the story, the film cuts back to that past moment, zooming in to a close-up of the tortilla basket, the object in focus in both the present and past scenes. In the historical scene the men threaten each other with their guns in plain sight, after Deeds refuses to obey Wade's instruction that he is to pick up the restaurant's monthly protection money, which is shown hidden among the tortillas in the basket. However, what is hidden in the tortilla basket is one among many secrets in the restaurant. Café Santa Barbara is a neocolonial establishment with much of its staff, undocumented Mexican employees, sequestered in the kitchen.

While the separation between the restaurant's kitchen and dining area constitutes an ethnic line of demarcation, adding to how the film thinks about such lines, the proprietress, Mercedes Cruz, is a former paramour of Sheriff Deeds, who unbeknownst to Pilar is her biological father, a secret that is not revealed to her until the very end of the film. Moreover, in addition to that ultimate revelation of Sam's investigation—Pilar, his former high school sweetheart and renewed romantic partner turning out to be his half-sister—are the many other generational tensions and paradoxes operating throughout the film's narrative. As for the immediate effect of Hollis's version of the story, Sam leaves that first encounter in Café Santa Barbara convinced that his father murdered Charley Wade. That adds to his vexation upon learning that soon to come is a public ceremony in front of the town

182 AESTHETICS OF EQUALITY

hall in which the plaque honoring his father will be unveiled (an event that is getting pushback from some of the town's Mexican American population).

The next two architectural sites the film narrative explores reveal another generational tension. Following the scene in the Café Santa Barbara is a cut to the town's army base where the spit and polish, by-the-book Colonel Delmore Payne (Joe Morton), an African American who was born in Frontera, is the commanding officer. Thinking that his philandering father, Otis Payne (Ron Canada) the proprietor of a bar in Frontera's dark town, had shown no interest in him after leaving his mother, Delmore has no plan to see him. In contrast, his high-school-age son Chet, curious about his grandfather, sneaks into the bar to get a glimpse of Otis, whom he has seen on a poster advertising the bar. His visit is brief because a fight breaks out, one soldier is wounded by a gun shot, and Otis hustles his grandson out the back, telling him, "You weren't here." Ultimately, big O's bar becomes a venue as significant as any other in the film—as a place where key investigation-relevant events in the past took place, as a place of family reconciliation, and as a space of interpretation of one of the film's major themes (in a conversation between Otis and his grandson Chet during a later visit, detailed below).

After a brief cut to Sam at his desk, looking at evidence, we're taken back to Pilar's school, where the already-noted curriculum battle is underway at a parent-teacher meeting. What is at stake is how the Texas-focused history curriculum will allocate historically based civic presence to all the peoples within what is a complex ethnoscape that has been subject to a dramatic cartographic shift in the history of the region's governance. The boisterous session begins with an angry Anglo mother's reaction to a more ethnically balanced account that Pilar has planned: "You're just tearin' everything down! Tearin' down our heritage, tearin' down the memory of people that fought and died for this land." During the give and take, after a Chicano father says, "We fought and died for this land, too!," the Anglo mother (noting her role on the textbook committee), counters, "it is not what we set as the standard." As Pilar and the principal try to offer reassurance (in vain) that they're just trying to broaden the historical perspective, an Anglo father angrily retorts that it's "propaganda."

LATINX VISIBILITY 183

What I want to emphasize from that scene is a remark by a Chicana mother that is cut off before it is complete. "We have the right," she says in response to the Anglo parents' insistence on sticking to the standard the text book committee had implemented. How can we construe the kind of right to which she is referring? At issue I suggest are what Leif Wener refers to as epistemic and affective rights. With respect to the former, he offers this distinction: "Epistemic and legal rights are in fact main representatives of the two major realms of rights . . . Epistemic rights form one domain in the larger realm of attitudinal rights—rights regarding judgment sensitive attitudes." And with respect to the latter, he states, "The other domain in this realm of attitudinal rights is the domain of affective rights . . . [for example] the right to *be proud* of what one has done."[88]

In *Lone Star* the epistemic and affective right issue has collective resonances for diverse modes of existence. In addition to the demands issued by Latino parents that their perspectives and sensibilities find their way into the school's history curriculum are several persons of color—Latino, Native American, and Black—whose perspectives and accounts of local history provide clues that enable Sam not only to solve the crime but also to uncover hidden histories, both personal and collective, that challenge an Anglo biopolitical hegemony that has maintained "lines of demarcation." As the film's narrative sequence moves through various sites and the encounters within them, Sayles evinces an implicit advocacy. He builds a case for the film's ultimate statement, "forget the Alamo," by lending diverse characters epistemic and affective rights; he gives them significant voices and qualifies their experiences and sensibilities as civically relevant. What emerges is not a "common world [but] a multiplicity of manners or gestures: manners of perceiving it, of appropriating it, or of exploring its potentialities." As Sam's investigatory itinerary draws on that multiplicity, there is no privileging of particular "manners or gestures."[89]

As the film's architectural itinerary proceeds and crucial divisions in Frontera's people-scape stand out—notably the ethno-racial and generational fault lines—seemingly marginal people, those with no authoritative "modes of existence,"[90] serve as key informants in Sam's simultaneous investigations of the crime and Frontera's interpersonal history. Two are particularly pertinent to an appreciation of the way

184 AESTHETICS OF EQUALITY

the film enfranchises those who have been outside civic recognition. One is literally outside, expressed in the film as someone "on the other side." After learning from a Latino jailed trustee, cleaning his office (what much of the Latino segment of the town already knew) that Sheriff Wade had murdered Eladio Cruz (Mercedes's Mexican husband), Sam takes a trip to what he refers to in a conversation with his deputy whom he leaves in charge, as "the other side," the Mexican town across the border.

After crossing the bridge into Mexico, he visits Chucho (Tony Amendola), who runs a tire shop in the adjacent Mexican border town after having lived on the US side for many years. He had been with Mercedes's husband, Eladio Cruz, the day he was murdered. After playfully describing himself as "El Rey de las Llantas, King of the Tires," he launches into a geopolitical lesson. Apart from his narration of the story (shown in a flashback) of the day he witnessed Sheriff Wade shooting Eladio is a critique he delivers about the relationship between space and authority. Drawing a line on the ground with an object that transcends geopolitical borders, a Coke bottle, he explains that once Sam has crossed over to the other side he's no longer the Sheriff of anything and adds, "Bird flying south—you think he sees that line? Rattlesnake, javelina—whatever you got—halfway across whatever you got—halfway across that line they don't start thinking different."

While the Sam-Chucho encounter speaks to the value of voices irrespective of their geography of enunciation, his encounter with Wesley, a Native American gift shop owner from whom he learns about his father's relationship with Mercedes, warrants the value of a voice that has been historically disqualified *within* the same geopolitical space. Before firm lines of demarcation had been drawn between Euro- and Native American spaces, settler and indigenous groups encountered each other on a frontier, which as William Cronon et al. point out was a space of negotiation, a space in which institutionalized regionalization had not yet been installed. Sharing a life world was in continual negotiation.[91] Once the Euro-American domination of the continent was completed and regional boundaries were established, domination replaced negotiation, and Native American voices lost their civic relevance on the continent.

LATINX VISIBILITY   185

It is therefore restorative that it is from Wesley Birdsong (Gordon Tootoosis), running a roadside giftshop, from whom Sam learns something that almost everyone in town already knew about: Buddy Deeds's extramarital relationship with Mercedes. Crucially, the encounter delivers a value lesson. Wesley jokes about the lack of value of his space, a "stretch of road [akin to barren reservation space that] runs between Nowheres and Nothin' Much," and points out that the artifacts available for tourists (which once had cultural value of Native American nations) are also without value. He has for example Buffalo chips and curios from Texas history that are reduced to kitschy icons. Helping to articulate the film's theme, one object Wesley sells is a parody of the Anglo's venerated myth: it's "a wooden radio carved to resemble the Alamo."

Subsequent to his conversation with Wesley, from whom he learns about an aspect of his family history, delivered by a voice that had been historically sidelined, Sam comes much closer to learning about the history he shares with Pilar. His and Pilar's paths cross for the first time when Pilar comes to fetch her son Amado. There is then a montage sequence that registers generational tensions. Pilar's first encounter with her former boyfriend Sam, years after they had been forcibly separated while at a drive-in movie by Sam's father Buddy, is followed by a cut back to the army base where Delmore, like Sam, remains at odds with *his* father (he's shown asking Mikey and Cliff about past trouble at O's, obviously still intending to make it off limits to his Black soldiers. The two generational misapprehensions proceed in parallel. While Sam pursues the murder case (in the next scene he's shown consulting a law enforcement colleague, having learned that the murder victim is Charley Wade), Delmore proceeds to visit his father's bar, while persisting in his feeling of alienation. Just as in a later scene, Delmore learns that his father had indeed followed his career assiduously (Delmore is shown a virtual shrine to his career in one of the bar's side-rooms), Sam is ultimately disabused of his assumption about *his* father. He learns in a later scene that his father was not the killer. In his last visit to Otis's bar, Otis and Hollis finally reveal the detail of Charley Wade's killing. It was Hollis who shot him to save Otis, whom Wade was about to murder (as he had many other non-Anglos).

186   AESTHETICS OF EQUALITY

Foregoing a rehearsal of all the encounters that clear up both the murder and other aspects of characters' personal histories, I want to highlight a few important venues where encounters, especially moments of intimacy, defy historically entrenched forms of divisiveness. One of the film's most telling sequences occurs in Otis's bar when his grandson Chet visits for the second time. Otis, like Chucho and Wesley, is one of the film's epistemological subjects, arguably the most important one. In contrast with his son Delmore's tendency toward tough love, what Chet describes as a steadfast avoidance of public displays of intrafamilial affection, Otis bonds warmly with Chet when he revisits the bar. While commiserating with his grandson's endurance of a rigid, judgmental father, Otis proceeds to impart a complex family history to Chet, who on entering the bar had wandered into a room containing Otis's display of Seminole artifacts. While Chet is staring at a picture of a Seminole warrior, Otis explains that Chet is looking at a picture of John Horse, who along with many other Seminoles left Florida for Oklahoma's Indian Territory and fought against a combination of "bandits, rustlers, Texas Red necks, Kiowas, Comanche." When Chet says to Otis, "So how come you got into this?" Otis replies, "These are our people. There were Paynes in Florida, Oklahoma, Piedras Ngeras."

When Chet's reacts to learning for the first time that he has Seminole ancestors, saying, "So I'm part Indian?," in response Otis delivers one of the film story's most important lines: "By blood you are, but blood only means what you let it." That remark sets up the film's last conversation between Sam and Pilar, who after learning that they are blood relatives (sharing the same father), decide not to let it mean that they can't be together romantically. Their decision, which weighs against forces at work in the town's local history (within and outside their families), distinguishes their generation's relationship to the Alamo myth that had divided the town's ethnic assemblages. At a personal level it's a radical departure from their parents' identity management, exemplified in scenes I want to explore before turning to their drive-in theater epiphany at the end of the film.

Mercedes's Café Santa Barbara's postcolonial structure reappears during an encounter she has with her daughter Pilar. Before heeding Pilar's presence, Mercedes is scolding a young kitchen worker: "*Donde estan sus guantes? Tonta! Quiere matar a mis clientes?*" (Where are you gloves? Stupid! You want to kill my customers?). After Mercedes continues muttering about her help, Pilar jumps in and refers to her hiring of illegals (which Mercedes against all evidence denies). When Pilar adds that she might do better with them by providing more training, Mercedes chides her for telling her how to run her restaurant. Pilar then turns to the topic of their Mexican origins, suggesting that Mercedes take a trip "down South," where she grew up. Mercedes rejects the suggestion, making it clear that she is wholly uninterested in her Mexican origins (despite having crossed into Frontera illegally herself as a young woman): "Why would I want to go there," she says. In contrast, a later scene in Café Santa Barbara hosts a moment of intimacy rather than contention. Sam and Pilar enter the restaurant after hours, hold each other closely as they slow dance to a Mexican song on the juke box, and then head to Sam's apartment to make love.

Earlier in the film, there's scene that hosts another intimate crossing of interethnic lines of demarcation. As Sam is conversing with Cody, the owner and bartender of the aforementioned redneck country and western bar, an interracial couple from the army base, the soldier Cliff and Priscilla, a Black officer, are in a booth discussing Cliff's marriage proposal. Referring to his bar as the last stand of Western civilization, Cody launches into a lament about ethnic mixing:

> We are in a state of crisis. The lines of demarcation have gotten fuzzy—to run a successful civilization you got to have lines of demarcation between right and wrong, between this one and that one—your Daddy understood that. He was like the whatchacallit—the referee for this damn menudo we got down here . . . Take that pair over in the corner [points toward Cliff and Priscilla] . . . Place like this, twenty years ago, Buddy woulda been, on them two—

Sam, who had personally experienced Buddy's refereeing, responds coolly with, "I bet he would."

That conversation prepares us for the scene in which Sam does not maintain his cool. The first of three crucial scenes take place at what I have referred to above as the architectural site that (obliquely) says "forget the Alamo," the local drive-in movie theater where at a personal

188   AESTHETICS OF EQUALITY

level intimacy interruptus becomes intimacy restored, at an allegorical level. The drive-in theater ruin demythologizes a story that Texas officials have used to preserve Anglo dominance. The first drive-in scene is a flashback to 1972, a drive-in theater date for the high school-aged Sam and his girlfriend Pilar. Apprised of the ongoing boundary-breaching romance between them, Buddy, along with his deputy Hollis, interrupts their romantic tryst. He opens the driver side door, flicks on the overhead light and sees Sam and Pilar half unclothed. Shouting "god dammit," he drags Sam's from the car by his ankles while Hollis pulls Pilar out from the other side. The verbal exchanges are loud and brief. Inventing a disingenuous excuse, Buddy says, "How old is that girl? Goddammit, where's your goddam sense," while a furious Sam shouts, "What the hell are you doing? You fucking asshole!" followed by "You got no fuckin' right! You stay out of my fuckin' life!" At the same moment, Pilar says to Hollis, "Let me go! *Pendejo!*" (stupid), while Hollis responds with, "Come on now, Missy, get your clothes."

The second drive-in scene takes place after twenty years have passed. It's dusk; as our eyes adjust we see Sam standing by his car in the parking lot of the long-abandoned drive-in with its ruined screen in the background. Recalling Tim Edensor's insight about ruins (quoted to illuminate the effect of the Boyle Heights ruins on Viramontes's characters in her novel *Dogs*), it applies as well to Sayles's film: "The objects, spaces and traces found in ruins highlight the radical undecidability of the past." Moreover, as regards the disorientation that this particular ruin creates, another of Edensor's observations is especially pertinent: "In ruins, instead of pre-arranged spectacles, the visual scene beheld is usually composed of no evident focal point but an array of apparently unrelated things . . . As a further consequence of this sensual disordering, the performative conventions of the city must be discarded in the ruin."[92]

Accordingly, as Sam and Pilar revisit the now ruined drive-in (in the third drive-in scene where the film ends), they agree to discard performative conventions. After Sam presents the incontrovertible evidence that Buddy was Pilar's father (with snapshots, letters, and official dates of birth), there's a silence broken by Pilar, who asks if the revelation means they can't be together. To that Sam responds, "If I met you for

Figure 5.1 Sam and Pilar at the drive-in in Sayes's *Lone Star*
Source: Castle Rock Entertainment

the first time today, I'd still want to be with you." They then proceed to evoke the problem of history, agreeing that the past that their parents had assiduously managed can no longer separate them. They can, as Pilar puts it, "start from scratch ... Everything that went before, all that stuff, that history—the hell with it, right?" An onscreen text, "Forget the Alamo," then affirms the film's allegorical level. The line of demarcation between Anglos and Latinos, policed by prior generations that have bought into the Alamo myth, must be effaced. The film's last shot seconds that statement: there's a wide shot of the drive-in from behind Sam and Pilar, who are sitting on the hood of Sam's car, holding hands while they look at the empty screen (Figure 5.1).

Notes

Introduction

1. Leo Lionni, *Frederick and His Friends* (New York: Knopf, 2002).
2. "60+ Best Eeyore Quotes and Saying from Winne the Pooh," Kidadl, last updated July 8, 2022, https://kidadl.com/articles/best-eeyore-quotes-and-sayings-from-winnie-the-pooh.
3. Gilles Deleuze and Claire Parnet, *Dialogues II*, trans. Hugh Tomlinson and Barbara Habberjam (New York: Columbia University Press, 2002), 57.
4. Michel Foucault, *Dits et Ecrits Vol. 11* (Paris: Gallimard, 1970–1975), 523 (my translation).
5. Cesare Casarino, "Philopoesis: A Theoretico-Methodological Manifesto," *boundary 2* 29, no. 1 (Spring 2002), 86.
6. See Gilles Deleuze and Felix Guattari, "Percept, Affect, Concept," in *What is Philosophy?*, trans. High Tomlinson and Graham Burchell (New York: Columbia University Press, 1994), 163–199.
7. Gilles Deleuouze, *Foucault*, trans. Sean Hand (Minneapolis: University of Minnesota Press, 1988), 86.
8. Kundera, *The Art of the Novel* (New York: HarperCollins, 2003), 71–72.
9. Jill Jarvis, *Decolonizing Memory: Algeria and the Politics of Testimony* (Durham, NC: Duke University Press, 2021), 61.
10. Theodor Adorno, "Commitment," *New Left Review* 87/88 (September/December, 1974), 77.
11. Jacques Rancière, *Disagreement*, trans. Julie Rose (Minneapolis: University of Minnesota Press, 1998), 60.
12. See for example Michel Foucault, *Society Must Be Defended: Lectures at the College De France 1975–1976*, trans. David Macey (New York: Picador, 2003), 70.
13. David Lapoujade, *The Lesser Existences: Etienne Souriau, an Aesthetics for the Virtual*, trans. Erik Beranek (Minneapolis: University of Minnesota Press, 2021), 35.
14. Daniel Alarcón, "Collectors," *The New Yorker*, July 22, 2003, https://www.newyorker.com/magazine/2013/07/29/collectors-3. The story is based on

192 NOTES

a historical event. Responding to prison riots in three Peruvian prisons. The military attacked and massacred more than 260 inmates. See Alan Riding, "Peru's Prison Massacres: Can the Facts Come Out?," *New York Times*, September 16, 1986, https://www.nytimes.com/1986/09/16/world/peru-s-prison-massacres-can-the-facts-come-out.html.

15. Lapoujade, *The Lesser Existences*, 11.
16. Thomas Mann, *Joseph and His Brothers*, trans. John E. Woods (New York: Everyman, 2005).
17. Ibid., 1265.
18. Thomas Mann, "Sixteen Years," in *Joseph and His Brothers*, xxxviii.
19. Referring to a prior novel, her *Beloved*, Morrison refers to how it "unleashed a host of ideas about how and what one cherishes under the duress and emotional disfigurement that a slave society imposes." Toni Morrison, Foreword to *Jazz* (New York: Vintage, 2007), xvi.
20. Morrison, *Jazz*, 120.
21. Ibid., 67.
22. Ibid., 51.
23. Ibid., 226–227.
24. Gayatri Spivak, *An Aesthetic Education in the Era of Globalization* (Cambridge, MA: Harvard University Press, 2012), 317.
25. Jacques Rancière, "Fictions of Time," in *Rancière and Literature*, ed. Grace Hwellyer and Julian Murphet (Edinburgh: Edinburgh University Press, 2017), 26.

Chapter 1

1. There are quotations around part of the chapter's subtitle because the phrase is borrowed from David Michael Hertz's *The Tuning of the Word: The Musico-Literary Poetics of the Symbolist Movement* (Carbondale: Southern Illinois University Press, 1987).
2. Thomas Mann, *Joseph and His Brothers*, trans. John E. Woods (New York: Everyman Library, 2005), 1081.
3. Roland Barthes, "From Work to Text," in *Image, Music, Text*, trans. Stephen Health (New York: Hill and Wang, 1977), 157.
4. Roland Barthes, *S/Z*, trans. Richard Howard (New York: Hill and Wang, 1974), 4.
5. Ibid., 5.

NOTES 193

6. Ibid., 4.
7. Erich Auerbach, "Odysseus' Scar," in *Mimesis*, trans. Willard R. Trask (Princeton, NJ: Princeton University Press, 1968), 3.
8. Ibid., 6.
9. Ibid., 7.
10. Ibid., 14.
11. Ibid., 15.
12. Mieke Bal, *Death & Dissymmetry: The Politics of Coherence in the Book of Judges* (Chicago: University of Chicago Press, 1988), 231.
13. "Parodia" ("παρῳδία" in Greek) translates as "countersong."
14. Thomas Mann, "Sixteen Years," in *Joseph and His Brothers*, trans. John E. Woods (New York: Knopf, 2005), xl.
15. Mann, *Joseph and His Brothers*, 90–91.
16. Ibid., 470.
17. John D. Yohannan, "Hebraism and Hellenism in Thomas Mann's Story of Joseph and Potiphar's Wife," *Comparative Literature Studies* 19, no. 4 (Winter 1982), 439.
18. Erich Auerbach, "The Brown Stocking," in *Mimesis*, 545.
19. Sam Anders, "Watch This Snowball Fight from 1897 for a Jolt of Pure Joy," *The New York Times Magazine*, November 5, 2020, https://www.nytimes.com/by/sam-anderson.
20. Morten Hoi Jensen, "Thomas Mann in America," *Europe Now Journal* April 3, 2017, https://www.europenowjournal.org/2017/04/03/thomas-mann-and-american-democracy/.
21. Linda Hutcheon, *A Poetics of Postmodernism: History, Theory, Fiction* (New York: Routledge, 1988), 124.
22. I am borrowing that phase from Kees van Hage's review of Mann's novella *The Tables of the Law*, accessed 10/15/20 at: https://keesvanhage.wordpress.com/4-23/.
23. Geog Lukács, quoted in Maire Kurrik, "The Novel's Subjectivity: Geog Lukács' Theory," *Salmagundi* 28 (Winter 1975), 119.
24. John T. Frederick, "Thomas Mann and 'Joseph the Provider,'" *College English* 6, no. 1 (October 1944), 4.
25. Mann, *Joseph and His Brothers*, 1265.
26. Mann, "Sixteen Years," xxxviii.
27. Ibid.
28. Frederick Morgan, "Notes on the Joseph Novels," *Hudson Review* 1, no. 4 (Winter 1949), 549.
29. Mann, *Joseph and His Brothers*, 410.
30. Ibid., 412.

194 NOTES

31. Ibid., 3.
32. The expression belongs to Milan Kundera, *Encounters*, trans. Linda Asher (New York: HarperCollins, 2009), 53.
33. Mann, *Joseph and His Brothers*, 94–95.
34. I am quoting Stacy Burton's succinct summary of Bakhtin's view in "Bakhtin, Temporality, and Modern Narrative: Writing the Whole Triumphant Murderous Unstoppable Chute," *Comparative Literature* 48, no. 1 (1996), 48.
35. See M. M. Bakhtin, "Discourse and the Novel," trans. Caryl Emerson, in *The Dialogic Imagination*, ed. Michael Holquist (Austin: University of Texas Press, 1981), 259–422.
36. M. M. Bakhtin, *Problems of Dostoevsky's Poetics*, trans. Caryl Emerson (Minneapolis: University of Minnesota Press, 1984), 203.
37. Mann, *Joseph and His Brothers*, 1065–1066.
38. Mann, "Sixteen Years," xxxix-xl.
39. Mann's letter of October 30–31, 1952 to Theodor Adorno, accessed 10/16/20 at: http://www.the-wagnerian.com/2016/08/a-letter-from-thomas-mann-to-theodor.html.
40. Mann, *Joseph and His Brothers*, 1492.
41. Friedrich Nietzsche, *Human All Too Human*, trans. R. J. Hollingdale (Cambridge: Cambridge University Press, 1996), 121.
42. Thomas Mann, quoted in Thomas Hollweck, "Mann's 'Work on Myth: The Uses of the Past,'" 2006, https://sites01.lsu.edu/faculty/voegelin/wp-content/uploads/sites/80/2015/09/Thomas-Hollweck1.pdf.
43. Mann, *Joseph and His Brothers*, 1042.
44. Ibid., 1088.
45. Ibid., 1117.
46. See Michael Minden, "Mann's Literary Techniques," in *The Cambridge Companion to Thomas Mann*, ed. Richie Robertson (New York: Cambridge University Press, 2002), 44.
47. Ibid., 53.
48. Goethe quoted in Thomas Hollweck, "Mann's 'Work on Myth.'"
49. Susan von Rohr Scaff, *History, Myth, and Music: Thomas Mann's Timely Fiction* (Columbia, SC: Camden House, 1998), 13.
50. Jacques Rancière, *The Flesh of Words*, trans. Charlotte Mandell (Stanford, CA: Stanford University Press, 2004), 73.
51. Jacques Rancière, *The Politics of Literature*, trans. Julie Rose (Cambridge: Polity, 2011), 26.
52. Ibid., 25–26.
53. Mann, *Joseph and His Brothers*, 541.

NOTES 195

54. Ibid.
55. Ibid.
56. Ibid., 546.
57. Ibid., 546–547.
58. Kundera, *Encounters*, 92.
59. Auerbach, "Odysseus's Scar," 15.
60. M. M. Bakhtin, "The *Bildungsroman* and its Significance in the History of Realism," in *Speech Genres and Other Late Essays*, trans. Vern W. McGee (Austen: University of Texas Press, 1986), 21.
61. Mann, *Joseph and His Brothers*, 544.
62. William E. McDonald, *Thomas Mann's Joseph and His Brothers* (Rochester, NY: Camden House, 1999), 185.
63. Mann, *Joseph and His Brothers*, 543.
64. Edmund Leach, "The Legitimacy of Solomon: Some Structural Aspects of Old Testament History," *European Journal of Sociology* 7, no. 1 (1966), 63.
65. Ibid., 80.
66. Ibid., 87.
67. Michael J. Shapiro, *Cinematic Geopolitics* (London: Routledge, 2009), 7.
68. Gilles Deleuze, *Cinema 1: The Movement Image*, trans. Hugh Tomlinson and Barbara Habberjam (Minneapolis: University of Minnesota Press, 1987), 64.
69. Thomas Mann, *The Theme of the Joseph Novels: Speech Delivered at the Library of Congress* (Washington, DC: Library of Congress, 1942), 11.
70. Among the emerging analyses of "slow movies" is Ira Jaffe's, *Slow Movies: Countering the Cinema of Action* (New York: Wallflower, 2014).
71. Mann, *Joseph and His Brothers*, 1077.
72. Andrei Tarkovsky, *Sculpting in Time*, trans. Kitty Hunter Blair (Austin: University of Texas Press, 2012), 183.
73. Mann, *Joseph and His Brothers*, 1121.
74. Ibid., 1119.
75. I am borrowing that apposite phrase from Minden's analysis of the "two opposed value-systems" in Mann's novella *Tonio Kroger*: "Mann's Literary Techniques," 50.
76. Mann, *Joseph and His Brothers*, 597.
77. Ibid., 1121.
78. Ibid., 612.
79. Ibid., 1122.
80. Ibid., 1056.
81. M. M Bakhtin, "Author and Hero in Aesthetic Activity," in *Art and Answerability*, trans. V. Liapunov (Austin: University of Texas Press, 1990), 13.

196 NOTES

82. Mann, *Joseph and His Brothers*, 1301.

83. Ibid., 607.

84. See Jacques Rancière, "Aesthetic Separation, Aesthetic Community: Scenes from the Aesthetic Regime of Art," *Art & Research* 2, no. 1 (2008), http://artandresearch.org.uk/v2n1/ranciere.html.

85. Michael J. Shapiro, "Go East, Go West, War's Exilic Subjects," *Security Dialogue* 44, no. 4 (2013), 315.

86. James Schmidt, "Mephistopheles in Hollywood: Adorno, Mann, and Schoenberg," accessed 10/17/20 at: https://www.researchgate.net/publ ication/237203986_Mephistopheles_in_Hollywood_Adorno_Mann_ and_Schoenberg/link/54cabea60cf2517b756009be.pdf.

87. From Frank Walter Steinmeier and Don Franzen's reprise of Mann' s democracy-promoting lecture tour in the United States: "A Talk About Democracy," *The Los Angeles Review of Books*, July 1, 2018, https://lare viewofbooks.org/article/a-talk-about-democracy/.

88. Evelyn Cobley, "Decentered Tonalities in *Doctor Faustus: Thomas Mann and Theodor Adorno*," *Modernist Cultures* 1, no. 2 (2005), https://www. semanticscholar.org/paper/Decentred-Totalities-in-Doctor-Faus tus%3A-Thomas-Mann-Cobley/588ed2f4fa3c558ad7a34ddc27c923090 02315c7.

89. Thomas Mann, *The Story of a Novel*, trans. Richard and Clara Winston (New York: Knopf, 1961), 45.

90. Hertz, *The Tuning of the Word*, 137. Hertz is quoting Theodor Adorno, *The Philosophy of Modern Music*, trans. Anne G. Mitchell and Wesley V. Blomster (New York: Continuum, 2002), 36–39.

91. Arnold Schoenberg, *Style and Idea* (New York: Philosophical Library, 1950), 104.

92. Hertz, *The Tuning of the Word*, 171.

93. Ibid., 14.

94. Adorno quoted in Sebastian Truskolaski, "Parataxis: Poetics and Politics in Adorno's Aesthetic Theory," accessed at: https://www.academia.edu/ 25891716/Parataxis_Poetics_and_Politics_in_Adornos_Aesthetic_The ory, 3.

95. Hertz, *The Tuning of the Word*, 7.

96. Schoenberg, *Style and Idea*, 104.

97. Ibid., 19.

98. Ibid., 17–18, 57.

99. Ibid., 30–31.

100. Ibid., 39.

NOTES 197

101. Mann quoted in Murray Ball, "A Troubling Passion," *The Manchester Guardian*, November 29, 2002, https://www.theguardian.com/books/2002/nov/30/classics.thomasmann.

102. Kelly quoted in H. A. Basilius, "Thomas Mann's Use of Musical Structure and Techniques in *Tonio Kroger*," *Germanic Review* 19, no. 4 (December 1944), 288–289.

103. I was alerted to that moment in the novel by Basilius, ibid., 301.

104. Alex Ross, *Wagnerism: Art and Politics in the Shadow of Music* (New York: FSG, 2020), 392.

105. The Mann quotation is a translation in William Kinderman, "Exploring the 'Temple of Initiation' on Thomas Mann's *Magic Mountain*: Wagnerian Affinities and 'Politically Suspect' Music," *Monatshefte* 109, no. 3 (2017), 404.

106. From Mann's writing on Wagner, quoted in ibid., 406.

107. Herman Broch, *The Sleepwalkers*, trans. Willa and Edwin Muir (New York: Vintage, 1996), 21.

108. Thomas Mann, *Doctor Faustus*, trans. John E. Woods (New York: Vintage, 1999), 10.

109. Adorno, *The Philosophy of Modern Music*, 45.

110. Mann, *Doctor Faustus*, 397.

111. Ibid., 207.

112. Reported in Adorno, *The Philosophy of Modern Music*, 39.

113. Ibid.

114. Georges Did-Huberman, "The Art of Not Describing: Vermeer—the Detail and the Patch," *History of the Human Sciences* 2, no. 2 (June 1989), 149.

115. Evelyn Cobley, "Avant Garde Aesthetics and Fascist Politics: Thomas Mann's Doctor Faustus and Theodor Adorno's 'Philosophy of Modern Music,'" *New German Critique* 66 (Spring–Summer 2002), 61.

116. Mann, *Doctor Faustus*, 354.

117. Ibid., 356.

118. See Ursula Mahlendorf, "Aesthetics, Psychology, and Politics in Thomas Mann's 'Doctor Faustus.'" *Mosaic* 11, no. 4 (1978), 1–18.

119. Mann, *Doctor Faustus*, 371.

120. Adorno, *Philosophy of Modern Music*, 45.

121. Mann, *Doctor Faustus*, 244.

122. Ibid., 200.

123. Ibid., 201.

124. Ibid.

198 NOTES

125. See Jean-François Lyotard, "The Sign of History," in *The Lyotard Reader*, ed. Andrew Benjamin (New York: Basil Blackwell, 1989), 93.

126. Ibid., 106. Lyotard provides an elaborate model in his *The Differend: Phrases in Dispute*, trans. G Van Den Abeele (Minneapolis: University of Minnesota Press, 1989), where he constructs a frame for analyzing situations that lack of a rule of judgment applicable to both sides of a discursive encounter.

127. Slavoj Žižek, "Kates Choice, or the Materialism of Henry James," in *Lacan: The Silent Partner*, ed. Slavoj Žižek (New York: Verso, 2006), 290.

128. Mann, *Joseph and His Brothers*, 1042.

129. Adorno on Schoenberg in his *Philosophy of Modern Music*, 59.

130. Mann, *Joseph and His Brothers*, 1116.

131. Ibid.

132. Ibid., 1117.

133. Peter Heller, "Some Functions of the Leitmotiv in Thomas Mann's Joseph Tetralogy," *Germanic Review* 22, no. 2 (April 1947), 130.

134. I am borrowing the expression from Jacques Rancière, *On the Shores of Politics*, trans. Liz Heron (London: Verso, 1995), 61.

135. That observation about the way Joseph becomes a political subject accords with Jacques Ranciere's analysis of a similar process of becoming political, that of French workers who write thereby stepping out of their assigned roles, become more than mere hands. See his *The Nights of Labor: The Workers' Dream in Nineteenth Century France*, trans. John Drury (Philadelphia: Temple University Press, 1989).

136. From Thomas Mann's commentary on his Joseph novels, quoted in Heller, "Some Functions of the Leitmotiv in Thomas Mann's Joseph Tetralogy," 137.

137. Gilbert Simondon, *Individuation in Light of Notions of Form and Information*, trans. Taylor Adkins (Minneapolis: University of Minnesota Press, 2020), 7.

138. James R. Martel, *The Misinterpellated Subject* (Durham, NC: Duke University Press, 2017), 6–7.

139. Mann, *Joseph and His Brothers*, 1122.

140. Ibid., 1379.

141. Pierre Klossowski, *Nietzsche and the victims circle*, trans. D. W. Smith (Chicago: University of Chicago Press, 1997), 216.

142. Rancière, *On the Shores of Politics*, 159.

143. Jacques Rancière, *Chronicles of Consensual Times* (London: Continuum, 2010), 6.

144. Mann, *Joseph and His Brothers*, 88.

NOTES   199

145. Ibid., 89.
146. Ibid., 92–93.

Chapter 2

1. Igor Stravinsky, *Chronicle of My Life* (London: Golancz, 1936), 91.
2. Theo van Leeuwen, "Music and Ideology: Notes Toward a Sociosemiotics of Mass Media Music," *Popular Music and Society* 22, no. 4 (1998), 26.
3. Lee B. Brown, "Adorno's Critique of Popular Culture: The Case of Jazz Music," *Journal of Aesthetic Education* 26, no. 1 (Spring 1992), 17.
4. Ibid., 19.
5. Frank Kofsky, "The Jazz Tradition: Black Music and Its White Critics," *Journal of Black Studies* 1, no. 4 (June 1971), 418.
6. Maurice Peress, *Dvorak to Duke Ellington* (New York: Oxford University Press, 2004), 182–183.
7. From my earlier analysis of the composition in Michael J Shapiro, *Deforming American Political Thought* (Lexington: University of Kentucky Press, 2006), 153.
8. See Ernest Callenbach, "When the Levees Broke: A Requiem in Four Acts," *Film Quarterly* 60, no. 2 (Winter 2006), 6.
9. Much of this discussion of the Lee-Blanchard documentary draws from my earlier reading of the Katrina event in Michael J. Shapiro, *Politics and Time: Documenting the Event* (Cambridge: Polity, 2017).
10. Michael J. Shapiro, *Punctuations: How the Arts Think the* Political (Durham, NC: Duke University Press, 2019), 31. And see Coltrane's remarks on his *Alabama* reported in Sasha Feinstein, "From *Alabama* to *A Love Supreme*: The Evolution of a John Coltrane Poem," *Southern Review* 23, no. 2 (April 1996), 315–327.
11. See Charles Leonard, "Political Songs | Alabama—John Coltrane," New Frame, March 8, 2019, https://www.newframe.com/political-songs-alab ama-john-coltrane/.
12. The expression, belonging to Laszlo Szekeley, is applied to music by Paul Garon, *Blues and the Poetic Spirit* (San Francisco, CA: City Lights, 1996), 165.
13. Nathaniel Mackey, "Other: From Noun to Verb," *Representations* 39 (Summer 1992), 51–70.
14. Shapiro, *Punctuations*, 31.
15. See the analysis of Black talk in Ben Sidran, *Black Talk* (New York: Da Capo, 1971), 31.

200 NOTES

16. Paul Gilroy, *The Black Atlantic: Modernity and Double Consciousness* (Cambridge, MA: Harvard University Press, 1993), 38.

17. See ibid., 253, where Gilroy characterizes that sphere as a "fragile community . . . composed of people who disagree with one another," albeit one in which a "fruitful mode of disagreement . . . grows with discipline and mutual respect."

18. For "microsyntax" see Leonard Meyer. *Emotion and Meaning in Music* (Chicago: University of Chicago Press, 1965); the next quotation is from Michael C. Finke's analysis of metapoesis in Russian literature, where the term applies to the way "authorial words engage "a very specific addressee or set of addressees": *Metapoesis* (Durham, NC: Duke University Press, 1995), 5; Shapiro, *Punctuations*, 32; the expression "structural hearing" belongs to Theodor W. Adorno, *Introduction to the Sociology of Music* (New York: Seabury Press, 1976), 4; Geneva Smitherman, *Talkin' and Testifyin': The Language of Black America* (Detroit: Wayne State University Press, 1977), 135.

19. See Toni Morrison's Tanner Lecture, "Unspeakable Things Unspoken: The Afro American Presence in American Literature," October 7, 1988, 147. https://tannerlectures.utah.edu/_resources/documents/a-to-z/m/mor rison90.pdf.

20. Ibid., 136.
    Toni Morrison, *Jazz* (New York: Vintage, 1992), 15. https://tannerlectu res.utah.edu/_resources/documents/a-to-z/m/morrison90.pdf.

21. I am borrowing the expression from Brent Hayes Edwards, *Epistrophies: Jazz and the Literary Imagination* (Cambridge, MA: Harvard University Press, 2017), 19.

22. Morrison, *Jazz*, xviii–xix.

23. Ibid., 208.

24. Shapiro, *Punctuations*, 53.

25. Gregory Clark, *Civic Jazz* (Chicago: University of Chicago Press, 2015), 31.

26. Ibid., 32.

27. Maurice Blanchot, *The Infinite Conversation*, trans. Susan Hanson (Minneapolis: University of Minnesota Press, 1993), 68.

28. I am borrowing that expression from Fumi Okiji because it captures the interactive, improvisational character of jazz performances. See her *Jazz as Critique: Adorno and Black Expression Revisited* (Stanford, CA: Stanford University Press, 2018).

29. The commentary is by Richard Davis, quoted in Ingrid Monson, *Saying Something: Jazz Improvisation and Interaction* (Chicago: University of Chicago Press, 1997), 32.

NOTES 201

30. Shapiro, *Deforming American Political Thought*, 157.
31. Gunther Schuller, *Early Jazz: Its Roots and Musical Development* (New York: Oxford University Press, 1968), 337.
32. Ibid., 338.
33. Monson, *Saying Something*, 27.
34. The Schoenberg-quoting commentary is by Christopher Lewis, "Morris and Metaphors: Reflections on Schoenberg and Nineteenth-Century Tonality," *19th-Century Music* 11, no. 1 (Summer 1987), 29.
35. Mackey, "Other: From Noun to Verb," 51.
36. Ibid., 53.
37. Houston A, Baker Jr., *Modernism and the Harlem Renaissance* (Chicago: University of Chicago Press, 1987), 51.
38. James Snead, "On Repetition in Black Culture," *Black American Literature Forum* 15, no. 4 (Winter 1981), 150.
39. See M. M. Bakhtin, "Discourse and the Novel," trans. Caryl Emerson, in *The Dialogic Imagination*, ed. Michael Holquist (Austin: University of Texas Press, 1981), 259–422.
40. Van Leeuwen, "Music and Ideology," 30.
41. See the explication "Tonal Harmony versus Modal Harmony," https://theja zzpianosite.com/jazz-piano-lessons/modern-jazz-theory/tonal-harm ony-vs-modal-harmony/.
42. Evelyn Cobley, "Decentered Tonalities in *Doctor Faustus*: *Thomas Mann and Theodor Adorno*," *Modernist Cultures* 1, no. 2 (2005), http://www.js-modcult.bham.ac.uk/articles/issue2_cobley.pdf.
43. Kofi Agawu, "Tonality as a Colonizing Force in Africa," in *Audible Empire: Music, Global Politics, Critique*, ed. Ronald Radano and Tejumola Olaniyan (Durham, NC: Duke University Press, 2016), ebook loc. 7782.
44. Ibid., loc. 7999.
45. For a brief but well focused review of the historical musical origins that have contributed to modern improvisational jazz, see Langston Hughes, *The First Book of Jazz* (New York: Franklin Watts, 1955).
46. Rodrigo Lazo, "Migrant Archives: Ne Routes In and out of American Studies," in *States of Emergency*, ed. Russ Castronovo and Susan Gillman (Chapel Hill: University of North Carolina Press, 2009), 36.
47. Ibid., 37.
48. Achille Mbembe, "The Power of the Archive and its Limit," in *Refiguring the Archive*, ed. Carolyn Hamilton, Verne Harris, and Michele Pickover (Dordrecht: Kluwer Academic Publishers, 2002), 19.

202 NOTES

49. Paul Naylor and Nathaniel Mackey, "Interview with Nathaniel Mackey," *Callaloo* 23, no. 2 (Spring 2000), 647.

50. Nathaniel Mackey, *From a Broken Bottle's Traces of Perfume Emanate* (New York: New Directions, 2010), 299.

51. Ibid., 300–303.

52. Naylor and Mackey, "Interview with Nathaniel Mackey," 647.

53. See the Jazz Advice blog "By Forrest": "Crazy John Coltrane Techniques Only For The Brave," February 25, 2018, https://www.jazzadvice.com/advanced-jazz-techniques-of-john-coltrane-in-transition/, and Per Aage Brandt, "On Tonal Dynamics and Musical Meaning," *Signata* 6 (2015). https://journals.openedition.org/signata/1089?lang=en.

54. Naylor and Mackey, "Interview with Nathaniel Mackey," 647.

55. Lars Eckstein, "A Love Supreme: Jazzthetic Strategies in Toni Morrison's 'Beloved,'" *African American Review* 10, no. 2 (Summer 2006), 271.

56. Ibid., 272.

57. Ibid., 276–277.

58. An interview with Toni Morrison, cited in Jurgen E. Grandt, "Kind of Blue: Toni Morrison, Hans Janowits and the Jazz Aesthetic," *African American Review* 38, no. 2 (Summer 2004), 304.

59. Morrison, Foreword to *Jazz*, xvi.

60. Garon, *Blues and the Poetic Spirit*, 39.

61. Morrison, *Jazz*, 176–177.

62. Angela Carabi, "Interview with Toni Morrison," *Belles Lettres* 10, no. 2 (1995), 42.

63. Ash Amin and Nigel Thrifty, *Reimagining the Urban* (Malden, MA: Polity, 20020, 84.

64. Andrew Scheiber, "'Jazz' and the Future Blues: Toni Morrison's Urban Folk Zone," *Modern Fiction Studies* 52, no. 2 (Summer 2006), 478, quoting Morrison, *Jazz*, 67.

65. Morrison, *Jazz*, 120.

66. Ibid., 5.

67. Ibid., 120.

68. Ibid., 90–94.

69. The passages and analysis are in Philip Page, *Dangerous Freedom: Fusion and Fragmentation in Toni Morrison's novels* (Jackson: University Press of Mississippi, 1995), quoted in Anne-Marie Paquet-Deyris, "Toni Morrison's Jazz and the City," *African American Review* 35, no. 2 (2001), 220.

70. Michael J. Shapiro, *Methods and Nations: Cultural Governance and the Indigenous Subject* (London: Routledge, 2004), 95.

NOTES 203

71. Ibid., 92.
72. Gilles Deleuze, *Difference and Repetition*, trans. Paul Patton (New York: Columbia University Press, 1994), 10.
73. Robin Small-McCarthy, "The Jazz Aesthetic in the Novels of Toni Morrison," *Cultural Studies* 9, no. 2 (1995), 298.
74. Scheiber, "'Jazz' and the Future Blues," 471.
75. I am borrowing that convenient summary from ibid., 294.
76. See Morrison, "Unspeakable Things Unspoken," 125.
77. Morrison, *Jazz*, 15.
78. Ibid.
79. Ibid., 44–49.
80. Ibid., 126–127.
81. Morrison, "Unspeakable Things Unspoken," 150.
82. Morrison, *Jazz*, 50.
83. Ibid., 67.
84. Ibid.
85. Ibid.
86. Ibid., 54.
87. Ibid., 30.
88. Garon, *Blues and the Poetic Spirit*, 25.
89. Ibid., 31.
90. From Dale Pattison's analysis of the novel's architecture in "Building Intimacy: The Erotic Architectures of Toni Morrison's *Jazz*," *Critique: Studies in Contemporary Fiction* 58, no. 2 (2017), 130.
91. Ibid., 131.
92. See Ralph Ellison, "An Extravagance of Laughter," in *Going to the Territory* (New York: Vintage, 1986), 148.
93. Anne-Marie Paquet-Deyris, "Toni Morrison's *Jazz* and the City," *African American Review* 35, no. 2 (2001), 219.
94. Ibid., 51.
95. Ibid., 11–12.
96. Ralph Ellison, "Richard Wright's Blues," in *Shadow and Act* (New York: New American Library, 1966), 60.
97. I am quoting from the Netflix version of the play, reported in Giovanni Russonello, "Jazz Onscreen, Depicted by Black Filmmakers at Last," *New York Times*, December 30, 2020, C1.
98. Ibid., 219.
99. See Amiri Baraka, *Blues People: Negro Music in White America* (New York: Harpers, 1999).

204 NOTES

100. Adam Gussow, "'Figuring the Jagged Edge': Ellison's Wright and the Southern Blues Violences," *boundary 2* 30, no. 2, 2003), 137.

101. I treat Smith-Sade on pain in Michael J. Shapiro, *Reading Adam Smith: Desire, History, and Value*, New Edition (Lanham, MD: Rowman & Littlefield, 2000), 116–118.

102. The observation about Wittgenstein on pain is in ibid., 115.

103. The concept of the "sociolect," the discursive practices of a social segment, belongs to M. M. Bakhtin, elaborated in his "Discourse and the Novel."

104. Morrison, *Jazz*, 226–227.

105. Roland Barthes, "To Write: An Intransitive Verb?," in *The Rustle of Language*, trans. Richard Howard (New York: Hill and Wang, 1986), 19.

106. Morrison, *Jazz*, 229.

107. Chad Jewett, "The Modality of Toni Morrison's 'Jazz,'" *African American Review* 48, no. 4 (Winter 2015), 446.

108. Toni Morrison, "Abrupt Stops and Unexpected Liquidity: The Aesthetics of Romare Bearden," in *The Romare Bearden Reader* (Durham, NC: Duke University Press, 2019), 188.

109. Morrison, *Jazz*, 229.

110. Clark, *Civic Jazz*, 87.

111. The expression is from Paquet-Deyris's reading of the novel, "Toni Morrison's *Jazz* and the City," 222.

112. Matthew M. Heard, "Tonality and Ethos," *Philosophy and Rhetoric* 46, no. 1 (2013), 47.

113. Ibid., 48. The expression "sonic subjectivity" is taken from Alexander G. Weheliye, *Phonographies: Grooves in Sonic Afro-Modernity* (Durham, NC: Duke University Press, 2005), 70.

114. See Jacques Derrida, "On a Newly Arisen Apocalyptic Tone in Philosophy," in *Raising the Tone of Philosophy*, ed. Peter Fenves (Baltimore: Johns Hopkins University Press, 1993), 117–171.

115. Heard, "Tonality and Ethos," 48.

116. Morrison, *Jazz*, 180–181.

117. Scheiber, "'Jazz' and the Future of Blues," 476; see also Dale Pattison's Tschumi-influenced analysis of the architectural aspects of Morrison's novel in "Building Intimacy: The Erotic Architecture of Toni Morrison's *Jazz*," *Critique: Studies in Contemporary Fiction* 58, no. 2 (2017), 129.

118. Pattison, "Building Intimacy," 130.

119. Gareth Milllington and Vladimir Rizov, "'What Makes City Life Meaningful is the Things We Hide': A Dialogue on Existential Space

between Marshall Berman and Orhan Pamuk," *City* 23, no. 6 (2019), 699. The quotation is from Marshall Berman, *On the Town: One Hundred Years of Spectacle in Times Square* (New York: Verso, 2006), xxiv.

120. Berman, *On the Town: One Hundred Years of Spectacle in Times Square*, 139.

121. Ellison, "An Extravagance of Laughter," 147.

122. Ibid., 149.

123. Ibid., 161.

124. See Michael J. Shapiro, "Blues & Politics," a review of Clyde Woods *Development Arrested* and Graham Lock, *Blutopia, Theory & Event* 4, no. 4 (2000).

125. On Lefebvre's lack of attention to race—his "glaring omission of any explicit discussion of racial identities"—see Eugene J. McCann, "Race, Protest, and Public Space," *Antipode* 31, no. 2 (1999), 164. See also Henri Lefebvre, "The Right to the City," in *Writings on Cities*, trans. Eleonore Kofman and Elizabeth Lebas (Malden, MA: Blackwell, 1996), 149.

126. Lefebvre, "The Right to the City," 150.

127. Ibid., 149.

128. Ibid., 158.

129. See Henri Lefebvre, *The Production of Space*, trans. Donald Nicholson-Smith (Malden, MA: Blackwell, 1991).

130. Andrej Zieleniec, "Lefebvre's Politics of Space: Planning the Urban as Oeuvre," *Urban Planning* 3, no. 3 (2018), 5–6.

131. Pattison, "Building Intimacy," 130.

132. From Daniel Kolitz, *Hope and Fears*, BoingBoing, August 22, 2016, https://bingboing.net/2016/08/22/robert-moses-wove-enduring-rac.html.

133. See Robert A. Caro, *The Power Broker: Robert Moses and the Fall of New York* (New York: Vintage, 1975). Also see this report on an exhibition that to a degree rehabilitates his legacy: "Rehabilitating Robert Moses," *New York Times*, January 23, 2007, https://www.nytimes.com/video/arts/1194817114315/rehabilitating-robert-moses.html.

134. Thomas J. Campanella, "Robert Moses and His Racist Parkway Explained," Bloomberg, July 9, 2017, https://www.bloomberg.com/news/articles/2017-07-09/robert-moses-and-his-racist-parkway-explained.

135. Bernard Tschumi, "Violence and Architecture," in *Architecture and Disjunction* (Cambridge, MA: MIT Press, 1994), 121.

136. Elizabeth Winter, *Black Past*, accessed 8/16/20 at: https://www.blackpast.org/student_historians/winter-elizabeth/.

206 NOTES

137. Pattison, "Building Intimacy," 129.
138. Charles Keil, "Participatory Discrepancies: A Progress Report," *Ethnomusicology* 39, no. 1 (1995), 4.
139. Shapiro, "Blues & Politics."
140. Altman quoted in David Sterritt, "Director Builds Metaphor for Jazz in *Kansas City*," in *Robert Altman: Interviews* (Jackson: University of Mississippi Press, 2000), 212.
141. Ibid., 213.
142. Ibid., 212.
143. Shapiro, "Blues & Politics."
144. LeRoi Jones/Amari Baraka, "Introduction," *Blues People* (New York: Quill, 1999), p. ix.
145. Allen J. Scott, "The Cultural Economy: Geography and the Creative Field," *Media, Culture & Society* 21, no. 6 (1999), 814.
146. Jennifer Lynn Stoever, *The Sonic Color Line: Race and the Cultural Politics of Listening* (New York: NYU Press, 2016), 3.
147. Macdonald Smith Moore, *Yankee Blues: Musical Culture and American Identity* (Bloomington: Indiana University Press, 1985), 5.
148. Ibid., 73.
149. Arthur Kempton, *Boogaloo: The Quintessence of American Popular Music* (New York: Pantheon, 2003), 17.
150. Pattison, "Building Intimacy," 139.
151. Ta-Nehisi Coates, *Between the World and Me* (New York: One World, 2015), 17–18.
152. Langston Hughes on James Baldwin's *Notes of a Native Son*, *New York Times*, November 15, 2019, https://www.nytimes.com/2019/11/15/books/review/langston-hughes-on-james-baldwins-notes-of-a-native-son.html.

Chapter 3

1. Edward Portes, "Immigration and the Metropolis: Reflections on Urban History," *Journal of International Migration and Integration* 1, no. 2 (Spring 2000), 161.
2. Ibid., 165.
3. Theodor W. Adorno, *Aesthetic Theory*, trans. C. Lenhardt (New York: Routledge & Kegan Paul, 1984), 34.
4. See Krzysztof Wodiczko, *Critical Vehicles: Writing, Projects, Interviews* (Cambridge, MA: MIT Press, 1999), 104. The original account of the

bâton d'étranger is in Krzysztof Wodiczko, *Art public, art critique: textes, propos, et documents* (Paris: École Normale Supérieure des Beaux-Arts, 1995).

5. Wodiczko, *Art public, art critique*, 212.
6. Ibid.
7. "Xenology and Identity: Krzysztof Wodiczko's Immigrant Instruments," legermi.typepad.com, October 2011, https://legermj.typepad.com/blog/2011/10/xenology-and-identity-krzysztof-wodiczkos-immigrant-instruments.html.
8. Ibid.
9. Patricia Phillips, "Creating Democracy: A Dialogue with Krzysztof Wodiczko," *Art Journal* 62, no. 4 (December, 2003), 35–36.
10. Described in Ermine Fişek, *Aesthetic Citizenship: Immigration and Theater in Twentieth-Century Paris* (Evanston, IL: Northwestern University Press, 2017), 31.
11. Ibid., 45, 121.
12. For an elaboration of the concept of the imperial gaze, see E. Ann Kaplan, *Looking for the Other: Feminism, Film and the Imperial Gaze* (London: Routledge, 1997).
13. Haneke quoted in Michael Lawrence, "Haneke's Stable: Death of an Animal and the Figuration of the Human," in *On Michael Haneke*, ed. Brian Price and John David Rhodes (Detroit: Wayne State University Press, 2010), 63.
14. John David Rhodes, "Haneke: The Long Take Realism," *Framework: The Journal of Cinema and Media* 47, no. 2 (Fall 2006), 20.
15. Michael Haneke, "Cowardly and Comfortable," interview with Dominik Kamalzadeh in *Eurozine*, January 30, 2006, http://www.signandsight.com/features/577.html.
16. Todd Herzog, "The Banality of Surveillance; Michael; Haneke's 'Cache' and life after the End of Privacy," *Modern Austrian Literature* 43, no. 2 (2010), 27, quoting David Sorfa, "Uneasy Domesticity in the Films of Michael Haneke," *Studies in European Cinema* 3, no. 2 (2006), 101–102.
17. From Brianne Gallagher's analysis of the film, "Policing Paris: Private Publics and Architectural Media in Michael Haneke's *Caché*," in *Genre and the City*, ed. Michael J. Shapiro (London: Routledge, 2011), 34.
18. The expression is from Giuliana Bruno's review of Sergei Eisenstein's cinematic approach to architecture. See her *Atlas of Emotion: Journeys in Art, Architecture, and Film* (New York: Verso, 2002), 56.
19. Kristin Ross, *May '68 and Its Afterlives* (Chicago: University of Chicago Press, 2002), 51.
20. Adam Shatz, Preface to a new edition of William Gardner Smith, *The Stone Face* (New York: New York Review Books, 2021), 13.

208 NOTES

21. Tzvetan Todorov, "'Race,' Writing and Culture," trans. Loulou Mack, in "*Race*," *Writing and Difference*, ed. Henry Louis Gates Jr. (Chicago: University of Chicago Press, 1986), 371–372.

22. Adam Gopnik, "The Trial of the Century: Revisiting the Dreyfus Affair," *The New Yorker*, September 28, 2009, https://www.newyorker.com/magaz ine/2009/09/28/trial-of-the-century.

23. Joy C. Schaefer, "The Spatial Affective Economy of (Post)colonial Paris: Reading Haneke's *Cache* (2005) through *Octobre a Paris* (1962)," *Studies in European Cinema* 14, no. 1 (2017), 52.

24. Gopnik, "The Trial of the Century."

25. Lewis R. Gordon, "Theory in Black: Teleological Suspension in Philosophy of Culture," *Qui* Parle 18, no. 2 (Spring/Summer, 2010), 196.

26. Achille Mbembe, "Provincializing France," *Public Culture* 23, no. 1 (2010), 88.

27. Ibid., 89.

28. Tariro Mzezewa, "We Wore What? Centuries of Global Fashion as a System of Power," *New York Times* Book Review, February 9, 2021, https://www. nytimes.com/2021/02/09/books/review/the-african-lookbook-catherine-e-mckinley-dress-codes-richard-thompson-ford.html?searchResultPosit ion=2.

29. Jorge Fernandes, *Challenging Euro-America's Politics of Indentity: The Return of the Native* (London: Routledge, 2008), 1.

30. See Andrei Tarkovsky, *Sculpting in Time*, trans. Kitty Hunter Blair (Austin: University of Texas Press, 2012).

31. Paul Schrader, *Transcendental Style in Film: Ozu, Bresson, Dreyer* (Berkeley: University of California Press, 2018), ebook loc. 121.

32. Pier Paolo Pasolini, "The Cinema of Poetry," in *Heretical Empiricism*, trans. Ben Lawton and Louise K. Bartnett (Washington, DC: New Academia, 2005), 184.

33. That observation about Antonioni's film work belong to Gilles Deleuze, *Cinema 2*, trans. Hugh Tomlinson and Robert Galeta (Minneapolis: University of Minnesota Press, 1989), 9.

34. Michelangelo Antonioni, quoted in Juhani Pallasma, *The Architecture of Vision: Existential Space in Cinema* (Helsinki: Rakennustieto Oy, 2001), 123.

35. The expression belongs to John David Rhodes, "The Spectacle of Skepticism: Haneke's Long Takes," in *On Michael Haneke*, ed. Price and Rhodes, 99.

36. Pascal Bonitzer quoted in Libby Saxton, "Secrets and Revelations: Off-Screen Space in Michael Haneke's *Caché*," *Studies in French Cinema* 7, no. 1 (2002), 5.

NOTES 209

37. Ibid., 9.
38. See Rhodes, "The Spectacle of Skepticism," 99.
39. From a Franz Grabner interview with Michael Haneke, translated in Niels Niessen, "The Staged Realism of Michael Haneke's *Caché*," *CiNeMas* 20, no. 1 (2009), 182.
40. Antonioni quoted in Joe McElhaney, *The Death of Classical Cinema: Hitchcock, Lang, Minelli* (Albany: SUNY Press, 2006), 239.
41. The expression belongs to Lisa Coulthard, "Haptic Aurality: Listening to the Films of Michael Haneke," *Film-Philosophy* 16, no. 1 (2012), 17.
42. The insight and quotation are borrowed from Eon Flannery's analysis of the film in "Postcolonial Passages: Migrations and Cinematic form in Michael Haneke's *Hidden* and Alan Gilsenan's *Zulu 9*," *Journal of Postcolonial Writing* 47, no. 1 (February 2011), 71.
43. Flannery, "Postcolonial Passages," 66.
44. See Fişek, *Aesthetic* Citizenship, 48–49.
45. Edouard Glissant, *Poetics of Relation*, trans. Betsy Wing (Ann Arbor: University of Michigan Press, 1997), 18.
46. Jacques Lacan, "The Eye and the Gaze," in *The Four Fundamental Concepts of Psycho-Analysis*, trans. Alan Sheridan (London: Penguin, 1979), 73.
47. Hugh S. Manon, "'*Comment ca rien*': Screening the Gaze in *Caché*," in *On Michael Haneke*, ed. Price and Rhodes, 109.
48. Ibid., 103.
49. Such is the case with the Sony Pictures, which uses the expression on the DVD case summary (2006).
50. As noted in Chapter 1, that genre designation has been developed by Linda Hutcheon. See her *A Poetics of Postmodernism: History, Theory, Fiction* (New York: Routledge, 1988).
51. Gallagher, "Policing Paris," 23.
52. Friedich Kittler, "The City Is a Medium," *New Literary History* 27, no. 4 (Autumn 1996), 718.
53. Ibid., 725.
54. Yves Cohen, "The Modernization of Production in the French Automobile Industry between the Wars: A Photographic Essay," *Business History Review* 65, no. 4 (Winter 1991), 754.
55. On the temporality of the advent of Fordist consumption in France, see Kristin Ross, *Fast Cars, Clean Bodies* (Cambridge, MA: MIT Press, 1993), 4–5.
56. Reuel Denny, *The Astonished Muse* (Chicago: University of Chicago Press, 1957), 142.

210 NOTES

57. Reuel Denny quoted in Randle W. Nelson, "Remembering Reuel Denny: Sociology as Cultural Studies," *American Sociologist* 24, no. 4 (2003), 35.

58. Gilles Deleuze, *Francis Bacon: The Logic of Sensation*, trans. Daniel W. Smith (Minneapolis: University of Minnesota Press, 2003), 14.

59. Michael J. Shapiro, *Cinematic Geopolitics* (London: Routledge, 2009), 100.

60. I am borrowing that expression from Pauline Guillemet, Margaux Eskenazi, and Alice Carré, "*Affronter les amnesies colonials: rencontre avec Margaux Eskenazi et Alice Carré, Creer: Experimenter les forms de l'histoire*," accessed 8/18/20 at: https://entre-temps.net/affronter-les-amnesies-coloniales-rencontre-avec-margaux-eskenazi-et-alice-carre/

61. Reported in Patrick Crowley, "When Forgetting is Remembering: Haneke's *Caché* and the Events of October 17, 1961," in *On Michael Haneke*, ed. Price and Rhodes, 269.

62. Reported by Roger Cohen, "In Reconciliation Act, Macron Acknowledges Truth of Algerian Lawyer's Death," *New York Times*, March 21, 2021, https://www.nytimes.com/2021/03/04/world/europe/macron-algeria-Ali-Boumendjel.html.

63. Gilles Deleuze, *Cinema 2: The Time Image*, trans. Hugh Tomlinson and Robert Galleta (Minneapolis: University of Minnesota Press, 1989), 272.

64. Jean Baudrillard, "Sign Function and Class Logic," in *For a Critique of the Political Economy of the Sign*, trans. Charles Levin (St. Louis, MO: Telos Press, 1981), 29.

65. Ibid., 38.

66. Alexandra Lloyd, "Songs of Innocence and Experience: Michael Haneke's Cinematic Visions of Childhood," *Modern Language Review* 111, no. 1 (January, 2016), 308.

67. Michael J. Shapiro, "Ingmar Bergman: Theatricality Contra Theology," in *The Phenomenology of Religious Belief: Media, Philosophy, and the Arts* (London: Bloomsbury, 2021), 101.

68. See Gilles Deleuze, "Postscript on Societies of Control," *October* 59 (Winter 1992), 3–7.

69. Gallagher, "Policing Paris," 25.

70. Jacques Rancière, *Disagreement: Politics and Philosophy*, trans. Julie Rise (Minneapolis: University of Minnesota Press, 1998), 29.

71. Rosalyn Deutsche, "Art and Pubic Space: Questions of Democracy," *Social Text* 33 (1992), 38.

72. Paul Gilroy, "Shooting Crabs in a Barrel," *Screen* 48, no. 2 (2007), 233.

73. Ibid.

74. Thornton Wilder, Letter to John Townley, "Afterword," in *The Bridge of San Luis Rey* (New York: Harper, 2014), 128.

NOTES 211

75. Nancy E. Virtue, "Memory, Trauma, and the French-Algerian War: Michael Haneke's *Caché* (2005)," *Modern & Contemporary France* 19, no. 3 (August 2011), 284–285.
76. Ibid., 284.
77. Ibid., 285.
78. Ibid.
79. The apropos expressions are taken from Deleuze's reading of Proust: Gilles Deleuze, *Proust & Signs*, trans. Richard Hamilton (Minneapolis: University of Minnesota Press, 2000), 20.
80. Haneke, "Cowardly and Comfortable."
81. In addition to Gilroy's moralistic review—already noted—is Dawn Fulton's "Unknown Knowns: Michael Haneke's *Caché* and the Failure of Allegory," *Modern Language Review* 114, no. 4 (October, 2019), 682–699 and Catherine Wheatley, *Michael Haneke's Cinema: The Ethic of the Image* (Oxford: Berghahn, 2009).
82. Haneke, "Cowardly and comfortable."
83. Pierre Nora, "Between Memory and History: *Les Lieux de Memoire*," *Representations* 26 (Spring 1989), 7.
84. Ibid., 8.
85. Ibid.
86. Ibid.
87. Ibid., 9.
88. Ibid.
89. Michel Foucault, *"Society Must Be Defended": Lectures at the College De France 1975–1976*, trans. David Macey (New York: Picador, 2003), 70.
90. The "image fact" expression is pervasive on the film analyses of Andrei Bazin. See for example his *What is Cinema, Volume Two*, trans. Hugh Gray (Berkeley: University of California Press, 1971).
91. Marcia Landy, *Cinema & Counter-History* (Bloomington: Indiana University Press, 2015), 2.
92. Schaefer, "The Spatial Affective Economy of (Post)colonial Paris," 60.
93. Ibid.
94. I am borrowing the quoted phrase from Fabiano Mielniczuk's reading the film (shared in a private conversation, July, 2021).
95. "Alou Won't Accept Radio Host's Apology," ESPN, August 6, 2005, https://www.espn.com/mlb/news/story?id=2127192.
96. I owe the discovery of that part of the soundtrack to the careful observing and listening of Niessen, "The Staged Realism of Michael Haneke's *Caché*," 187.
97. Michael Haneke, "The World That Is Known: An Interview with Michael Haneke by Christopher Sharrett," *Cineaste* 28, no. 3 (2003), 31.

212 NOTES

98. Jacques Rancière, *The Flesh of Words: The Politics of Writing*, trans. Charlotte Mandell (Stanford, CA: Stanford University Press, 2004), 159.

Chapter 4

1. Kazuo Ishiguro, *The Remains of the Day* (New York: Vintage, 1989), 3.
2. Laura van Staaten, "Diverse Portraits," *New York Times* May 1, 2022, 24.
3. Miss Rosen, "Dazed Interview with The Portrait is Political Artist," BRIC Studio Space, May 9, 2019, https://www.bricartsmedia.org/dazed-interv iew-portrait-political-artists.
4. Jenny Edkins, *Face Politics* (London: Routledge, 2015), 2.
5. From Richard Powers's novelistic treatment of Sander's photographic project, *Three Farmers on Their Way to a Dance* (New York: William Morrow, 2001), 39.
6. The concept was initiated by the Nazi anthropologist Alfred Hoche. See *Arztliche Bemerkungen* in Karl Binding and Alfred Hoche, *De Freigabe der Vernichtung Lebensunwerten Lebens: Ihr Mass und ihre Form* (Leipzig, 1920), 61–62.
7. Marley Marius, "'The Past Doesn't Stay in the Past': Inside Photographer Dawound Bey's Stirring New Retrospective," *Vogue*, April 14, 2021; https://www.vogue.com/article/dawoud-bey.
8. From a report on Bey's Whitney Museum exhibition, "Art History from Home: Whitney Museum Presents *Dawoud Bey: An American Project*," April 19, 2021, https://flash---art.com/2021/04/whitney-museum-daw oud-bey-american-project/.
9. Jacqueline Karp, "A Tale of Two Paintings: Orhan Pamuk and Turkey's Troubled Identity," *Agni*, July 1, 2007, https://agnionline.bu.edu/essay/a-tale-of-two-paintings-orhan-pamuk-and-turkeys-troubled-identity.
10. Ibid.
11. Orhan Pamuk, *Istanbul: Memories and the City* (New York: Vintage, 2006), 10.
12. Ibid., 29.
13. Orhan Pamuk, *My Name is Red* (New York: Vintage, 2002).
14. The observation belongs to Carl Abbott, "Beyond Blade Runner: Community in Cities of the Future," *Los Angeles Review of Books*, February 10, 2017, https://lareviewofbooks.org/article/beyond-blade-runner/.
15. Anna Secor, "'There Is an Istanbul That Belongs to Me': Citizenship, Space, and Identity in the City," *Annals of the Association of American Geographers* 94, no. 2 (2004), 357.

NOTES 213

16. Françoise Vergès, Capitalocene, "Waste, Race, and Gender," e-flux Journal 100 (May 2019), https://www.e-flux.com/journal/100/269165/capitaloc ene-wasterace-and-gender/.

17. That situation is reported in Dell Upton, *Another City: Urban Life and Urban Space in the New American Republic* (New Haven, CT: Yale University Press, 2008), 191.

18. Marion Weiss, "The Politics of Underestimation," in *The Sex of Architecture*, ed. Dana Agrest, Patricia Conway, and Leslie Kanes (New York: Henry N. Abrams, 1996), 253.

19. Fergus M, Bordewich, *Washington: The Making of an American Capital* (New York: Amistad, 2008), 269.

20. Edward P. Jones, *Lost in the City* (New York: Amistad, 2005), 148.

21. Abby Shultz, "The Understated Master of Gordon Parks," *Barron's Daily*, July 15, 2020, https://www.barrons.com/articles/the-understated-mast ery-of-gordon-parks-51592222401.

22. See Jesse Green, "Reanimating Cabaret' One Frame at a Time," New York Times, April 14, 2021, https://www.nytimes.com/interactive/2021/04/14/ arts/recreating-cabaret.html.

23. Andre Bazin, "The Ontology of the Photographic Image," *Film Quarterly* 13, no. 4 (Summer 1960), 8.

24. Ibid.

25. Gilles Deleuze, *Bergsonism*, trans. Hugh Tomlinson and Barbara Habberjam (New York: Zone Books, 1990), 25–26.

26. Gilles Deleuze and Felix Guattari, *A Thousand Plateaus*, trans. Brian Massumi (Minneapolis: University of Minnesota Press, 1987). 179.

27. The expression is from a book review by John Williams, "A Meditation on Albecht Dürer and His Art," *New York Times* May 6, 2021, C4.

28. Upon reading Jean Marc Gaspard Itard's account of the difficulty he had "to train the wolf-boy to fix his gaze, the Japanese novelist Kōbō Abe, reflects on the difference between socialized humans and that feral boy: "Having built a bulwark against the contingencies of nature through the formation of society, man [*sic*] gained the freedom to gaze and concentrate on individual things. Wild animals are constantly exposed to contingent dangers, however, and so it is much more natural for them to pay close attention to all that takes place around them." In "Artistic Revolution: Theory of the Art Movement," quoted in Abe Kōbō, *The Frontier Within*, trans. Richard Calichman (New York: Columbia University Press, 2013), 67.

29. Michael J. Shapiro, *The Political Sublime* (Durham, NC: Duke University Press, 2018), 15–16.

30. James Wood, "Moveable Types," *The New Yorker*, November 26, 2007, https://www.newyorker.com/magazine/2007/11/26/movable-types.

214 NOTES

31. Leo Tolstoy, *Anna Karenina*, trans. Louise and Aylmer Maud (Mineola, NY: Dover, 2004), ebook 1621.

32. Cyril Béghin, "The Long Take, Mastery," *Film Quarterly* 70, no. 1 (Fall 2016), 48.

33. Wieslaw Godzic, "Iconological Method in Film Research," *Aritubus et Historae*, 2, no. 3 (1981), 152.

34. Gilles Deleuze, *Cinema 1: The Movement Image*, trans. Hugh Tomlinson and Barbara Haberjam (Minneapolis: University of Minnesota Press, 1986), 100.

35. I am quoting Richard Rushton's distillation of Deleuze's perspective: "What Can a Face Do: On Deleuze and Faces," *Cultural Critique* 51 (Spring 2002), 224.

36. Ibid., 228.

37. Andreja Zevnik, "The Politics of the Face: The Scopic Regime and the (Un-)masking of the Political Subject," *Journal for Cultural Research* 20, no. 2 (2016), 122.

38. The expression belongs to Jacques Derrida, "'Geopsychoanalysis' . . . and the Rest of the World," *American Imago* 48, no. 2 (Summer 1991), 199.

39. See Stefania Pandolfo, *Knot of the Soul* (Chicago: University of Chicago Press, 2018).

40. Nathan Gorelick, "Becoming Revolution: From Symptom to Act in the 2011 Arab Revolts," in *Islamic Psychoanalysis and Psychoanalytic Islam*, ed. Ian Parker and Sabah Siddiqui (New York: Routledge, 1029), 97.

41. Pandolfo, *Knot of the Soul*.

42. Brecht's *Gesammelte Werke*, quoted in Roswitha Mueller, "Montage in Brecht," *Theater Journal* 39, no. 4 (December 1987), 475.

43. Esther Da Costa Meyer, "La Donna e Mobile: Agoraphobia, omen and Urban Space," in *The Sex of Architecture*, ed. Agrest, Conway, and Weisman, 146.

44. That aesthetic is described in Mueller, "Montage in Brecht," 475.

45. David Bordwell, "Nordisk and the Tableaux Aesthetic," David Bordwell's Website on Cinema, June 2010, https://www.davidbordwell.net/essays/nordisk.php, 1.

46. See Gilles Deleuze, *Cinema 2: The Time Image*, trans. Hugh Tomlinson and Robert Galeta (Minneapolis: University of Minnesota Press, 1989).

47. Fahri Karakas, "'Ethos' Is the Best Turkish Series Netflix has Ever Commissioned," Medium, accessed 3/15/21 at: https://medium.com/an-idea/ethos-is-the-best-turkish-series-netflix-has-ever-commissioned-fdc1b129a5c8.

48. Tolstoy, *Anna Karenina*, loc. 229.

NOTES 215

49. Eray Alpay Özdemir, "A Truthful, Excellent, Striking Turkish Original Series: Ethos on Netflix," DoYouKnow Turkey.com, November 21, 2020, https://www.doyouknowturkey.com/an-excellent-turkish-series-ethos-on-netflix/.

50. John le Carré, *A Perfect Spy* (New York: Penguin, 2011), 315.

51. The expression belongs to Georg Lukács, *Theory of the Novel*, trans. Anna Bosock (Cambridge, MA: MIT Press, 1971), 84.

52. The quotation belongs to the architect Sanford Kwinter. See his *Requiem for the City at the End of the Century* (New York: ACTAR, 2010), 58.

53. Lynda Bundtzen, "Bergman's 'Fanny and Alexander': Family Romance or Artistic Allegory?" *Criticism* 29, no. 1 (Winter 1987), 95.

54. From Philip Mosley, *Ingmar Bergman: The Cinema as Mistress* (London: Marion Boyars, 2000), 65.

55. Wanda Corn, "The Birth of a National Icon: Grant Wood's 'American Gothic,'" *Art Institute of Chicago Museum Studies* 10 (1983), 255–256.

56. The concept of a building as an event space belongs to the architectural theorist Bernard Tschumi. See his *Architecture and Disjunction* (Cambridge, MA: MIT Press, 1994).

57. The concept/figure of the conceptual persona belongs to Gilles Deleuze and Felix Guattari, *What is Philosophy?*, trans. Hugh Tomlinson and Graham Burchell (New York: Columbia University Press, 1994), 61–83.

58. Michael J. Shapiro, *Studies in Trans-Disciplinary Method: After the Aesthetic Turn* (London: Routledge, 2012), xiv.

59. Àlvar Peris Blanes, "Imagining the Nation Through Television Fiction: Memory, Proximity and Daily Life," *Debates: Journal on Culture, Power and* Society 1 (2016), 34.

60. Jacob Kingsbury Downs, "Acoustic Territories of the Body: Headphone Listening, Embodies Space, and the Phenomenology of Sonic Homeliness," *Journal of Sonic Studies*, https://www.researchcatalogue.net/view/1260 374/1260375.

61. See Cathy Caruth, *Unclaimed Experience Trauma, Narrative and History* (Baltimore: Johns Hopkins University Press, 2016).

62. Michael J. Shapiro, *Cinematic Geopolitics* (London: Routledge, 2009), 60, .

63. Michel Foucault, "What Is critique?," in *The Politics of Truth*, trans. Lysa Hochroth (New York: Semiotext(e), 1997), 47.

64. Michael J. Shapiro, *For Moral Ambiguity: National Culture and the Politics of the Family* (Minneapolis: University of Minnesota Press, 2011), 27, quoting Pierre Bourdieu, *The Middle Brown Art*, trans. Shaun Whiteside (Stanford, CA: Stanford University Press, 1990), 26.

65. Bourdieu, *The Middle Brow Art*, 29.

216   NOTES

66. Nagihan Haliloğlu, "Revelation on 'Ethos': Secrets and Lies in Berkun Oya's New Series," Daily Sabah, December 13, 2020, https://www.dailysabah.com/arts/reviews/revelation-on-ethos-secrets-and-lies-in-berkun-oyas-new-series.

67. Matthew M. Heard, "Tonality and *Ethos*," *Philosophy and Rhetoric* 46, no. 1 (2013), 44.

68. Aafke Komter, "Gifts and Social Relations," *Journal du Mauss*, April 10, 2007, http://journaldumauss.net/?GIfts-and-Social-Relations.

69. Mark Twain, *Adventures of Huckleberry Finn* (Berkeley: University of California Press, 1988), 155.

Chapter 5

1. Laura Bliss, "The Shimmering Private Pools of Los Angels Country, Mapped," *Bloomsbury News*, April 11, 2016, https://www.bloomberg.com/news/articles/2016-04-11/ken-schwencke-maps-the-swimming-pools-of-los-angeles-county.

2. Jeff Wiltse, *Contested Waters: A Social History of Swimming Pools in America* (Chapel Hill: University of North Carolina Press, 2009), 2.

3. John Cheever, "The Swimmer," *The New Yorker*, July 18, 1964, https://www.newyorker.com/magazine/1964/07/18/the-swimmer.

4. Michael Kimmelman, "Los Angeles Has a Housing Crisis. Can Design Help?," *New York Times*, June 23, 2021, https://www.nytimes.com/2021/06/22/arts/design/los-angeles-housing-crisis.html.

5. Alastair Sooke, "The Bewitching Allure of Hockney's Swimming Pools," BBC, February 23, 2017, https://www.bbc.com/culture/article/20170210-the-bewitching-allure-of-hockneys-swimming-pools.

6. Matthew Sperling, "The Pull of Hockney's Pool Paintings," *Apollo*, February 4, 2017, https://www.apollo-magazine.com/david-hockney-pool-paintings/.

7. Gomez, interviewed in K. L. Sullivan, "Striking Images Reveal What It Really Takes to Live a Life of Luxury," *Mic*, January 2, 2004, https://www.mic.com/articles/77863/striking-images-reveal-what-it-really-takes-to-live-a-life-of-luxury.

8. Hockey remarked, "LA was the first city I ever painted. I started painting the architecture." Quoted in Frances Anterton, "David Hockney: Still Inspired by LA After 50 Years," *Design and Architecture*, April 19, 2016,

https://www.kcrw.com/culture/shows/design-and-architecture/david-hockney-still-inspired-by-l-a-after-50-years.

9. Lawrence Weschler, "Ramiro Gomez's Domestic Disturbances," *New York Times Magazine*, August 16, 2015, https://www.nytimes.com/2015/08/16/magazine/ramiro-gomezs-domestic-disturbances.html.

10. Avishay Artsy, "Ramiro Gomez Seeks to 'Make the Invisible Visible,'" *Design and Architecture*, April 20, 2016, https://www.kcrw.com/culture/shows/design-and-architecture/ramiro-gomez-seeks-to-make-the-invisible-visible.

11. Crescencio López González, *The Latinx Urban Condition: Trauma, Memory, and Desire in Latinx Urban Literature and Culture* (Lanham, MD: Lexington Books, 2021), 7.

12. Martin Hammer, "The Photographic Source and Artistic Affinities of David Hockney's 'A Bigger Splash,'" *Burlington Magazine* 159, no. 1370 (2017), https://www.burlington.org.uk/archive/article/the-photographic-source-and-artistic-affinities-of-davidhockneys-a-bigger-splash.

13. Mike Davis, *City of Quartz: Excavating the Future in Los Angeles* (New York: Vintage, 1990), 223.

14. Michael J. Shapiro, *The Time of the City: Politics, Philosophy and Genre* (London: Routledge, 2010), 50.

15. Ibid., Chapter 4.

16. "California As I Saw It: First Person Narratives of California's Early Yeats, 1849–1900," Library of Congress, November 25, 2021. https://www.loc.gov/collections/california-first-person-narratives/?fa=online-format:web+page.

17. The quotation about that part of the Californios story is from Joy M. Lynch, "'A Distinct Place in America Where all *Mestizos* Reside': Landscape and Identity in Ana Castillo's *Sapogonia* and Dana Chang's *The Frontiers of Love*," *Melus* 26, no. 3 (Fall, 2001), 120.

18. Judith A. Bense, "Introduction: Presidios of the North American Borderlands," *Historical Archaeology* 38, no. 3 (2004), 1.

19. Davis, *City of Quartz*, 231.

20. Henri Lefebvre, "The Everyday and Everdayness," trans. Christine Levich, *Yale French Studies* 73 (1987), 8.

21. Henri Lefebvre, *The Production of Space*, trans. Donald Nicholson-Smith (Cambridge, MA: Blackwell, 1991), 165.

22. Ivan Illich, *Tools for Conviviality* (New York: Marion Boyars, 2001), 58.

23. Stephen Graham, *Vertical: The City from Satellites to Bunkers* (London: Verso, 2016), 260.

218 NOTES

24. Anne Friedberg, "Urban Mobility and Cinematic Visuality: The Screens of Los Angeles—Endless Cinema or Private Telematics," *Journal of Visual Culture* 1, no. 2 (2002), 184.

25. Michel de Certeau, *The Practice of Everyday Life*, trans. Steven Rendall (Berkeley: University of California Press, 1984), 93.

26. The expression belongs to Dale Pattison, "Trauma and the 710: The New Metropolis in Helena Viramontes's *Their Dogs Came with Them*," *Arizona Quarterly* 70, no. 2 (Summer 2014), 116.

27. Helena María Viramontes, *Their Dogs Came with Them* (New York: Washington Square Press, 2007), 2.

28. The *La Bloga* staff, "Interview with Helena Maria Viramontes," July 8, 2007, https://www.popmatters.com/their-dogs-came-with-them-by-helena-maria-viramontes-2496230784.html.

29. Ibid.

30. Pattison, "Trauma and the 710," 117.

31. Stephan Graham and Simon Martin, *Splintering Urbanism* (London: Routledge, 2001), 383.

32. Viramontes, *Their Dogs Came with Them*, 61.

33. Susan Bickford, "Constructing Inequality: City Spaces and the Architecture of Citizenship," *Political Theory* 28, no. 3 (June 2000), 363–364. The phrase "privacy-related liberty" is from Anita L. Allen, "Privacy at Home: The Twofold Problem," in *Revisioning the Political*, ed. Nancy J. Hirschmann and Christine Di Stefano (Boulder, CO; Westview Press, 1996), 193–212.

34. Hsuan L. Hsu "Fatal Contiguities: Metonymy and Environmental Justice," *New Literary History* 42, no. 1 (2011), 154.

35. Pattison, "Trauma and the 710," 124.

36. Viramontes, *Their Dogs Came with Them*, 168.

37. Ibid., 274.

38. I am quoting from my earlier reading of the film in Shapiro, *The Time of the City*, 58.

39. The expression belongs to David Bordwell, *Planet Hong Kong: Popular Cinema and the Art of Entertainment* (Cambridge, MA: Harvard University Press, 2000), 89.

40. Elena Zilberg, "Falling Down in El Norte: A Cultural Politics & Spatial Poetics of the ReLatinization of Los Angeles," *Wide Angle* 20, no. 3 (1998), 185.

41. Gilles Deleuze, *Cinema 1: The Movement Image*, trans. High Tomlinson and Barbara Habberjam (Minneapolis: University of Minnesota Press, 1986), 64.

NOTES 219

42. Michel de Certeau, *The Practice of Everyday Life*, trans. Steven Rendall (Berkeley: University of California Press, 1988), 37.
43. Ibid., 36. Emphasis in the original.
44. For a survey see Crescencio López González, *The Latinx Urban Condition* (Lanham, MD: Lexington Books, 2020).
45. David R. Diaz, *Barrio Urbanism: Chicanos, Planning, and American Cities* (New York: Routledge, 2005), 45.
46. The quotation is from the documentary film, *East LA Interchange* July 21, 2021 https://eastlainterchangefilm.com/about-film/boyle-heights-history/.
47. Kean O'Brien, Leonardo Vilchis, and Corina Maritescu, "Boyle Heights and the Fight Against Gentrification as State Violence," *American Quarterly* 17, no. 2 (June 2019), 390.
48. Rojas quoted in Amanda Merck, "James Rojas: How Latino Urbanism Is Changing Life in American Neighborhoods," *Salud America!*, January 14, 2020, https://salud-america.org/james-rojas-how-latino-urbanism-is-changing-life-in-american-neighborhoods/.
49. Ibid.
50. Michael Rios, "Pubic Space Praxis: Cultural Capacity and Political Efficacy in Latina/o Placemaking," *Berkeley Planning Journal* 22 (2009), 95.
51. Henri Lefebvre, "The Right to the City," in *Writings on Cities*, trans. Eleonore Kofman and Elizabeth Lebas (Malden, MA; Blackwell, 1996), 152.
52. Jorge N. Leal, "Mapping from Below: Approaches in Charting Out Latinx Historical and Quotidian Presence in Metropolitan Los Angeles, 1990–2020," *European Journal of American Culture* 40, no. 1 (2021), 7.
53. Merck, "James Rojas."
54. Ibid.
55. Anthony Vidler. "Aftermath; A City Transformed: Designing 'Defensible Space,'" *New York Times*, September 23, 2001, https://www.nytimes.com/2001/09/23/weekinreview/aftermath-a-city-transformed-designing-defensible-space.html.
56. Karla Cornejo Villavicencio, "The Spectacle of Latinx Colorism," *New York Times*, July 30, 2021, https://www.nytimes.com/2021/07/30/opinion/latino-racism-colorism-latinx.html.
57. Johanna Londoño, *Abstract Barrios: The Crises of Latinx Visibility in Cities* (Durham, NC: Duke University Press, 2020), 103.
58. Daniel D. Arreola, "Mexican American Housescapes," *Geographical Review* 78, no. 3 (July 1988), 305.

220 NOTES

59. Camilo Vergara, *The New American Ghetto* (New Brunswick, NJ: Rutgers University Ores, 1995), 11.

60. Michael J. Shapiro, *Deforming American Political Thought: Challenging the Jeffersonian Legacy*, 2nd ed. (New York: Routledge, 2016), 135; Chrysanthe B. Broikos, "Urban Portraiture: The Persona of Place in the Work of Camilo Jose Vergara," *National Building Museum*, October 27, 2009, https://www.nbm.org/urban-portraiture-persona-place-work-camilo-jose-vergara/.

61. Londoño, *Abstract Barrios*, 103, quoting Sandra Cisneros in Kathy Lowry, "The Purple Passion of Sandra Cisneros," *Texas Monthly*, October 1, 1997, https://www.texasmonthly.com/articles/the-purple-passion-of-sandra-cisneros/.

62. Londoño, *Abstract Barrios*, 104.

63. Adrian Nathan West, *The Aesthetics of Degradation* (New York: Repeater, 2016), 56.

64. Charles P. Coffey, "Louis Carlos Bernal's *Barrios*: The Politics of Domesticity in the Wake of the Chicano Movement," master's degree essay, American University, Washington, DC, 2021, 12.

65. Bryan Burrough, Chris Tomlinson, and Jason Stanford, *Forget the Alamo* (New York: Penguin, 2021), 269.

66. Ibid., 342.

67. Viramontes, *Their Dogs Came with Them*, 9.

68. Tim Edensor, *Industrial Ruins: Space, Aesthetics and Materiality* (New York: Berg, 2005), 101.

69. Ibid., 164.

70. Pierre Nora, "Between Memory and History: *Les Lieux de Memoire*," *Representations* 26 (Spring 1989), 7.

71. Ibid., 8.

72. Ibid.

73. Ibid.

74. Ibid., 9.

75. Simon Romero, "Texas Pushes to Obscure the State's History of Slavery and Racism," *New York Times*, May 5, 2021, https://thepn.org/2021/05/21/texas-pushes-to-obscure-the-states-history-of-slavery-and-racism-simon-romero-new-york-times/.

76. Jacob Asmussen, "Monument on Battlefield," *Texas Scorecard*, September 23, 2020, https://texasscorecard.com/tag/alamo-master-plan/.

77. I treat the political significance of the future anterior in Michael J. Shapiro, *Politics and Time* (Cambridge: Polity, 2017).

78. Dave Davies, "Forget the Alamo Author Says We Have the Texas Origin Story Wrong," transcript of NPR's "Fresh Air" broadcast, June 16, 2021,

https://www.npr.org/2021/06/16/1006907140/forget-the-alamo-texas-history-bryan-burrough.

79. Burroughs et al., *Forget the Alamo*, 340.

80. Pauline Adamek, "John Sayles Interviewed for 'Lone Star,'" *Artsbeat LA*, https://www.artsbeatla.com/2020/04/john-sayles-lone-star/ (first published June 1996).

81. Vincent Perez, "Remembering the Alamo, Post-9/11," *American Quarterly* 55, no. 4 (December 2003), 772.

82. Ibid.

83. Neil Campbell, "'Forget the Alamo': History, Legend and Memory in John Sayles' *Lone Star*," Deleuzecinema.com, September 30, 2018, http://deleuzecinema.com/2018/09/30/forget-the-alamo-history-legend-and-memory-in-john-sayles-lone-star/, 162, quoting Diane Carson, ed., *John Sayles Interviews* (Jackson: University of Missouri Press, 1999), 203.

84. Campbell, "Forget the Alamo," 167.

85. Dave Hookstra, "John Sayles Roots Music," July 24, 1996, http://www.davehoekstra.com/wp-content/uploads/2014/03/john_sayles_roots_music.pdf.

86. Friedberg, "Urban Mobility and Cinematic Visuality," 187.

87. Roberto Calasso, *K.* (New York: Knopf, 2005), 33.

88. Leif Wener, "Epistemic Rights and Legal Rights," *Analysis* 63, no. 2 (2003), 144.

89. From David Lapoujade's analysis of Etienne Souriau's politics of aesthetics in *The Lesser Existences: Etienne Souriau, an Aesthetics for the Virtual* (Minneapolis: University of Minnesota Press, 2021), 35.

90. That expression is central to Souriau's politics of aesthetics, elaborate on in ibid.

91. See William Cronon, George Miles, and Jay Gitlin, "Becoming West," in *Under an Open Sky: Re-thinking America's Western Past*, ed. William Cronon, George Miles, and Jay Gitlin (New York: Norton, 1992), 3–27.

92. Edensor, *Industrial Ruins*, 169.

Index

For the benefit of digital users, indexed terms that span two pages (e.g., 52–53) may, on occasion, appear on only one of those pages.

Figures are indicated by *f* following the page number

Abraham, (Biblical), 11, 18–19, 20, 33, 35–36
Adderley, Cannonball, 59–60
Adorno, Theodor, 6–7, 38–40, 44–45, 48–49, 55–56, 89–91
Affaire du Foulard, 97
Aguwa, Kofu, 63
Akerman, Chantal, 130–31
Alamo (The), 16–17, 174–78, 180, 183, 185, 186, 187–89
Alarcón, Daniel, 7–8, 9–10
allegory
    in Mann, 42, 44–45
    in Sayles's *Lone Star*, 179
    in the series *Ethos*, 141–42
Alou, Felipe (baseball manager), 119–20
Althusser, Louis, 51
Altman, Robert, 82–83, 85–86
Antonioni, Michelangelo, 98–100
apocalypse/apocalyptic
    Derrida on tone, 78–79
    in Mann, 43–45
architecture
    in Altman's *Kansas* City, 85–86
    in California's, 159–74
    Egyptian, 35–36, 59
    in Haneke's *Caché*, 92–93
    as Media, 102–3
    in Morrison's *Jazz*, 80–81, 82–83, 87
    in Moses (Robert) legacy, 81–82
    narrative of, 15
    as public history, 173–74
    in Sayles's *Lone Star*, 174–84, 187–88
    in the series *Ethos*, 140–43, 140*f*, 144–45
    in Texas, 174–75

Tschumi on, 82–83
archives
    jazz as, 63–65
    Lazo on, 63–64
    Mbembe on, 63–64
Auerbach, Erich, 19–20, 21–22, 27–28, 30, 32
Automobility, in France, 103
    in Haneke's *Caché*, 103, 114
    Lefebvre on, 163
    in Los Angeles, 163–70, 172–73
    in Paris, 103–65
    in the United States, 103

Bacon, Francis (painter), 105, 152–53
Baker, Houston A, Jr., 62–63
Bakhtin, M. M., 26–27, 36–37, 46–47, 62–63
Bal, Mieke, 20–21, 22–23
Baldwin, James, 87–88
Baraka, Amiri (Leroy Jones), 76–85–
Barthes, Roland, 19, 39, 77
Baudrillard, Jean, 110–11
Bazin, Andrei, 130
Beethoven, Ludwig von, 38, 41, 43–45
Bellini, Giovanni, 124
Beloved (Morrison novel), 66–67
Bergman, Ingmar, 110*f*, 112, 131–32, 133*f*, 138–39
Berman, Marshall, 80–81
Bey, Dawoud, 123–24
Bickford, Susan, 165, 166
Blakey, Art, 60
Blanchard, Lee, 56–57
Bliss, Laura, 159
Bonitzer, Pascal, 98–99

224 INDEX

Bordwell, David, 137–38
Boumendjel, Ali, 107
Brecht, Bertolt, 135f
Broch, Herman, 42

Calasso, Roberto, 180
Campbell, Neil, 177–78
Carney, Harry, 61–62
Caro, Robert, 81–82
Casarino, Cesare, 4–5
Cheever, John, 159–60
cinema, Altman on, 83–84
    Antonioni on, 99–100
    Bonitzer on, 98–99,
    Deleuze on, 34–35, 107–8, 118, 131–32, 137–38, 169
    Haneke on, 116–17
    Pasolini on, 98–99
    Schrader on, 98
    Tarkovsky on, 35, 97–98
Cisneros, Sandra, 173–74
cities Baltimore, 2
    Barcelona, 89–91
    Ferrara, 97–98
    Istanbul, 124, 125–27, 135–36, 148, 149
    Kansas City, 82–88
    Los Angeles, 160, 161, 163–64, 171, 172–73, 174
    New Orleans, 56–57
    New York, 11–12, 72, 73–74, 80 ––83, 86, 87–88, 91–92, 123–24
    Paris, 12–13, 87–88, 91, 93, 95–96, 98, 102–4, 113–14, 117, 124–25, 175–76, 178
    Washington DC, 127–28
citizenship
    aesthetic, 91
    French, 91
    obligations of, 29
    public, 73–74, 80
civic
    action, 87
    assertion, 87–88
    bodies, 89–91
    contribution, 1–2
    encounter, 60–61
    expression, 57–58, 78–79, 83
    jazz, 60, 79–80
    participation, 87
    presence, 4, 58, 182

recognition, 100, 183–84
relevance, 9–10, 184
responsibility, 29
significance, 14, 29
value, 9–10
virtue, 29
voice, 2
Clark, Gregory, 60–61, 78, 79–80
class
    automobility and, 103–4
    Baudrillard on, 110–11
    bigotry, 126–27
    codes, 9–10, 160–61
    differences, 125
    distinction, 174
    divides, 135–36
    markers of, 110–11
    middle, 98, 159, 173–74
    politics of, 159
    pressures of, 108–9
    privileged, 125
    profiles, 159–60
    semiotics of, 162–63
    signs of, 108–9
    weapon, 174
    working, 81, 125
Cobley, Evelyn, 62–63
Code Unknown (Haneke film), 107–8
Collectors (Alarcon story), 7–10
colonialism (French), 95, 116–17
Coltrane, John, 57–58, 65–67, 69, 95, 116–17
Crockett, Davy, 177
Cronon, William, 185
culture
    African American, 69, 77
    American, 69
    Black, 86, 87
    body, 59
    dominant, 177–78
    hierarchical, 148–49
    media, 93
    musical, 86, 87
    Ottoman, 124–25
    popular, 148, 173
    Turkish, 126–27, 141–43, 149–50, 154
    Urban, 172–73
    white, 69

Davis, Mike, 162–63

INDEX 225

Davis, Miles, 59–62
De Certeau, Michel, 164, 170
Deleuze, Gilles, 4–5, 34–35, 105, 107–8,
    113, 117, 130, 131–32, 137–38,
    152–53, 169
Deutsche, Rosalyn, 114
Diaz, David, 170
Didi-Huberman, Georges, 181–82
discourse
    Bakhtin on, 45–46
    Christian, 45–46
    coded, 57–58
    democratization of, 44–45
    domains of, 84–85
    double-voiced, 22
    egalitarian, 26
    faith-based, 166–67
    historical, 22
    politics of, 26, 30–31
    psychiatric, 126–27
    psychoanalytic, 156–57
    psychological, 46
    theoretical, 16–17
    of truth, 153–54
    verbal, 64
Dostoyevsky, 26
Dreyfus Affair, 94–95
Drumont, Édouard, 94–95
Dürer, Albrecht, 130, 131*f*

Eckstein, Lars, 66–67
Edensor, Tim, 175–76, 188
Ellington, Duke, 55–57, 61–62, 70–71
Ellison, Ralph, 73–74, 75, 76, 80–81
Ethnography, 126
ethos
    of attunement, 156
    of civic recognition, 100
    democratic, 35, 61–62, 155
    egalitarian, 1, 2, 39, 61–62, 63,
        74, 78–80
    of *Ethos* series, 14–15, 157–58
    in Henry James, 47–48
    political, 171–72
    of reciprocity, 100, 150, 157
existence
    bourgeois, 96
    in Harlem, 72
    human, 29
    Lapoujade on, 7

lessor, 7
    modes of, 7, 8, 14–15, 183–84

Falling Down (Schumacher film), 166–70
Fanny and Alexander (Bergman film),
    111, 138–39
Fernandes, Jorge, 97–98
Flannery, Eon, 100
Flaubert, Gustave, 41
Ford, Henry, 102–3
Foucault, Michel, 4–5, 7, 117, 118, 153–54
Frederick (Lionni story), 1 --2
Freud, Sigmund, 46–47, 50–51, 132–
    34, 146–47
Friedberg, Anne, 164, 180

Gallagher, Brianne, 102–3, 113
Garrison, Jimmy, 57, 66–67
gender
    bias in France, 91
    equality (in Mann), 11
    policing in Turkey, 126, 149–50
Genesis (Book of), 10–12, 18–19, 23–24,
    25–26, 33, 35–36, 53–54, 55
genres
    artistic, 6, 44–45, 86
    Auerbach on, 32
    biographical, 44–45
    constraints of, 22
    cultural, 58
    discursive, 167
    historiographic metafiction as, 10, 22,
        83, 102–3, 118, 164
    literary, 22
    low, 30
    narrative, 15
    novel as, 30
    poetry as, 30
    politics of, 29
    scriptures as, 19–20
    stories as, 6
    textual, 15, 125, 126–27, 174–75
    the whodunit, 96, 115, 118
geopolitics, 15–16
Gilroy, Paul, 56–57, 114–15
Glissant, Edouard, 100
Godzic, Wieslaw, 131–32
Goethe, Johann Wolfgang von, 30
Gomez, Ramiro, 160–61
Gopnik, Adam, 94–95

226 INDEX

Gorelick, Nathan, 133–34
Graham, Stephen, 164
Great Migration, 69–70, 72, 85–86
Green, Jessie, 130
Griffith, D. W., 176–77
Guattari, Felix, 4–5, 130

Haneke, Michael, ix, 12–13, 91–93, 95–
  100, 102–3, 107–9, 111, 112, 113,
  114–17, 118, 120–21, 178
Heard, Matthew M, 78–79
Hertz, David Michael, 40
history
  African American, 10–11, 64–65, 76–77
  of the Alamo, 174–75
  American, 70–71, 128–29
  architectural, 173–74
  of the archive, 63–64
  art, 1
  Auerbach on, 21–22
  of automobility, 103
  Black, 56–57, 74
  collective, 16–17, 175
  counter, 7, 17, 117
  of dispossessed, 6
  European, 94–95, 115
  versus fiction, 22
  of forms, 4–5
  French, 91–92, 93, 97, 115–16, 118
  institutionalized, 6
  jazz, 58, 85–86
  linear, 89–91
  in Mann, 22, 24, 30, 52–53
  versus memory, 117, 175–76, 177–78
  musical, 56–57, 62–63, 85
  New York, 81–82
  Nora on, 116–17, 175–76
  personal, 6–7, 166–67, 179, 185
  political, 83
  popular, 118
  portraiture as, 122–23
  as protagonist, 12–13
  public, 159, 173–74
  of race struggle, 117
  of the racial order, 93
  of ruins, 175
  Sayles on, 177–78
  of slavered, 176–77
  Texas, 15–16, 176–77, 182, 183–84,
    185, 188–89
Hitchcock, Alfred, 99–100

Hockney, David, 160–61
Homer, 19–20, 32
Hughes, Langston, 67, 87
Huis Clos (Sartre play), 6
Hutcheon, Linda, 22
hypotactic/hypotaxis, 3, 30, 40–41, 52–
  53, 61, 132–33, 148–49

identity
  Black, 73–74
  cultural, 124–25
  Egyptian (of Joseph), 43
  ethnic, 173–74
  ethno-racial ethno-religious, 94, 97–98
  as fortuitous, 51–52
  French, 97
  journeys of (Joseph's), 51–52
  management of, 186
  markers of, 103
  matrices of, 91–92, 100
  multiplicities of, 18–19
  national, 118
  stigmatized, 177–78
ideology
  of form, 93–94
  social, 93–94
Ishiguro, Kazuo, 122
Ives, Charles, 86

James, Henry, 47–48
Jarvis, Jill, 6
Jones, Edward P, 127–28
Jones, Elvin, 57, 66–67
Jones, LeRoi, 85. See also Amiri Baraka
Jung, Carl, 14–15, 146–47

Kafka, Franz, 180
Kandinsky, Wassily, 44–45
Kansas City (film), 82–85
Kant, Immanuel, 35–36, 47–48
Karp, Jacqueline, 124
Kassovitz, Mathieu (director), 95–96, 97–98
Katrina, Hurricane, 56–57
Kelly, J. A., 41
Kemalist, 125, 132–33, 135–36, 154
King, Martin Luther, 57
Kittler, Friedrich, 102–3
Kundera, Milan, 5–6, 32

L'Enfant, Peter Charles, 127–28
La Haine (film), 95–96, 97–99

INDEX 227

Lacan, Jacques, 101–2
Landy, Marcia, 118
La Penn, Marine, 94
Lapoujade, David, 7
Lazo, Rodrigo, 63–64
L'Carré, John, 137–38
Leach, Edmund, 33–35
Leal, Jorge, 172–73
Lee, Spike, 56–57
Lefebvre, Henri
  on automobility, 164–65
  on "right to the city," 33–34, 81–82
  on space, 6–7, 172–73
Leo Lionni, 1
Lenox Avenue: Midnight (Langston
  Hughes poem), 67
Leon-Portilla, Miguel, 164
Levi-Strauss, Claude, 156–57
Lloyd, Alexandra, 111
Lone Star (Sayles film), 15, 17, 177, 178–89
Lyotard, Jean François, 47–48

Machiavelli, Nicolo, 29
Mackey, Nathaniel, 57–58, 62, 64–66
Macron, President Emmanuel, 107
Ma Rainey's Black Bottom (August
  Wilson play), 75–76
Martel, James, 51
Mason, William, 86
Mbembe, Achille, 63–65, 97
Mehmet II, (Turkish Sultan), 124
Middle Passage, 55–56, 76–77
Milne, A. A., 4
Minden, Michael, 29
Monk, Thelonious, 57–58
Moore, Macdonald Smith, 86
Moses, Robert, 81–82, 87–88

Nietzsche', Friedrich, 27–28, 38–39,
  45–46, 48
Nora, Pierre, 116–17, 175–76, 177–78
novel forms
  Bildungsroman, 24, 32
  Mann's essayistic, 18–19, 25–26, 27–28,
    32–33, 42
  Morisons jazzthetic, romantic, 29

Odyssey, Homer's, 19
ontologies, Adorno's of chaos, 45
  Egypt's aesthetic, 37
  image, 128–29

Mann's geographic, 32
Morrison's blues/music, 67, 75–76
Oya, Berkun Ethos director), 146, 150,
  154–55, 156–57, 158

pain
  as democratic, 137–38
  Morrison's jazz, 76–77
  Sade on, 76
  Adam Smith on, 76
  Wittgenstein on, 76–77
Pamuk, Orhan, 124–25
Papon, Maurice, 93–94, 95–96, 105–
  6, 114–15
paratactic/parataxis, 1–2, 3, 13, 35–36, 40,
  41, 52–53, 61–62, 83, 109–10, 120–
  21, 132, 147–48
Parker, Charlie (Bird), 55–56, 82–83, 86
Parks, Gordon, 128–29, 129f
Pattison, Dale, 80–81, 87
Paul (apostle), 46–47
Philopoesis, 4–5
Pocock, J G A, 29
Portes, Edward, 89–91
postcolonial, 13, 89–92, 97–98, 100–1,
  116–17, 186–87
Potiphar's wife (biblical), 10–11, 23–24,
  35, 43, 53–54
psychoanalysis
  European, 13–14
  Jungian, 138, 146–47
  in Turkey, 132–34, 142–43

racism, 73, 92–96, 176
reciprocity (ethos of)
  In Ethos series, 147, 150, 156–58
  Levi-Strauss on, 156–57
Rhodes, David, 91–92
right(s)
  affective, 183
  to the city, 6–7, 11–12, 33–34, 80, 81,
    82, 87, 89, 126, 127–28, 162–63, 164,
    165, 171–72
  epistemic, 183
  to history, 183
  to the Holy Land, 11–12, 26
  legal, 183
  to space, 6–7, 11–12
  to urban life, 12, 81
Rios, Michael, 171–73
Rojas, James, 171–73

228 INDEX

Roosevelt, President Franklin D, 38

Sade, Marquis de, 76
Sander, August, 123–24
Sartre, Jean-Paul, 6
Sayles, John, 15, 17, 177–78, 180–81,
183, 188
Schoenberg, Arnold, 38, 39–41, 44–47,
48–49, 53–54, 55, 61–62
Schrader, Paul, 98
Schuller, Gunther, 60–61
Schumacher, Joel, 164, 166–67, 169
scopic field, 1–2, 13, 98–99, 100–2, 111–
12, 130
Shakespeare, William, 39–40, 45–46
Silence, The (Bergman film), 111, 112
Simondon, Gilbert, 50–51
Smith, Adam, 76
Smith, Mamie, 85–86
Smith, William Garner, 93
Smitherman, Geneva, 57–58
Snead, James, 62–63
Soja, Edward, 162
sovereignty
commercial, 168
history of, 92
Mexican, 162
shared, 162–63
Spivak, Gayatri, 17
Stoever, Jennifer Lynn, 86
Stravinsky, Igor, 55
subjectivity, 43–44, 80
individual, 122
inter- 47–48
sonic, 78
stability of, 132–33

Tamar (biblical), 10, 11, 22–23, 24, 33–
34, 53–54
Taylor, Frederick W, 103
temporality
Adorno on, 89–91
in Caché, 91–92, 102–3, 118
cinematic, 131–32
Deleuze on, 118, 130
in Ethos series, 137–38
Latinx, 170

Machiavelli's, 29
Mann's, 21–22
Morrison's, 65–66
textual
explorations, 126–27
form, 6–7
genres, 6, 7, 17, 122, 159–60
Joseph, 28–29
Morrison's jazz as, 59
objects, 4–6
past, 22
space, 33, 164
strategy, 66–67
work, 57–58
Thrift, Nigel, 67–68
Todorov, Tzvetan, 93–94
Tolstoy, Leo, 130–31, 137–38, 139
Tschumi, Bernard, 82–83
Twain, Mark, 157
Tyner, McCoy, 57, 66–67

Vallejo, Mariano Guadalupe, 162–63
Vermeer, Johannes, 44–45
Vidler, Anthony, 172–73
Villavicencio, Karla Cornejo, 172–73
Viramontes, Elena Maria, 164, 165, 166–
67, 170, 174, 175–76, 188
Virtue, Nancy, 115–16

Wagner, Richard, 11–12, 39–41, 42,
43–44, 45
Watson, Ella May, 128–29
Wayne, John (actor/director), 177
Wener, Leif, 183
When the Levees Broke (Spike Lee
film), 56–57
Wilson, August, 75–76
Wire, The HBO series, 2
Wittgenstein, Ludwig, 76–77
Wodiczko, Krzysztof, 89–91
Woo, John, 98
Wood, Grant, 128–29, 140–41
Wood, James, 130–31

Zevnik, Andreja, 131–32
Zilberg, Elena, 169
Žižek, Slavoj, 47–48